Get the eBook FREE!

(PDF, ePub, Kindle, and liveBook all included)

We believe that once you buy a book from us, you should be able to read it in any format we have available. To get electronic versions of this book at no additional cost to you, purchase and then register this book at the Manning website.

Go to https://www.manning.com/freebook and follow the instructions to complete your pBook registration.

That's it!
Thanks from Manning!

Kubernetes Native Microservices with Quarkus and MicroProfile

JOHN CLINGAN
AND KEN FINNIGAN

MANNING
SHELTER ISLAND

For online information and ordering of this and other Manning books, please visit www.manning.com. The publisher offers discounts on this book when ordered in quantity. For more information, please contact

Special Sales Department
Manning Publications Co.
20 Baldwin Road
PO Box 761
Shelter Island, NY 11964
Email: orders@manning.com

Manning Publications Co.
20 Baldwin Road
PO Box 761
Shelter Island, NY 11964

Development editor:	Elesha Hyde
Technical development editor:	Raphael Villela
Review editor:	Aleksandar Dragosavljević
Production editor:	Keri Hales
Copy editor:	Pamela Hunt
Proofreader:	Katie Tennant
Technical proofreader:	Mladen Knežić
Typesetter:	Dennis Dalinnik
Cover designer:	Marija Tudor

ISBN: 9781617298653
Printed in the United States of America

contents

preface

We, the authors, have been involved in the Enterprise Java industry for more than a decade. We started working together at Red Hat in 2016, during the founding of MicroProfile to create Java microservices specifications, and with WildFly Swarm, now called Thorntail, as a runtime to implement those specifications.

Since then, Kubernetes has continued to grow as a container orchestration platform. Given Red Hat's integral involvement with Kubernetes and OpenShift—its enterprise distribution—our job was to facilitate Thorntail deployments on Kubernetes. We also worked with the MicroProfile community, who also recognized the growth of Kubernetes, to evolve its specifications to add support for Java microservices deployments on Kubernetes.

We also recognized the limitations of Java and runtimes like Thorntail deployed to Kubernetes, consuming hundreds of megabytes of RAM for each microservice instance. Resource utilization can put Java at a considerable disadvantage, compared with other runtimes like Node.js or Golang, for shared deployment environments like Kubernetes clusters. To address this, Red Hat introduced Supersonic Subatomic Java—in other words, Quarkus!

Quarkus is a unique runtime. It supports MicroProfile and other industry-leading specifications and frameworks, helping developers become productive quickly. Kubernetes is a first-class deployment platform for Quarkus, with built-in tooling that reduces native compilation and Kubernetes deployment to a single command. We have to say that working together with a couple of dozen other Red Hat employees crammed into a conference room in Neuchâtel, Switzerland, on Quarkus's "launch day" was one of the most memorable and rewarding days of our professional careers.

We recognize that plenty of books are available for MicroProfile, Kubernetes, and, more recently, Quarkus. We set out to write a book that reflects how the three used together are greater than the sum of their parts. Deploying to Kubernetes is not an afterthought; it is integral to each chapter. We wanted to go beyond developing an application locally by deploying it (implemented as a collection of microservices) to Kubernetes as it evolves throughout the book. We wanted to show how MicroProfile-based APIs interoperate with backend services while running in a Kubernetes cluster, like Prometheus and Grafana, Jaeger, and Kafka. We wanted a balance between demonstrating the step-by-step Quarkus live coding iterative development style with MicroProfile and Quarkus APIs like JUnit 5 and WireMock for automated testing of MicroProfile applications.

The challenge is to bring microservices development with Quarkus, MicroProfile, and Kubernetes together in a single book and make it feel like the natural experience it truly is. Hopefully, we have met this challenge, and you learn as much from reading this book as we did in writing it. Happy reading (and coding)!

acknowledgments

We would like to thank Elesha Hyde, our development editor, for being so understanding of our delays in finishing the writing. In addition, we'd like to thank all the reviewers: Alain Lompo, Alessandro Campeis, Andres Sacco, Asif Iqbal, Daniel Cortés, David Torrubia Iñigo, DeUndre' Rushon, John Guthrie, Kent R. Spillner, Krzysztof Kamyczek, Michał Ambroziewicz, Mladen Knežić, Ramakrishna Chintalapati, Sergio Britos, and Yogesh Shetty. Their suggestions helped make this a better book.

Also, a thank-you goes to the entire Manning team for all their efforts on the project: Raphael Villela, technical development editor; Aleksander Dragosavljević, review editor; Keri Hales, production editor; Pamela Hunt, copyeditor; Mladen Knežić, technical proofreader; Katie Tennant, proofreader; as well as the rest of the production team. It's been greatly appreciated, and the book wouldn't be here today without them.

JOHN CLINGAN: I'd like to thank my wife, Tran, and daughters, Sarah and Hailey, who had a part-time spouse and father, respectively, while working on this book in the home office, car, and hotel during many weekend soccer tournaments. I also thank my coauthor, Ken, as an experienced author and friend, for his patience and guidance while authoring my first book.

KEN FINNIGAN: I will be forever indebted to Erin, my wife, for her continued understanding and support throughout the process. I would also like to thank my sons, Lorcán and Daire, for understanding their dad disappearing to work on the book in the evenings or weekends.

about this book

Over the last couple of years, Quarkus has exploded in popularity as a framework for developing microservices, and Eclipse MicroProfile is continuing to grow as a set of APIs for developing microservices with Java. This book details how to create, build, debug, and deploy Quarkus microservices with MicroProfile and Spring APIs to Kubernetes.

Building and deploying a microservice is not the end of the story. To that end, this book also covers related aspects of microservices on Kubernetes, such as application health, monitoring and observability, security, and visualizing endpoints.

Who should read this book?

The audience for the book includes Java EE and Jakarta EE developers with a few years of experience who may have some knowledge of microservices but are looking for guidance on best practices and the latest developments. Developers will gain insight into Eclipse MicroProfile and how to use the APIs within Quarkus, as well as how to deploy their Quarkus microservices to Kubernetes.

How this book is organized: A road map

Chapter 1 introduces the reader to microservices by covering what they are, what a microservices architecture is, and why specifications for microservices are needed. Then it introduces Eclipse MicroProfile, Quarkus, and Kubernetes. Lastly, it introduces some characteristics of Kubernetes-native microservices.

Chapter 2 delves deeper into Quarkus, starting with how to create a Quarkus project. It covers important topics such as live coding, writing tests, native executables, and how to package a Quarkus application and deploy it to Kubernetes.

Chapter 3 introduces configuration with Eclipse MicroProfile in Quarkus, including how to set and retrieve it. Then it covers how to use a ConfigSource to define a new source of configuration for Quarkus.

Chapter 4 covers database interactions with Panache. It explains how data sources work in Quarkus before covering three different patterns for database access with Panache: JPA, active record, and data repository. Lastly, it explains how to deploy a PostgreSQL database to Kubernetes.

Chapter 5 introduces how Quarkus enables the consumption of external services with MicroProfile by using the REST Client and defines type-safe representations for them. It explains how to use CDI or a programmatic API to use the REST Client, and how it can be mocked for testing. Lastly, it covers how to add headers to the client request, or additional filters and providers used in processing the request.

Chapter 6 introduces the concept of application health and how MicroProfile Health integrates with the Kubernetes Pod life cycle. It covers how to combine similar checks into a custom group and how to see the checks in a convenient manner in the UI.

Chapter 7 covers all the resilience strategies offered by MicroProfile Fault Tolerance, including bulkheads, fallbacks, retries, and circuit breakers. It then covers how to override the settings of each strategy through properties.

Chapter 8 introduces reactive streams, explaining what they are and how they are constructed from publishers, subscribers, and processors. It then explains how to create Reactive Streams in Quarkus with Reactive Messaging, as well as bridging imperative and reactive code with an emitter. Lastly, it covers deploying Apache Kafka to Kubernetes and deploying a reactive system consisting of microservices using it as a backbone.

Chapter 9 covers how existing Spring developers can convert their applications to Quarkus with minimal changes. It then explains how to use the Spring Config Server as a ConfigSource in Quarkus. Lastly, it details what is compatible between Spring and Quarkus, without modification, for web and data access.

Chapter 10 explains the importance of metrics in monitoring applications, especially in microservices architectures. It covers how to use Prometheus and Grafana for visualizing metrics, whether from MicroProfile Metrics or Micrometer.

Chapter 11 introduces how to trace microservices with MicroProfile and OpenTracing. It then explains how to deploy Jaeger to Kubernetes, send traces from microservices to Jaeger, and view them in the UI. Next, it covers how to customize span names and inject a tracer to create custom spans. Lastly, the chapter covers how to trace database calls and messages sent to or from Apache Kafka.

Chapter 12 examines API visualization with MicroProfile OpenAPI and how to view the generated documents with Swagger UI. Then it covers how to customize the OpenAPI document with application information, schema information, and specific details of the operations for REST endpoints. Lastly, it covers a design-first approach and how to use an existing OpenAPI document.

Chapter 13 explains authentication and authorization for microservices, first with file-based authentication and also when using OpenID Connect with Keycloak. Then it covers protecting specific resources and how to test the authorization flow. Next, it explains JSON Web Tokens (JWT) and the APIs included for retrieving different parts of the token. Lastly, it covers how to secure a microservice with JWT and propagate tokens between microservices.

About the code

This book contains many examples of source code both in numbered listings and in line with normal text. In both cases, source code is formatted in a `fixed-width font` `like this` to separate it from ordinary text.

In many cases, the original source code has been reformatted; we've added line breaks and reworked indentation to accommodate the available page space in the book. In some cases, even this was not enough, and listings include line-continuation markers (➡). Additionally, comments in the source code have often been removed from the listings when the code is described in the text. Code annotations accompany many of the listings, highlighting important concepts.

All the code from the book can be found in the source code accompanying the book. You can get executable snippets of code from the liveBook (online) version of this book at https://livebook.manning.com/book/kubernetes-native-microservices-with-quarkus-and-microprofile. The complete source code can be downloaded free of charge from the Manning website at https://www.manning.com/books/kubernetes-native-microservices-with-quarkus-and-microprofile and is also available via the GitHub repository at https://github.com/jclingan/manning-kube-native-microservices. The sample code is structured as a series of Maven modules for each chapter, or part of a chapter.

liveBook discussion forum

Purchase of *Kubernetes Native Microservices with Quarkus and MicroProfile* includes free access to liveBook, Manning's online reading platform. Using liveBook's exclusive discussion features, you can attach comments to the book globally or to specific sections or paragraphs. It's a snap to make notes for yourself, ask and answer technical questions, and receive help from the author and other users. To access the forum, go to https://livebook.manning.com/#!/book/kubernetes-native-microservices-with-quarkus-and-microprofile/discussion. You can also learn more about Manning's forums and the rules of conduct at https://livebook.manning.com/#!/discussion.

Manning's commitment to our readers is to provide a venue where a meaningful dialogue between individual readers and between readers and authors can take place. It is not a commitment to any specific amount of participation on the part of the authors, whose contribution to the forum remains voluntary (and unpaid). We suggest you try asking the authors some challenging questions lest their interest stray! The forum and the archives of previous discussions will be accessible from the publisher's website as long as the book is in print.

about the authors

JOHN CLINGAN has more than 30 years of experience in the enterprise software industry as a developer, system administrator, consultant, technical sales engineer, and product manager. He has been a product manager for Java EE and the GlassFish reference implementation and is a founding member of Micro-Profile. He is currently an active member of the Jakarta EE and MicroProfile communities and a member of the Quarkus team, where he focuses on the Quarkus community and its partners.

KEN FINNIGAN has been a consultant and software engineer for more than 20 years with enterprises throughout the world. Ken has a history of delivering projects on time and on budget across many industries, providing key customer value. Ken is currently focused on all things observability, while also looking to innovate with Kubernetes-native development. Ken is part of the team developing Quarkus to be Supersonic Subatomic Java. He has previously served as the project lead for SmallRye, Thorntail, and LiveOak, with more than 10 years of experience contributing to open source. Ken is an author of several books in the tech space, including *Enterprise Java Microservices* (Manning, 2018).

Part 1

Introduction

What are microservices? When should I use Quarkus? Why is Kubernetes so important? These are a few of the questions we will address in part 1.

Part 1 also takes the reader through creating their first Quarkus application and describes some key features of Quarkus, such as live reload and deployment to Kubernetes.

Introduction to Quarkus, MicroProfile, and Kubernetes

This chapter covers

- Microservices overview
- Overview and history of MicroProfile
- Quarkus introduction
- Kubernetes introduction

Entire books are available on Quarkus, microservices, MicroProfile, Spring, and Kubernetes. However, they tend to focus only on each specific topic. This book covers how to combine these topics into an effective and integrated development and deployment stack. Kubernetes-native microservices utilize and integrate with Kubernetes features naturally and efficiently. The result is a productive developer experience that is consistent with the expectations of Kubernetes platform administrators.

This chapter begins by defining microservices and how and why they have evolved over the last decade as a popular enterprise software architecture. We then provide a brief history and overview of MicroProfile and its growth into a significant collection of microservices-related specifications. With a baseline understanding of microservices and MicroProfile, we introduce Quarkus as a Java runtime that supports these technologies. Last, we introduce some core Kubernetes concepts and why they make Kubernetes an ideal microservice deployment platform.

> **NOTE**   A "runtime" is an execution environment that includes a collection of packaged frameworks that collectively support a developer's application logic. Java EE (now Jakarta EE [https://jakarta.ee/]) application servers, Spring Boot, and Quarkus are all examples of Java runtimes: each is a Java execution environment with Java frameworks that support application logic.

1.1   *What is a microservice?*

An internet search will result in hundreds of microservice definitions. There is no industry consensus on a single definition, but some common and well-understood principles exist. We are using a definition that aligns with those principles but with a particular emphasis on one principle—*isolation*. As defined in *Enterprise Java Microservices* (https://livebook.manning.com/book/enterprise-java-microservices), a microservice consists of a single deployment executing within a single process, isolated from other deployments and processes, that supports the fulfillment of a specific piece of business functionality.

We are going to put a bit more emphasis on the runtime aspect of isolation than most other writings. With Kubernetes as the target deployment platform, we have an opportunity for optimizing code and the Java runtime itself. Although a microservice is isolated business functionality, it nearly always interacts with other microservices. That is the basis of many code examples for this book. There are a couple of useful points to make when breaking down the selected definition.

First, a microservice implements a specific piece of business functionality, known as a *bounded context* (as explained by Eric Evans; https://www.amazon.com/Domain-Driven-Design-Tackling-Complexity-Software/dp/0321125215), which is a logical separation of multiple business problem domains within an enterprise. By logically breaking down a business domain into multiple bounded contexts, each bounded context more accurately represents its specific view of the business domain and becomes easier to model.

As represented in figure 1.1, the set of bounded contexts for a small business accounting application may include accounts receivable, accounts payable, and invoicing. A traditional monolithic application would implement all three bounded contexts. Multiple bounded contexts within in a single monolith can result in "spaghetti code" as a result of unnecessary interdependencies and unplanned intermixing of contexts. In a microservices architecture, each of these capabilities is modeled individually as a bounded context and implemented as a microservice that addresses each specific bounded context.

Next, a microservice executes within a single isolated process. Although this is not a concrete requirement, it has become a preferred architectural approach. There are some practical reasons behind this, based on more than a decade of experience of deploying applications to Java EE application servers and servlet containers like Apache Tomcat. We refer to these synonymously as "application servers."

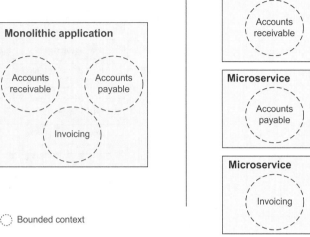

Bounded context

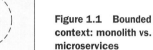

Figure 1.1 Bounded context: monolith vs. microservices

From a technical perspective, application servers can host multiple microservices. However, this deployment model has fallen out of favor for the following reasons:

- *Resource management*—One microservice can starve other microservices of resources. The Java Virtual Machine (JVM) does not have built-in resource management to limit resource consumption by different applications within the same JVM instance.
- *Patching/upgrading*—Patching or upgrading an application server negatively impacts the availability of all hosted microservices simultaneously.
- *Versioning*—Each microservice development team may want to evolve at a different pace, causing an application server versioning-requirements mismatch. Some may want to leverage new features of the latest version, whereas others may prefer to avoid introducing risk because the current version is stable in production.
- *Stability*—One poorly written microservice can cause stability issues for the entire application server, impacting the availability of the remaining stable applications.
- *Control*—Developers rightfully cede control of shared infrastructure, like application servers, to a separate DevOps team. This limits developer options like JDK version, tuning for a specific microservice's optimal performance, application server version, and more.

Figure 1.2 shows that these issues have driven the industry toward adopting a *single-application stack* for microservices, which is a one-to-one mapping between a microservice application and its runtime. This began nearly a decade ago by deploying a single microservice per application server, and shortly thereafter evolved into specialized microservice runtimes like Dropwizard, Spring Boot, and, more recently, Quarkus to

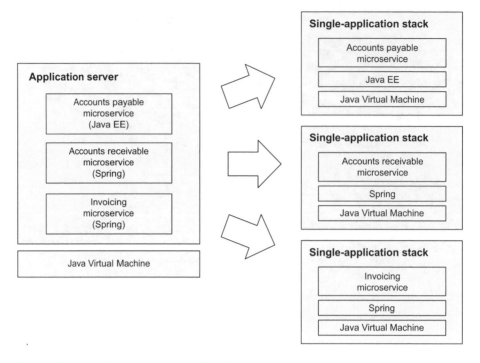

Figure 1.2   Application servers vs. single-application stacks

improve the developer and administrator experience. We refer to these single-application stacks as *Java microservice runtimes* and cover this concept in more detail later in the chapter. Note that with microservices, it is easier to split out and optimize the stack for a particular runtime like Java EE or Spring. An added benefit of the single-application stack is that it can also be implemented in non-Java technologies like Node.js or Golang, although this is out of scope of this discussion.

1.1.1   *The rise of microservices*

Early microservices tended to directly communicate with one another, an approach sometimes referred to as "smart services with dumb pipes." A possible downside to this approach is the encoding within each service of the knowledge of *what happens next*. Tightly coupling this knowledge into the code makes it inflexible to dynamic change—and a potentially tedious task for engineers if it experiences regular change. If the knowledge around *what happens next* changes frequently, consider implementing the functionality using a business rules engine or utilizing events as part of an event-driven architecture. We will use both approaches in the example application.

   With the popularity of Netflix, with its thousands of microservices, and other unicorns like them, the popularity and thrall of microservices exploded. Microservices became *the thing* everyone wanted to develop for their next project.

The rise of microservices led to perceived benefits in delivery speed, better utilization of resources with smaller teams, and shifting of operational concerns to the team developing the code. This last item we now refer to as *DevOps*.

However, microservices were not the panacea that everyone hoped they would be. The benefits we mentioned previously don't come automatically by virtue of developing a microservice. It takes organizational change for all the benefits to be achieved. It's often forgotten that not all implementation patterns, such as microservices, are right for every organization, team, or even group of developers. Sometimes we must acknowledge that although microservices are not appropriate for a given situation, they would be perfect for another. As with everything in software engineering, do your homework, and don't blindly adopt a pattern because *it's cool*. That is the path to disaster!

1.1.2 *Microservices architecture*

So, what is a microservices architecture, and what does it look like?

Figure 1.3 shows just one example of many possible architectures that are applicable when developing microservices. We can have microservices calling databases, microservices calling other microservices, microservices communicating with external services, or microservices passing messages, or events, to brokers and streaming services. For example, to add a user experience, a frontend web UI microservice has been added whose purpose is to add, update, delete, and view relevant information in the accounts payable and accounts receivable microservices. The freedom of architecting microservices in any desired manner offers limitless options, which is also its downside. It becomes difficult to chart a path toward a meaningful microservices architecture. The key is to start with the smallest possible piece of functionality and begin building out from there. When it's the first time a team is developing microservice architectures, it's even more critical to not create a "big picture" up front. Taking the time to create that big picture without previous experience of microservices architecture design will consume time when it's likely the final architecture will actually be very different. During the process of gaining experience with microservices, the architecture will shift over time toward a more appropriate one.

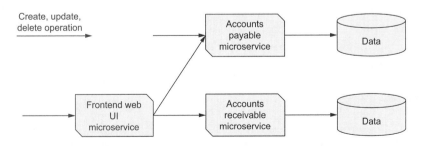

Figure 1.3   Microservices architecture: collaborating microservices

NOTE An alternative approach is to develop a monolith of loosely coupled components that can then be extracted out into microservices, strangling the monolith if deemed necessary down the road.

In short, a microservices architecture can be almost anything that incorporates the coordination of services into a cohesive application that meets business requirements.

Granted, with a limitless set of options for what can constitute a microservices architecture, architects and developers can benefit tremendously from having patterns and recommendations for how they can be designed.

This is where microservices specifications come to the aid of enterprise Java developers.

1.1.3 The need for microservices specifications

Java EE has been the standard-bearer for Enterprise Java specifications for roughly 20 years. However, Java EE has been traditionally focused on three-tier monolithic architecture with a steady, measured evolution and a strong focus on backward compatibility. Java EE stopped evolving between 2014 and 2017, just as the industry began to heavily adopt microservices.

During that pause, the Java EE community began to experiment and deliver early microservices APIs. The risk of API fragmentation across Java runtimes that had been known for application portability increased. In addition, there was a risk of losing reusable skills. For example, Java EE APIs like JPA and JAX-RS are used with non-Java EE platforms like Spring and Dropwizard, making it easier to switch to a Java runtime that better meets business criteria. To avoid fragmentation and loss of reusable skills, the community decided to collaborate on microservice specifications.

1.2 MicroProfile

To avoid Java API fragmentation and to leverage the collective vendor and community knowledge and resources, IBM, London Java Community (LJC), Payara, Red Hat, and Tomitribe founded MicroProfile in June 2016. The tagline, "Optimizing Enterprise Java for a Microservices Architecture," recognizes that Java offers a solid foundation for building microservices. MicroProfile extends that foundation through the creation and evolution of Java API specifications for well-understood microservices patterns and cloud-related standards. These common APIs can be used by multiple frameworks and implementations or runtimes.

Today, 12 specifications have been developed by the MicroProfile community, listed in table 1.1 and table 1.2. Most of the specifications in table 1.1 will be covered in future chapters.

NOTE MicroProfile has grown to include 12 specifications. Some are concerned that including too many specifications in the overall platform is a barrier to entry for new implementations. For this reason, any new specification is outside the existing platform and referred to as a "standalone" specification.

The MicroProfile community plans to review how to organize specifications in the future.

Table 1.1 MicroProfile platform specifications

Specification	Description
Config	Externalizes application configuration
Fault Tolerance	Defines multiple strategies to improve application robustness
Health	Expresses application health to the underlying platform
JWT RBAC	Secures RESTful endpoints
Metrics	Exposes platform and application metrics
Open API	Java APIs for the OpenAPI specification that documents RESTful endpoints
OpenTracing	Defines behaviors and an API for accessing an OpenTracing-compliant Tracer object
REST Client	Type-safe invocation of REST endpoints

Table 1.2 MicroProfile standalone specifications

Specification	Description
Context propagation	Propagates contexts across units of work that are thread-agnostic
GraphQL	Java API for the GraphQL query language
Reactive Streams operators	Allows two different libraries that provide asynchronous streaming to be able to stream data to and from each other
Reactive Streams messaging	Provides asynchronous messaging support based on Reactive Streams

1.2.1 History of MicroProfile

MicroProfile is unique in the industry. Whereas specification organizations tend to evolve in an intentionally slow and measured manner, MicroProfile delivers industry specifications that evolve rapidly. In four short years, MicroProfile has released 12 specifications with nearly all having multiple updates and some having major updates. These updates deliver new features that work across multiple implementations in the hands of developers up to three times per year. In other words, MicroProfile keeps pace with changes in the industry.

Figure 1.4 puts this in perspective. MicroProfile 1.0 was released in September 2016, adopting three Java EE specifications to define its core programming model, specifically, Java API for RESTful Services (JAX-RS) 2.0, Contexts and Dependency Injection (CDI) 1.2, and JSON Processing (JSON-P) 1.0. The MicroProfile founders looked to expand the vendor and community members, while also beginning specification development. The community immediately recognized that hosting MicroProfile

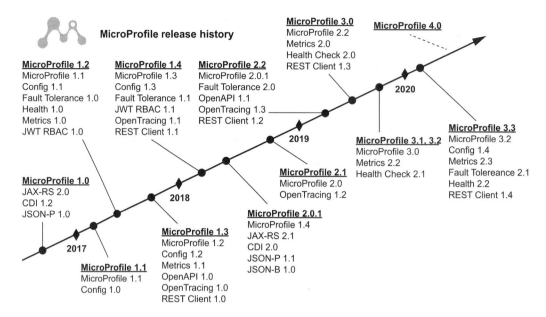

Figure 1.4   MicroProfile releases

in a vendor-neutral foundation would facilitate these goals. After considering the options, the Eclipse Foundation became the home of MicroProfile in December 2016. Over the next four years, MicroProfile released three major releases and nine minor releases that adopted JSON-B from Java EE and defined 12 "homegrown" specifications outlined in table 1.1 and table 1.2.

1.2.2   *MicroProfile community core principles*

As an Eclipse Foundation working group, MicroProfile follows some of the Foundation's core tenets like open source, vendor neutrality, and community engagement and collaboration. The MicroProfile Working Group Charter (https://www.eclipse.org/org/workinggroups/microprofile-charter.php) extends those tenets with the following additional principles:

- *Limited processes*—MicroProfile uses the Eclipse Development Process and the MicroProfile Specification Process. Any additional processes specific to Micro-Profile are created only when necessary.
- *Experiment and innovate*—MicroProfile as a community provides an industry proving ground to incubate and experiment with well-established problems needing cross-Java-runtime APIs, gather user feedback, and adapt and iterate at a fast pace.
- *No backward-compatibility guarantee*—Major versions of a specification developed within MicroProfile may break backward compatibility.

- *Implementation first*—MicroProfile specifications are released only after an implementation has been created and both the specification and implementation have had sufficient time for community review.
- *Encourage brand adoption*—Define guidelines that would allow usage of the MicroProfile brand without charge.
- *Openness*—Transparency, inclusiveness, and eliminating barriers to participate are highly valued principles. Public meetings and lists are preferred. Lists are favored for key decisions. Specifications have been managed in a way that provides open access to all MicroProfile committers.
- *Low barrier to entry*—It is MicroProfile's intent to operate a low-cost working group. Budget will be evaluated annually and as membership changes for opportunities to maintain low fees and costs.

These tenets make MicroProfile somewhat different from most organizations that create specifications. For example, MicroProfile considers itself an agile project and is willing to break backward compatibility. This willingness results from a rapid-moving specification project, and any breaking changes are well thought out with strong justification and as narrow a scope as possible.

1.3 *Quarkus*

Quarkus is a Java microservice runtime. Does the industry really benefit from yet another Java microservice runtime? Yes! To understand why, let's take a look at some inherent problems with existing runtimes.

Most Java microservice runtimes use existing frameworks that were developed for shared environments like application servers, where each application has its own set of requirements. These frameworks are mature and still relevant but haven't fundamentally changed since the mid-2000s and continue to rely heavily on dynamic runtime logic using Java reflection. More specifically, no substantive optimizations have been made to these frameworks for Java microservice runtimes. The result is high RAM utilization and slower startup time due to a large amount of work at application startup.

Another pain point is that developer productivity often suffers with Java microservice runtimes. Every time a developer makes a change, they have to save the file, rebuild the application, restart the application, and refresh the browser. This can take tens of seconds, significantly impacting the productivity of the developer. Multiply that by the number of developers in a team over time, and it quickly equates to a large sunk resource cost for an enterprise.

Developers and DevOps teams began to feel the pain of developing and deploying Java microservices and have been increasingly considering alternatives like Node.js and Golang due to their reduced RAM requirements and fast startup time. These alternatives can also achieve a 5- to 10-times deployment density on the same hardware, significantly reducing cost.

Quarkus is a Java runtime that takes a fresh look at the needs of the modern Java microservice developer. It is designed to be as productive as Node.js for developers and consume as few resources as Golang. To many developers, Quarkus feels both new and familiar at the same time. It includes a lot of new, impactful features while supporting the APIs that developers are already familiar with.

When developing microservices, runtimes often do not consider the target environment. Most runtimes are deployment-environment agnostic to be broadly relevant. Although Quarkus is used in a wide variety of deployment environments, it has specific enhancements and optimizations for Linux containers and Kubernetes. For this reason, Quarkus is referred to as *Kubernetes-native Java.*

1.3.1   *Developer joy*

Developer joy is a top priority for Quarkus. Developers are rightfully enamored with the productivity of dynamic language runtimes like Node.js, and Quarkus is driving to deliver that experience, even though Java is a "static" (precompiled) language.

The top developer joy feature is live coding, where code changes are detected, recompiled, and reloaded without having to restart the JVM. Live coding is enabled when Quarkus is started in developer mode using `mvn quarkus:dev`. Specifically, Quarkus checks for code changes when it receives external events like HTTP requests or Kafka messages. The developer simply makes code changes, saves the file, and refreshes the browser for near-instant updates. Live coding even works with pom.xml changes. The Quarkus Maven plugin will detect pom.xml changes and restart the JVM. It is not uncommon for Quarkus developers to start Quarkus in developer mode and then minimize the terminal window, never having to restart the JVM during a coding session.

> **NOTE**   Quarkus supports both Maven and Gradle. This book references Maven commands and features, but equivalent capabilities are available with Gradle.

Another developer joy feature is a unified configuration. Quarkus supports APIs and concepts from multiple ecosystems like Java EE, Eclipse Vert.x, and even Spring. Each of these ecosystems defines its own collection of configuration files. Quarkus unifies configuration so that all configuration options can be specified in a single application .properties configuration file. Quarkus supports MicroProfile Config, an API specification that includes support for multiple configuration sources. Chapter 3, "Configuring microservices," discusses this in more detail.

Future chapters discuss additional developer joy features as they are used. For example, chapter 4, "Database access with Panache," discusses how to replace boilerplate database access code with a simplified data access API layered on the Java Persistence API (JPA) and Hibernate.

1.3.2 MicroProfile support

Quarkus is a Java runtime with a focus on developing microservices to run on Kubernetes. MicroProfile is a collection of Java specifications for developing microservices. Therefore, it is a natural fit for Quarkus to implement MicroProfile specifications to facilitate microservices development. Also, developers can rehost their existing MicroProfile applications on Quarkus for improved productivity and runtime efficiency. Quarkus is continually evolving to stay current with MicroProfile releases. At the time of this writing, Quarkus supports MicroProfile 4.0 as described in section 1.2, MicroProfile, and all standalone MicroProfile specifications. Besides CDI and MicroProfile Config, which are included in the Quarkus core, each MicroProfile specification is available as a Quarkus extension that can be included using Maven dependencies.

1.3.3 Runtime efficiency

Quarkus has become known for its fast startup time and low memory usage, earning its "Supersonic, Subatomic Java" marketing tagline. Quarkus can run applications on the JVM. It can also compile the application to a native binary using GraalVM Native Image (https://graalvm.org/). Table 1.3 compares Quarkus startup times with a traditional cloud-native Java stack, packaged and run as uber-JARs.

Table 1.3   Startup plus time to first HTTP response (seconds)

	Traditional cloud-native Java stack	Quarkus JVM	Quarkus native
REST application	4.3	.943	.016
CRUD application	9.5	2.03	.042

The REST application replies to HTTP REST requests, and the CRUD application creates, updates, and deletes data in a database. This table demonstrates that Quarkus can start significantly faster than traditional Java runtimes. Next, let's look at the memory usage, as shown in table 1.4.

Table 1.4   Memory usage (megabytes)

	Traditional cloud-native Java stack	Quarkus JVM	Quarkus native
REST application	136	73	12
CRUD application	209	145	28

Quarkus achieves compelling RAM and startup time improvements over traditional cloud-native Java runtimes. It achieves this by rethinking the problem. Traditional cloud-native Java runtimes do a lot of work when they boot. Each time an application boots, it scans configuration files, scans for annotations, and instantiates and binds annotations to build an internal metamodel before executing application logic.

Quarkus, on the other hand, executes these steps during compilation and records the results as bytecode that executes at application startup. In other words, Quarkus executes application logic immediately upon startup. The result is rapid startup time and lower memory utilization.

1.4   Kubernetes

During the 2000s, virtual machines were the go-to platform for hosting Java application servers, which in turn often hosted dozens of monolithic applications. This was sufficient until the adoption of microservices within the enterprise, which caused an explosion in the number of application instances to hundreds, thousands, and up to tens of thousands for large organizations. Virtual machines use too many compute and management resources at this scale. For example, a virtual machine contains an entire operating system image, consuming more RAM and CPU resources than needed by the microservice, and must be tuned, patched, and upgraded. This was typically managed by a team of administrators, leaving little flexibility to developers.

These limitations led to the popularity of Linux containers, in part due to their balanced approach to virtualization. Containers, like virtual machine images, include the capability of packaging an entire application stack in container images. These images can be run on any number of hosts and instantiated any number of times to achieve horizontal scalability for service reliability and performance. Linux containers are significantly more efficient than virtual machines because all containers running on the same host share the same Linux operating system kernel.

Although containers offer efficient execution of microservices, managing hundreds to thousands of container instances and ensuring proper distribution across container hosts to ensure scalability and availability is difficult without help from an orchestration platform for containers. Kubernetes has become that platform, and it is available from popular cloud providers and can also be installed locally within a datacenter.

This also redraws the boundary between developers and those who manage the Kubernetes clusters. Developers are no longer required to utilize the Java version, application server version, or even the same runtime that had been dictated to them in the past. Developers now have the freedom to choose their own stack, as long as it can be containerized.

1.4.1   Introduction to Kubernetes

Kubernetes is a container orchestration platform that offers automated container deployment, scaling, and management. It originated at Google in various forms as a means to run internal workloads, was publicly announced in mid-2014, and version 1.0 was released mid-2015. Coinciding with the 1.0 release, Google worked with the Linux Foundation to form the Cloud Native Computing Foundation (CNCF), with

Kubernetes being its first project. Today, Kubernetes has more than 100 contributing organizations and well over 500 individual contributors. With such large, varied, and active contributions, Kubernetes has become the de facto standard enterprise container orchestration platform. It is quite broad in functionality, so we'll focus on the underlying Kubernetes features and concepts that are most relevant when developing and deploying a microservice.

Kubernetes was not available before 2015, so early microservice deployments had to not only manage microservices but also manage infrastructure services to support a microservices infrastructure. Kubernetes offers some of these infrastructure services out of the box, making Kubernetes a compelling microservices platform. Although we are focusing on Java microservices, the following built-in features are runtime agnostic:

- *Service discovery*—Services deployed to Kubernetes are given a stable DNS name and IP address. For a microservice to consume another microservice, it only has to locate the service by a DNS name. Unlike early microservice deployments, Kubernetes does not need a third-party service registry to act as an intermediary to locate a service.
- *Horizontal scaling*—Applications can be scaled out and scaled in manually or automatically based on metrics like CPU usage.
- *Load balancing*—Kubernetes load-balances across application instances. This removes the need for client-side load balancing that became popular during the early days of microservices.
- *Self-healing*—Kubernetes restarts failing containers and directs traffic away from containers that are temporarily unable to serve traffic.
- *Configuration management*—Kubernetes can store and manage microservice configuration. Configurations can change without updating the application, removing the need for external configuration services used by early microservice deployments.

The Kubernetes architecture enables these features and is outlined next in figure 1.5, illustrating this summary of each architectural component:

- *Cluster*—A Kubernetes cluster abstracts hardware or virtual servers (nodes) and presents them as a pool of resources. A cluster consists of one or more administration ("master") servers used to manage the cluster and any number of worker nodes used to run workloads (pods). The administration server exposes an API server used by administration tools, like `kubectl`, to interact with the cluster. When a workload (pod) is deployed to the cluster, the scheduler schedules the pod to execute on a node within the cluster.
- *Namespace*—A means to divide cluster resources between projects or teams. A namespace can span multiple nodes in a cluster, so the diagram is a bit oversimplified for readability. Names defined within a namespace must be unique but can be reused across namespaces.

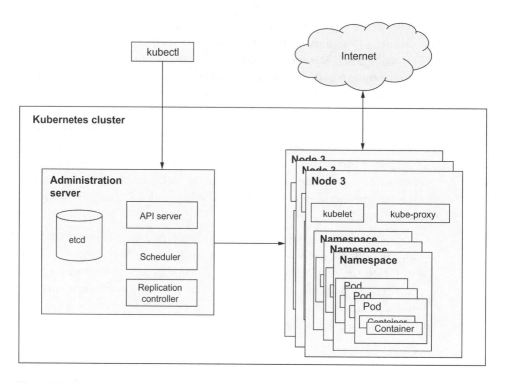

Figure 1.5   Kubernetes architecture

- *Pod*—A pod is one or more containers that share the same storage volumes, network, namespace, and life cycle. Pods are atomic units, so deploying a pod deploys all containers within that pod to the same node. For example, a microservice may use a local out-of-process cache service. It may make sense to place the microservice and the caching service in the same pod if they are tightly coupled. This ensures they are deployed to the same node and have the same life cycle. The pods in the exercises consist of one container per pod, so it will "feel" as if a pod is the same thing as a container, but that is not the case. A pod is ephemeral, meaning a pod's state is not maintained between destruction and any subsequent creation.
- *Replication controller*—Ensures the number of running pods matches the specified number of replicas. Specifying more than one replica improves availability and service throughput. If a pod is killed, then the replication controller will instantiate a new one to replace it. A replication controller can also conduct a rolling upgrade when a new container image version is specified.
- *Deployment*—A deployment is a higher-level abstraction that describes the state of a deployed application. For example, a deployment can specify the container image to be deployed, the number of replicas for that container image, health check probes used to check pod health, and more.

- *Service*—A stable endpoint used to access a group of like pods that brings stability to a highly dynamic environment.

  Microservices are deployed within pods, and pods come and go, each with their own IP address. This is reflected in figure 1.6. For example, the replication controller scales the number of pods, either up or down, to meet the specified number of replicas (running pods). The Accounts Payable service has three replicas. The pod at IP address 172.17.0.4 is failing and needs to be replaced with a new pod. The pod at IP address 172.17.0.5 is running and receiving traffic. The pod at IP address 172.17.0.6 is starting and will be able to serve traffic once booted. This example shows quite a bit of instability with pods, each with its own IP address, failing and starting. Any service, such as the Frontend Web UI microservice described earlier, needs a stable IP address to connect to. A service creates a single IP address and a DNS name within the cluster so other microservices can access the service in a consistent manner, and requests are proxied to one of the replicas.

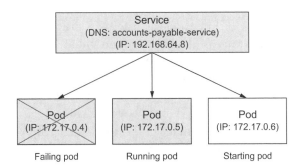

Failing pod   Running pod   Starting pod   **Figure 1.6   Kubernetes service**

- *ConfigMap*—Used to store microservice configuration, separating configuration from the microservice itself. ConfigMaps are clear text. As an option, a Kubernetes Secret can be used to store confidential information.

With the exception of the cluster, each of these concepts is represented by a Kubernetes object. Kubernetes objects are persistent entities that collectively represent the *current* state of the cluster. We can manipulate the cluster by creating, manipulating, and deleting Kubernetes objects. By manipulating the state, we are defining what we want the *desired* state to be. We manipulate objects by invoking APIs on the Kubernetes API server running on an administration server. The three most popular means of invoking the API server is by using a web UI such as the Kubernetes Dashboard, by using the `kubectl` CLI to directly manipulate state, or by defining the state in YAML and applying the desired state with `kubectl apply`.

Once a desired state is defined, a Kubernetes cluster updates its *current* state to match the *desired* state. This is done by using the *controller pattern*. Controllers monitor the state of the cluster, and when a controller is notified of a state change, it reacts to that change by updating the *current* state to match the *desired* state. For example, if a replication controller sees a change to a `ReplicationController` object from a current state of three replicas to a desired state of two replicas, the replication controller will kill one of the pods.

Defining Kubernetes objects using YAML and applying object state with `kubectl` is very popular among administrators, but not all Java developers have embraced YAML. Luckily, we can avoid YAML by using the Quarkus Kubernetes extension that lets us define the desired state using a property file. When building the application, the Kubernetes deployment YAML is generated automatically. The YAML can be applied automatically as a part of the Quarkus build process, or it can be applied manually using `kubectl`.

1.5   *Kubernetes-native microservices*

What does it mean to develop Kubernetes-native microservices? It's developing a microservice with the understanding that Kubernetes is the underlying deployment platform and is facilitated by having a Kubernetes runtime like Quarkus. How is this different from any other microservice, or the frequently mentioned "cloud-native Java"? Some differentiating characteristics follow:

- *Low memory consumption*—A Kubernetes cluster is a shared infrastructure, and organizations want to extract as much value out of their Kubernetes investment by consolidating as many services across as many departments on a Kubernetes cluster as possible. Reduced memory consumption is a gating factor. Until runtimes like Quarkus, organizations were considering leaving Java runtimes for Node.js or Golang to better utilize their Kubernetes clusters.

- *Fast startup*—Kubernetes can automatically create new microservice instances to meet demand. Without fast startup, existing instances can become overloaded and fail before new instances come online, impacting overall application stability. This potential complication can also impact rolling upgrades when a new version of a service is incrementally deployed to replace an existing one.

- *Minimize operating system threads*—A Kubernetes node may be running hundreds of microservice instances, each of which may have up to hundreds of threads. It is not uncommon for a thread to consume a megabyte of memory. In addition, the operating system scheduler works increasingly harder as the number of threads increases. Quarkus runs its asynchronous, reactive, and (by default) traditional thread-blocking imperative APIs on an event loop, which significantly reduces the number of threads.

- *Consume Kubernetes ConfigMaps*—Services deployed to Kubernetes can be configured using a Kubernetes ConfigMap. A ConfigMap is a file that is typically mounted to a pod filesystem. However, Quarkus can seamlessly use the Kubernetes client API to access a ConfigMap without mounting the filesystem in the pod, simplifying configuration.

- *Expose health endpoints*—A service should always expose its health so Kubernetes can restart an unhealthy service or redirect traffic away from a pod that is temporarily unavailable. In addition to supporting custom health checks, Quarkus has built-in data source and messaging client (ActiveMQ and Kafka) readiness health checks to automatically pause traffic when those backend services are unavailable.

- *Support CNCF projects*—CNCF is the Cloud-Native Computing Foundation, which is responsible for the evolution of Kubernetes and related projects like Prometheus monitoring (using the OpenMetrics format) and Jaeger (using OpenTracing/OpenTelemetry).
- *Inherent Kubernetes deployment support*—Quarkus has built-in support for deploying to Kubernetes. It enables a developer to compile, package, and deploy a microservice to Kubernetes using a one-line Maven (or Gradle) command. In addition, Quarkus requires no Kubernetes YAML expertise. Kubernetes YAML is generated automatically and can be customized using Java properties.
- *Kubernetes client API*—Quarkus includes a Java-friendly API for interacting with a Kubernetes cluster, enabling programmatic access to any Kubernetes capability to extend or tailor it for enterprises needs.

Summary

- A microservice models and implements a subset of business functionality called a bounded context.
- A microservices architecture is a collection of evolving, collaborating microservices.
- MicroProfile is a collection of microservice specifications that facilitate the creation of portable microservices across multiple implementations.
- Microservices have evolved from running in a shared environment, like an application server, to running on a single-application stack.
- Kubernetes has replaced the application server as the shared application environment.
- Quarkus is a Java single-application stack that can efficiently run MicroProfile applications on Kubernetes.

Your first Quarkus application

This chapter covers

- Creating a Quarkus project
- Developing with Quarkus live coding
- Writing tests for a Quarkus microservice
- Deploying and running a microservice to Kubernetes

Throughout the book we will use the domain of banking to create microservice examples, highlighting key concepts from each chapter. The example will be an Account service. The purpose of the Account service is to manage bank accounts, holding information like customer name, balance, and overdraft status. In developing the Account service, the chapter will cover the ways to create Quarkus projects, developing with *live coding* for real-time feedback, writing tests, building native executables for an application, how to package an application for Kubernetes, and how to deploy to Kubernetes.

There's a lot to cover; let's dive into creating the Account service!

2.1 *Creating a project*

We can create a microservice using Quarkus in the following ways:

1 With the project generator at https://code.quarkus.io/
2 In a terminal with the Quarkus Maven plugin
3 By manually creating the project and including the Quarkus dependencies and plugin configuration

Of these options, option 3 is the more complicated and prone to errors, so we won't cover it in this book.

NOTE Examples work with JDK 11 and Maven 3.8.1+.

Option 2 would use a command such as the following:

```
mvn io.quarkus:quarkus-maven-plugin:2.1.3.Final:create \
    -DprojectGroupId=quarkus \
    -DprojectArtifactId=account-service \
    -DclassName="quarkus.accounts.AccountResource" \
    -Dpath="/accounts"
```

For the Account service, we will use option 1, using the project generator at https://code.quarkus.io/.

Figure 2.1 is a view of the Quarkus project generator, at the time the screenshot was taken. The top left of the page contains fields for customizing project information, such as the group and artifact ids, and the build tool for the project.

The bottom of the page shows all the possible extensions that can be selected for the application.

TIP The Quarkus project generator lists hundreds of extensions. Use the search box to filter the list of available extensions to more quickly locate a particular set of extensions.

Select the RESTEasy JAX-RS extension, and leave Starter Code set to Yes.

Figure 2.2 shows all the changes we've made to the generator for the Account service. The group has been set to quarkus, the artifact to account-service, and the RESTEasy JAX-RS extension selected. Also notice the number next to Generate Your Application. The number shows how many extensions are selected, and hovering over the rocket displays a pop-up with them listed.

Once the changes have been made, hover over the arrow next to Generate Your Application, as seen in figure 2.3.

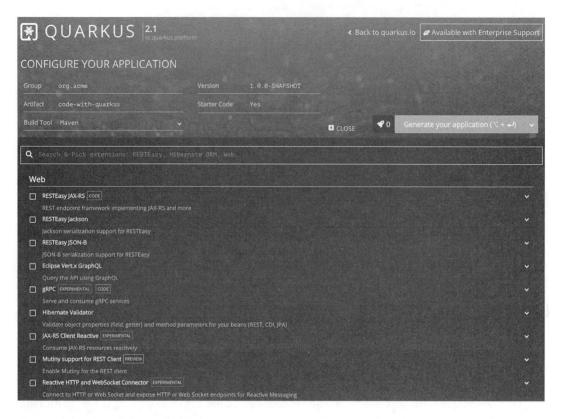

Figure 2.1   Quarkus project generator

Figure 2.2   Quarkus project generator: selected extension

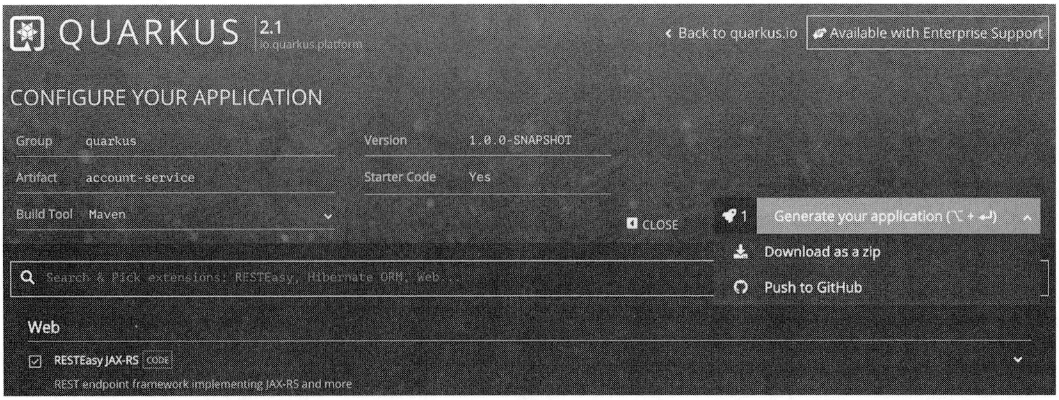

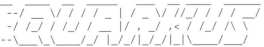

Figure 2.3 Quarkus project generator: generate application

Figure 2.3 highlights the following options we have for generating the project:

- Download as a Zip
- Push to GitHub

Select Download as a Zip, and a zip file containing the project source will be created and downloaded.

Once the zip file has downloaded, extract the contents into a directory. We explain the generated contents shortly, but first open a terminal window and change into the directory where the zip file was extracted. In that directory, run the following command:

```
mvn quarkus:dev
```

Maven artifacts and their dependencies must be downloaded the first time a particular version of Quarkus is used, as shown in listing 2.1.

Listing 2.1 contains the console output when Quarkus starts the project. The output includes the version used, in this case 2.1.3.Final, and installed features include cdi and resteasy.

Listing 2.1 Quarkus startup

```
__  ____  __  _____   ___  __ ____  _____ 
 --/ __ \/ / / / _ | / _ \/ //_/ / / / __/
 -/ /_/ / /_/ / __ |/ , _/ ,< / /_/ /\ \  
--_____/_/ |_/_/|_/_/|_|\____/___/  
INFO  [io.quarkus] (Quarkus Main Thread) account-service 1.0.0-SNAPSHOT on
JVM (powered by Quarkus 2.1.3.Final) started in 1.653s. Listening on:
     http://localhost:8080
INFO  [io.quarkus] (Quarkus Main Thread) Profile dev activated. Live Coding
activated.
```

```
INFO  [io.quarkus] (Quarkus Main Thread) Installed features: [cdi, resteasy,
smallrye-context-propagation]
```

Once started, the application can be accessed at http://localhost:8080, as shown in figure 2.4.

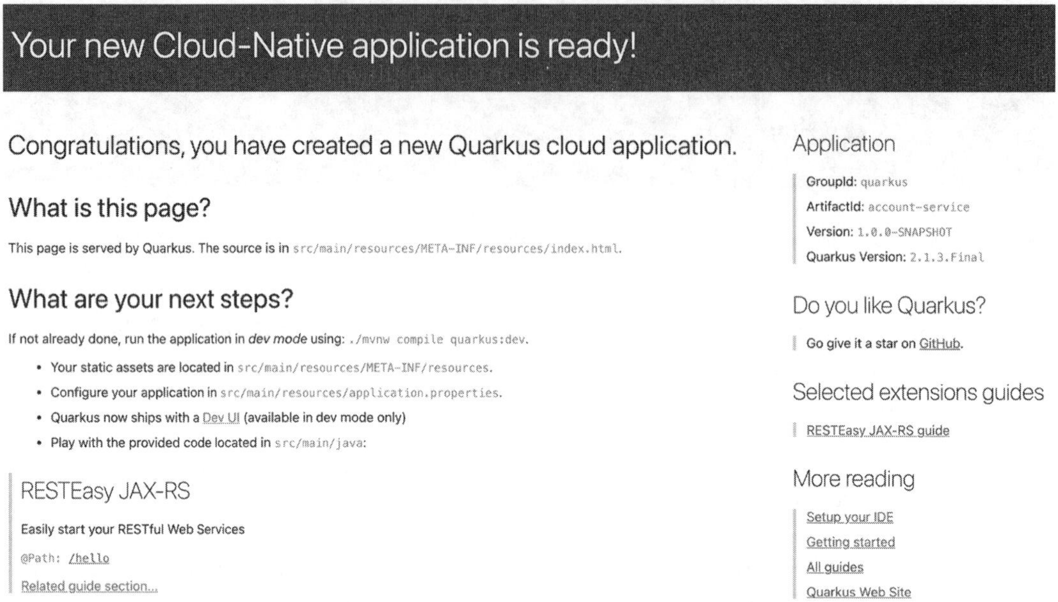

Your new Cloud-Native application is ready!

Congratulations, you have created a new Quarkus cloud application.

What is this page?

This page is served by Quarkus. The source is in `src/main/resources/META-INF/resources/index.html`.

What are your next steps?

If not already done, run the application in *dev mode* using: `./mvnw compile quarkus:dev`.

- Your static assets are located in `src/main/resources/META-INF/resources`.
- Configure your application in `src/main/resources/application.properties`.
- Quarkus now ships with a Dev UI (available in dev mode only)
- Play with the provided code located in `src/main/java`:

RESTEasy JAX-RS

Easily start your RESTful Web Services

`@Path: /hello`

Related guide section...

Application

GroupId: `quarkus`
ArtifactId: `account-service`
Version: `1.0.0-SNAPSHOT`
Quarkus Version: `2.1.3.Final`

Do you like Quarkus?

Go give it a star on GitHub.

Selected extensions guides

RESTEasy JAX-RS guide

More reading

Setup your IDE
Getting started
All guides
Quarkus Web Site

Figure 2.4   Quarkus default index page

The default page of the generated application provides some pointers on what can be done next for creating REST endpoints, servlets, and static assets.

In addition to the default index page, open http://localhost:8080/hello to be greeted by the generated JAX-RS resource. With the generated application running, take a look through what the project includes from the generation process as shown in figure 2.5. Open up the project in an editor or whatever tool might be preferred.

The project root contains the build file, in this case pom.xml, a README.md with information on how to run the project, and Maven wrappers for those who may not have Maven installed already.

Looking in src/main, we see directories for Docker files, Java source files, and other resources. In the docker directory are Dockerfiles for the JVM, native executable, native executable with a distroless base image, and legacy-jar format. Native executables will be discussed in "Creating a native executable," section 2.4.

Figure 2.5   Quarkus-generated project structure

Each of the Docker files uses the Red Hat Universal Base Image (UBI) as their base. Full details on the image content can be found here: http://mng.bz/J6WQ.

Within the Java source directory, src/main/java, is the quarkus package. Inside the package is the GreetingResource class, containing a JAX-RS resource endpoint, as shown in the next listing.

Listing 2.2   GreetingResource

```
@Path("/hello")
public class GreetingResource {

    @GET
    @Produces(MediaType.TEXT_PLAIN)
    public String hello() {
        return "Hello RESTEasy";
    }
}
```

◁ Defines the JAX-RS resource to respond at /hello-resteasy

◁ The method responds to an HTTP GET request.

◁ Responds to the browser to set the content type to TEXT_PLAIN

◁ Returns "Hello RESTEasy" as the HTTP GET response

Take a look at the next directory, src/main/resources. The first file is application.properties. This is where any configuration packaged within the application should be placed. Configurations can also reside outside the application, but these are restricted to aspects we can configure at runtime.

> **NOTE** We discuss the different types of configuration in chapter 3, including the ability to use application.yaml instead of a properties file.

Currently, there is no configuration in application.properties, but we will add that soon.

Also in src/main/resources is the META-INF/resources directory. Any static assets for the application should be placed in this directory. Inside the directory is the static index.html that created the page seen in figure 2.4.

Moving on from what was generated in src/main/, next is src/test. Here there are two classes, GreetingResourceTest and NativeGreetingResourceIT. The first uses @QuarkusTest to run a unit test on the JVM, verifying the endpoint returns hello as expected, as shown in the next listing.

Listing 2.3 GreetingResourceTest

```
@QuarkusTest                                    ◁────    Tells JUnit to use the Quarkus
public class GreetingResourceTest {                      extension, which starts the
    @Test                                ◁──              application for the test
    public void testHelloEndpoint() {
        given()
          .when().get("/hello")          ◁──      A regular JUnit test
          .then()                                 method marker
            .statusCode(200)
            .body(is("Hello RESTEasy"));  ◁──     Uses RestAssured
    }                                             to access the /hello-
}                 Verifies the response had a body    resteasy URL
                  that contained Hello RESTEasy
```

NativeGreetingResourceIT runs the same tests, but with the native executable of the application, as shown next.

Listing 2.4 NativeGreetingResourceIT

```
@NativeImageTest                              ◁────    Tells JUnit to use
public class NativeGreetingResourceIT                  the Quarkus-native
    extends GreetingResourceTest {        ◁──          executable extension
    // Execute the same tests but in native mode.
}
                  Extends from the JUnit
                  unit tests to reuse them
```

> **NOTE** It's not required to run the same set of tests with a native executable and the JVM. However, it is a convenient means of testing on the JVM and a native executable with a single set of common tests.

Having looked through what the project generator creates, all Java source files—and the index.html file—can be deleted. Don't modify the Dockerfiles, application.properties, or Java packages for now.

2.2 Developing with live coding

With a blank application, it's time to develop the Account service. For developing the service, we use the live coding functionality of Quarkus.

Using live coding enables us to update Java source, resources, and configuration of a running application. All changes are reflected in the running application automatically, enabling developers to improve the turnaround time when developing a new application.

Live coding enables hot deployment via background compilation. Any changes to the Java source, or resources, will be reflected as soon as the application receives a new request from the browser. Refreshing the browser or issuing a new browser request triggers a scan of the project for any changes to then recompile and redeploy the application. If any issues arise with compilation or deployment, an error page provides details of the problem.

To begin, create a minimal JAX-RS resource as shown here.

Listing 2.5 AccountResource

```
@Path("/accounts")
public class AccountResource {
}
```

There's not much there right now, just a JAX-RS resource that defines a URL path of /accounts. There are no methods to respond to any requests, but restart live coding if it had been stopped as follows:

```
mvn quarkus:dev
```

> **TIP** Live coding handles the deletion and creation of new files without issue while it's still running.

In the terminal window, output similar to the following appears.

Listing 2.6 Account service startup

```
Listening for transport dt_socket at address: 5005

__  ____  __  _____   ___  __ ____  _____
--/ __ \/ / / / _ | / _ \/ //_/ / / / __/
-/ /_/ / /_/ / __ |/ , _/ ,< / /_/ /\ \
--_____/_/ |_/_/|_/_/|_|\____/___/
INFO  [io.quarkus] (Quarkus Main Thread) chapter2-account-service
1.0.0-SNAPSHOT on JVM (powered by Quarkus 2.1.3.Final) started in 1.474s.
Listening on: http://localhost:8080
INFO  [io.quarkus] (Quarkus Main Thread) Profile dev activated. Live Coding
activated.
INFO  [io.quarkus] (Quarkus Main Thread) Installed features: [cdi, resteasy,
smallrye-context-propagation]
```

Notice the first line indicates that a debugger has been started on port 5005. This is an added benefit to using live coding—Quarkus opens the default debug port for the application.

Figure 2.6 shows the result of opening a browser to http://localhost:8080.

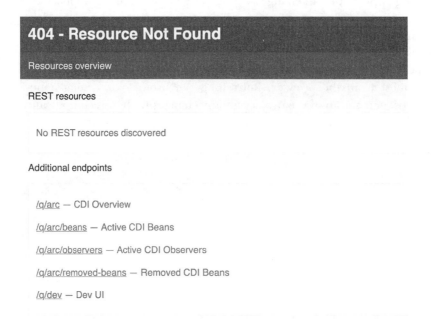

Figure 2.6   Account service no resources

Don't be concerned with the error: it makes sense because the JAX-RS resource defined a URL path and no methods to process HTTP requests. If we access http://localhost:8080/accounts, the same error message is in the browser.

Notice some additional endpoints are available, even without application code. These endpoints are provided by the installed extensions of the application. Most of the endpoints are related to Arc, the CDI container for Quarkus, which provides information about CDI Beans and CDI in general.

The last endpoint for Dev UI contains extension-specific behavior, such as editing configuration, and links to the guides for each installed extension. The Dev UI for the application can be seen in figure 2.7.

Now it's time to start developing some code. While live coding is still running, create the Account POJO to represent a bank account in the system, as shown in listing 2.7.

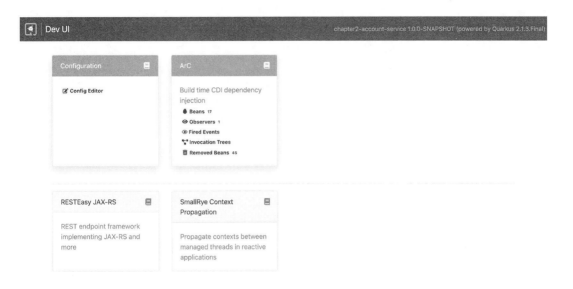

Figure 2.7 Quarkus Dev UI

Listing 2.7 Account

```java
public class Account {
  public Long accountNumber;
  public Long customerNumber;
  public String customerName;
  public BigDecimal balance;
  public AccountStatus accountStatus = AccountStatus.OPEN;

  public Account() {
  }

  public Account(Long accountNumber, Long customerNumber, String
      customerName, BigDecimal balance) {
    this.accountNumber = accountNumber;
    this.customerNumber = customerNumber;
    this.customerName = customerName;
    this.balance = balance;
  }

  public void markOverdrawn() {
    accountStatus = AccountStatus.OVERDRAWN;
  }
}
```

```
public void removeOverdrawnStatus() {
  accountStatus = AccountStatus.OPEN;
}

public void close() {
  accountStatus = AccountStatus.CLOSED;
  balance = BigDecimal.valueOf(0);
}

public void withdrawFunds(BigDecimal amount) {
  balance = balance.subtract(amount);
}

public void addFunds(BigDecimal amount) {
  balance = balance.add(amount);
}

public BigDecimal getBalance() {
  return balance;
}

public Long getAccountNumber() {
  return accountNumber;
}

public String getCustomerName() {
  return customerName;
}

public AccountStatus getAccountStatus() {
  return accountStatus;
}
}
```

Account has some fields to hold data about the account: account number, customer number, customer name, balance, and account status. It has a constructor that takes values to populate the fields, except for the account status because that defaults to OPEN. After are methods for setting and clearing the overdrawn status, closing the account, adding and withdrawing account funds, and, lastly, some getters for balance, account number, and customer name.

Not a lot to it, but it's a foundation to build from. Right now it won't compile, because AccountStatus needs to be created, as shown in the next code listing.

Listing 2.8   AccountStatus

```
public enum AccountStatus {
  OPEN,
  CLOSED,
  OVERDRAWN
}
```

There's nothing there yet, but open up http://localhost:8080/accounts to show the error page. With live coding running, open pom.xml and change the quarkus-resteasy dependency to quarkus-resteasy-jsonb. Doing this adds support for returning JSON objects in the endpoints.

> **NOTE** Instead of quarkus-resteasy-jsonb, quarkus-resteasy-jackson could also be used.

> **IMPORTANT** Modifying dependencies in pom.xml can be done with live coding, but the delay before restarting is complete is longer if new dependencies need to be downloaded.

To begin creating the Account service, open up AccountResource and add the following code.

> **Listing 2.9** `AccountResource`

```
@Path("/accounts")
public class AccountResource {
  @GET
  @Produces(MediaType.APPLICATION_JSON)        ← Indicates the response is converted to JSON
  public Set<Account> allAccounts() {          ← Returns a Set of Account objects
    return Collections.emptySet();
  }
}
```

To add some data, add the code snippet shown in the next listing to AccountResource.

> **Listing 2.10** `AccountResource`

```
@Path("/accounts")
public class AccountResource {
  Set<Account> accounts = new HashSet<>();      ← Creates a Set of Account objects to hold the state

  @PostConstruct                                ← @PostConstruct indicates the method should be called straight after creation of the CDI Bean.
  public void setup() {
    accounts.add(new Account(123456789L, 987654321L, "George Baird", new
      BigDecimal("354.23")));
    accounts.add(new Account(121212121L, 888777666L, "Mary Taylor", new
      BigDecimal("560.03")));
    accounts.add(new Account(545454545L, 222444999L, "Diana Rigg", new
      BigDecimal("422.00")));
  }
  ...
}
```

setup() prepopulates some data into the list of accounts.

> **NOTE** Though the JAX-RS resource does not specify a CDI Scope annotation, Quarkus defaults JAX-RS resources to @Singleton. The JAX-RS resource can utilize whatever is the preferred CDI Scope: @Singleton, @Application-Scoped, or @RequestScoped.

Right now allAccounts() returns an empty Set. Change it to return the accounts field, as shown next.

Listing 2.11   AccountResource

```
@Path("/accounts")
public class AccountResource {
  ...
  @GET
  @Produces(MediaType.APPLICATION_JSON)
  public Set<Account> allAccounts() {
    return accounts;
  }
  ...
}
```

Refresh the browser window open to http://localhost:8080/accounts, as shown in figure 2.8. The page has reloaded to show all the accounts that are stored in the service.

```
[
  {
      "accountNumber": 121212121,
      "customerNumber": 888777666,
      "customerName": "Mary Taylor",
      "balance": 560.03,
      "accountStatus": "OPEN"
  },
  {
      "accountNumber": 123456789,
      "customerNumber": 987654321,
      "customerName": "George Baird",
      "balance": 354.23,
      "accountStatus": "OPEN"
  },
  {
      "accountNumber": 545454545,
      "customerNumber": 222444999,
      "customerName": "Diana Rigg",
      "balance": 422,
      "accountStatus": "OPEN"
  }
]
```

Figure 2.8   Account service: all accounts

NOTE   Figure 2.8 uses the JSON Formatter extension for Chrome to format the JSON response. Such an extension provides a better means of viewing the structure of the JSON document.

Listing 2.12 creates a method for retrieving a single Account instance.

Listing 2.12 AccountResource

```
@Path("/accounts")
public class AccountResource {
    ...
    @GET
    @Path("/{accountNumber}")
    @Produces(MediaType.APPLICATION_JSON)
    public Account getAccount(@PathParam("accountNumber") Long accountNumber) {
        Optional<Account> response = accounts.stream()
            .filter(acct -> acct.getAccountNumber().equals(accountNumber))
            .findFirst();

        return response.orElseThrow(()
            -> new NotFoundException("Account with id of " + accountNumber + "
        does not exist."));
    }
    ...
}
```

Defines the name of the parameter on the URL path

@PathParam maps the accountNumber URL parameter into the accountNumber method parameter.

Returns a NotFoundException if no matching account is present

Streams the accounts, filters by accountNumber, and finds the first account, if there is one

With these changes, open http://localhost:8080/accounts/121212121 in a browser to see the account details in a JSON document.

Quarkus has a nice feature with live coding for showing available URLs when accessing a URL that doesn't exist. This feature isn't present when running the application with java -jar. Open http://localhost:8080/accounts/5 in a browser. The error page is shown in figure 2.9.

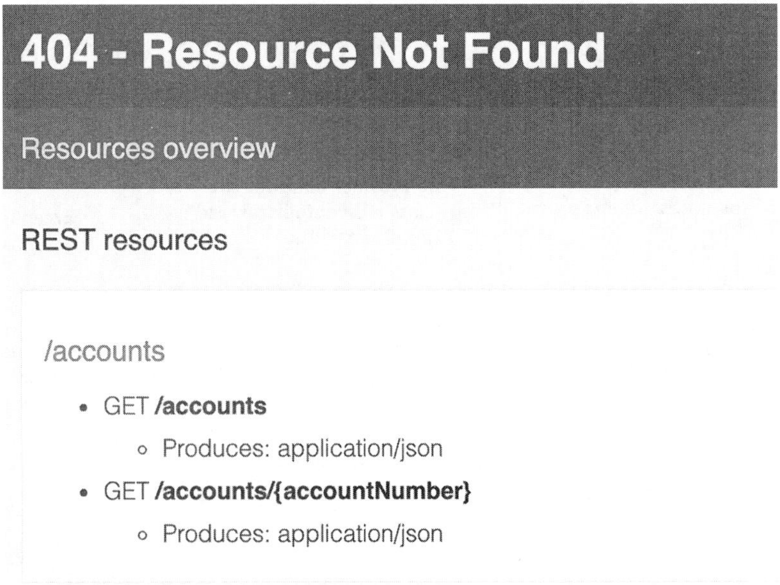

404 - Resource Not Found

Resources overview

REST resources

/accounts

- GET **/accounts**
  - Produces: application/json
- GET **/accounts/{accountNumber}**
  - Produces: application/json

Figure 2.9 Quarkus error page

Not finding an account number, the response is an HTTP 404, but the page offers useful information about what endpoints are available. In this case, there is the main /accounts/ URL path, and the two URL paths within it that have been created.

Because the endpoint we accessed was valid, but the requested record was not found, there is a nicer 404 response that we can create to provide more details. Instead of `getAccount()` throwing a `NotFoundException` when no record is found, change it to `WebApplicationException` and pass `404` as the response code, as shown in the next listing.

Listing 2.13   `AccountResource.getAccount()`

```
return response.orElseThrow(()
    -> new WebApplicationException("Account with id of " + accountNumber + "
    does not exist.", 404));
```

To convert the exception into a meaningful response, create a JAX-RS exception mapper in `AccountResource`, as shown in listing 2.10 and in figure 2.10.

```
{
    "exceptionType": "javax.ws.rs.WebApplicationException",
    "code": 404,
    "error": "Account with id of 5 does not exist."
}
```

Figure 2.10   Account not found

Listing 2.14   `AccountResource`

```
@Path("/accounts")
public class AccountResource {            @Provider indicates the              Implements
    ...                                   class is an autodiscovered       ExceptionMapper for
    @Provider                ◁            JAX-RS Provider                   all Exception types
    public static class ErrorMapper implements ExceptionMapper<Exception> {   ◁

        @Override                                                  Overrides the toResponse
        public Response toResponse(Exception exception) {   ◁      method for converting the
                                                                   exception to a Response
            int code = 500;
            if (exception instanceof WebApplicationException) {   ◁
                code = ((WebApplicationException)
            exception).getResponse().getAccountStatus();
            }
                                             Checks for WebApplicationException,
                                             and extracts the HTTP status code;
                                             otherwise defaults to 500
```

```
          JsonObjectBuilder entityBuilder = Json.createObjectBuilder()
              .add("exceptionType", exception.getClass().getName())
              .add("code", code);

          if (exception.getMessage() != null) {
            entityBuilder.add("error", exception.getMessage());
          }

          return Response.status(code)
              .entity(entityBuilder.build())
              .build();
        }
      }
    }
```

If there is a message, adds it to the JSON object →

Uses builder to construct JSON-formatted data containing exception type and HTTP status code

Returns a Response with the HTTP status code and JSON object

As an exercise for the reader, add methods to AccountResource for creating accounts, withdrawing funds, depositing funds, and deleting accounts. The full code for AccountResource is in /chapter2/account-service.

2.3 Writing a test

The Account service has methods for the following tasks:

- Retrieving all accounts
- Retrieving a single account
- Creating a new account
- Updating an account
- Deleting an account

However, no verification exists that what has been coded actually works. Only retrieving all accounts and retrieving a single account have been verified, by accessing specific URLs from a browser to trigger HTTP GET requests. Even with manual verification, any additional changes that might be made are not verified, unless manual verification follows every change.

It's important to ensure the developed code has been tested and verified appropriately against expected outcomes. For that, we must add, at a minimum, some level of tests for the code.

Quarkus supports running JUnit 5 tests with the addition of @QuarkusTest onto a test class. @QuarkusTest informs JUnit 5 of the extension to use during the test. The extension performs the necessary augmentation of the service being tested, equivalent to what happens during compilation with the Quarkus Maven or Gradle plugin. Prior to running the tests, the extension starts the constructed Quarkus service, just as if it was constructed with any build tool.

To begin adding tests to the Account service, add the following dependencies in the pom.xml:

```
<dependency>
    <groupId>io.quarkus</groupId>
```

```
        <artifactId>quarkus-junit5</artifactId>
        <scope>test</scope>
    </dependency>
    <dependency>
        <groupId>io.rest-assured</groupId>
        <artifactId>rest-assured</artifactId>
        <scope>test</scope>
    </dependency>
```

If we generate the project from https://code.quarkus.io, the Account service already includes the testing dependencies.

> **NOTE**   rest-assured is not a required dependency for testing, but it offers a convenient means of testing HTTP endpoints. It would be possible to use different testing libraries for the same purpose, but the examples that follow all use rest-assured. In addition, using rest-assured has a dependency on Hamcrest for asserting and matching test data.

The project generator also sets up the Maven Surefire plugin for testing, as shown next:

```
<plugin>
    <artifactId>maven-surefire-plugin</artifactId>
    <version>${surefire-plugin.version}</version>        ⊲──┐   Sets to a version of the
    <configuration>                                              Surefire plugin that works
        <systemPropertyVariables>                                with JUnit 5. A minimum of
            <java.util.logging.manager>org.jboss.logmanager.LogManager</java.util   3.0.0-M5 is required.
            .logging.manager>                ⊲──┐   Sets a system property
        </systemPropertyVariables>                to ensure the tests use
    </configuration>                              the correct log manager
</plugin>
```

A test case to verify retrieving all accounts returns the expected result, as shown in the next listing.

Listing 2.15   AccountResourceTest

```
@QuarkusTest
public class AccountResourceTest {              Declares the method
    @Test                              ⊲────    as a test method
    void testRetrieveAll() {           ⊲────    With JUnit 5, test methods
        Response result =                        don't need to be public.
            given()
               .when().get("/accounts")    ⊲────    Issues an HTTP GET
               .then()                               request to /accounts URL
  Verifies the    ⊢─▷ .statusCode(200)
  response had        .body(                            Verifies the body contains
  a 200 status            containsString("George Baird"),   ⊲──── all customer names
  code, meaning           containsString("Mary Taylor"),
  it returned             containsString("Diana Rigg")
  without problem      )
               .extract()             Extracts the
               .response();    ⊲────  response
```

```
    List<Account> accounts = result.jsonPath().getList("$");
    assertThat(accounts, not(empty()));
    assertThat(accounts, hasSize(3));
  }
}
```

> Extracts the JSON array and converts it to a list of Account objects

> Asserts the array of Account objects is not empty

> Asserts the array of Account objects has three items

One test method is not sufficient to ensure the prevention of future breakages. The next code snippet displays a test method for verifying the retrieval of a single `Account`.

Listing 2.16 `AccountResourceTest`

```
@Test
void testGetAccount() {
  Account account =
      given()
          .when().get("/accounts/{accountNumber}", 545454545)
          .then()
            .statusCode(200)
            .extract()
            .as(Account.class);

  assertThat(account.getAccountNumber(), equalTo(545454545L));
  assertThat(account.getCustomerName(), equalTo("Diana Rigg"));
  assertThat(account.getBalance(), equalTo(new BigDecimal("422.00")));
  assertThat(account.getAccountStatus(), equalTo(AccountStatus.OPEN));
}
```

> Passes the ID of the account to be retrieved as a URL path parameter

> Verifies the account response object with expected values

The tests written so far do not verify updating or adding data with the Account service; they only verify that existing data returns with the correct values. Next, add a test to verify that the creation of a new account succeeds.

Testing account creation covers multiple facets. In addition to verifying the creation of the new account, the test needs to ensure that the list of all accounts includes the new account. When including tests for mutating the state within a service, it becomes necessary to order the execution sequence of tests.

Why is it necessary to order the test execution? When there is a test to create, delete, or update the state within a service, it will impact any tests that read the state. For instance, in the earlier test to retrieve all accounts, listing 2.15, the expectation is it returns three accounts. However, when the test method execution order is nondeterministic, that is, not in a defined order, it's possible for the test creating an account to execute before listing 2.15, causing it to fail by finding four accounts.

To define the test method execution order, add `@TestMethodOrder(Order-Annotation.class)` to the test class definition, as shown in listing 2.17. Above or below `@QuarkusTest` is fine. `@Order(x)` is added to each test method, where x is a number to indicate where in the execution sequence of all tests is this particular test. `testRetrieveAll()` and `testGetAccount()` can either be `Order(1)` or `Order(2)`; they don't mutate data, so it does not matter.

Listing 2.17   AccountResourceTest

```
@Test
@Order(3)              ◄────┐       Defines the test execution order to
void testCreateAccount() {          be third, after the retrieve all and
    Account newAccount = new Account(324324L, 112244L, "Sandy Holmes", new
        BigDecimal("154.55"));      get account tests

    Account returnedAccount =                  Sets the content type to
        given()                                JSON for the HTTP POST
            .contentType(ContentType.JSON)  ◄──┐    Sets the new account object
            .body(newAccount)      ◄─────────────── into the body of the HTTP POST
            .when().post("/accounts")   ◄───────┐
            .then()                             Sends the HTTP POST
                .statusCode(201)    ◄───┐       request to /accounts URL
                .extract()
                .as(Account.class);         Verifies the HTTP status code returned is
                                            201, indicating it was created successfully

    assertThat(returnedAccount, notNullValue());      ◄─────┐   Asserts that the account
    assertThat(returnedAccount, equalTo(newAccount));        from the response was
                                                             not null and equals the
    Response result =                                        account we posted
        given()
            .when().get("/accounts")   ◄────────┐
            .then()                             Sends an HTTP GET
                .statusCode(200)                request to /accounts URL,
                .body(                          for retrieving all accounts
                    containsString("George Baird"),
                    containsString("Mary Taylor"),
                    containsString("Diana Rigg"),        Verifies the response
                    containsString("Sandy Holmes")  ◄─── contains the name of
                )                                        the customer on the
                .extract()                               new account
                .response();

    List<Account> accounts = result.jsonPath().getList("$");
    assertThat(accounts, not(empty()));
    assertThat(accounts, hasSize(4));   ◄────┐   Asserts there are
}                                            now four accounts
```

Open a terminal window in the directory where the Account service is located and run the next test:

```
mvn test
```

Figure 2.11 shows the error when running the tests.

Though creating an account should have returned a 201 HTTP status code, the test received 200 instead. Though the request succeeded, it didn't return an expected HTTP status code.

To fix it, instead of returning the created `Account` instance, the method should return a `Response` to enable the appropriate HTTP status code to be set. The next listing contains the updated create method.

```
[ERROR] Tests run: 3, Failures: 1, Errors: 0, Skipped: 0, Time elapsed: 3.817 s <<< FAILURE! -
in quarkus.accounts.AccountResourceTest
[ERROR] quarkus.accounts.AccountResourceTest.testCreateAccount  Time elapsed: 0.079 s  <<< FAIL
URE!
java.lang.AssertionError:
1 expectation failed.
Expected status code <201> but was <200>.

    at quarkus.accounts.AccountResourceTest.testCreateAccount(AccountResourceTest.java:72)
```

Figure 2.11 Create account test failure

Listing 2.18 `AccountResource`

```
@Path("/accounts")
public class AccountResource {
  ...
  @POST
  @Consumes(MediaType.APPLICATION_JSON)
  @Produces(MediaType.APPLICATION_JSON)
  public Response createAccount(Account account) {
    if (account.getAccountNumber() == null) {
      throw new WebApplicationException("No Account number specified.", 400);
    }

    accounts.add(account);
    return Response.status(201).entity(account).build();   ⟵
  }                                              Constructs a Response with status code
  ...                                            201 containing the new account entity
}
```

Running mvn test again shows a different error. Now it fails because the two accounts, the one sent in the HTTP POST request and the one returned, are not equal. The test failure follows:

```
Expected: <quarkus.accounts.repository.Account@22361e23>
    but: was <quarkus.accounts.repository.Account@46994f26>
    at quarkus.accounts.activerecord.AccountResourceTest.testCreateAccount(
    AccountResourceTest.java:77)
```

Account doesn't have any equals or hashcode methods, making any equality check use the default object comparison, which in this case means they are not the same object. To fix it, update Account with equals and hashcode methods, as shown here.

Listing 2.19 `Account`

```
public class Account {
  ...
  @Override
  public boolean equals(Object o) {
    if (this == o) return true;
```

```
    if (o == null || getClass() != o.getClass()) return false;
    Account account = (Account) o;
    return accountNumber.equals(account.accountNumber) &&
        customerNumber.equals(account.customerNumber);
}

@Override
public int hashCode() {
    return Objects.hash(accountNumber, customerNumber);
}
...
}
```

NOTE The equality check and hashcode creation use only the account and customer numbers. All the other data on Account can change, and it still represents the same instance. It's very important to ensure objects have an appropriately unique business key.

Run `mvn test` again; all tests now pass.

In future sections and chapters, we discuss additional aspects of testing, including running tests with native executables and defining required resources for tests.

2.4   Creating a native executable

Java programs require a Java Virtual Machine (JVM) as their operating system for execution. The JVM includes all the low-level Java APIs wrapping operating system libraries, as well as convenience APIs to simplify Java programming. The JVM, including all the APIs it provides, is not small. It occupies large parts of memory, measured by its resident set size (RSS), when running Java programs.

Native executables are files containing programs to be executed directly on an operating system, only relying on operating system libraries to be present. Embedded within them are all the necessary operating system instructions required by a particular program. The key difference between a native executable and Java programs is that there is no requirement for a JVM to be present during runtime execution.

The ability to compile a Java program down into a native executable significantly reduces the file size of the program because the JVM is no longer required. It also significantly reduces the amount of RSS memory used while executing and shortens the time required to start the program.

WARNING The reduction in the program size is a result of the *dead code elimination* process. Several aspects of this impact how code can execute inside a native executable. A key difference is that dynamic class loading will not work, because nondirectly referenced code is removed from the native executable. Full details of what won't work in a native executable can be found on the GraalVM website: https://www.graalvm.org/reference-manual/native-image/.

Over the last couple of years, a part of the GraalVM project offering compilation to native executable has become popular. GraalVM might sound familiar because of the

Truffle compiler subproject offering polyglot programming on the JVM, but the compilation of Java down to native executable is from a different subproject.

Native executables are particularly beneficial in serverless environments where processes need to start promptly and require as few resources as possible. Quarkus offers first-class support for native executable creation and optimization. Such optimization is possible through *ahead-of-time* (AOT) compilation, build-time processing of framework metadata, and native image preboot.

> **NOTE** *Ahead-of-time* refers to the process of compiling Java bytecode to a native executable. The JVM offers only *just-in-time* compilation.

Metadata processing at build time ensures any classes required for initial application deployment are used during the build and are no longer required during runtime execution. This reduces the number of classes needed at runtime, providing the dual benefits of reduced memory utilization and faster startup time.

> **NOTE** Examples of metadata processing include processing persistence.xml, and defining required processing based on annotations in the code.

Quarkus further reduces the number of classes needed at runtime in a native executable by performing a preboot when building the native image. During this phase, Quarkus starts as much of the frameworks as possible within the application and stores the serialized state within the native executable. The resulting native executable has therefore already run most, if not all, of the necessary startup code for an application, resulting in further improvement to startup time.

In addition to what Quarkus does, GraalVM performs dead code elimination on the source and packaged libraries. This process traverses the code to remove methods and classes that aren't actually on the execution path. Doing so reduces both the size of the native executable and the memory required to run the application.

How does a project create a native executable? In the pom.xml for the project, the profile for the native executable creation was added by the generator as follows:

```
<profile>
  <id>native</id>                    ← Specifies the ID of the
  <activation>                         profile when activating
    <property>                         with -Pnative
      <name>native</name>          ←
    </property>                        Defines a flag that
  </activation>                        when present will
  <build>                              activate the profile,
    <plugins>                          -Dnative
      <plugin>                                             Includes the
        <artifactId>maven-failsafe-plugin</artifactId>  ← Failsafe plugin to
        <version>${surefire-plugin.version}</version>     run integration
        <executions>                                      tests with a native
          <execution>                                     executable
            <goals>
```

```
            <goal>integration-test</goal>
            <goal>verify</goal>
        </goals>
        <configuration>
            <systemPropertyVariables>
```

Defines the path
to the native
executable for use
when testing

```
<native.image.path>${project.build.directory}/${project.build.finalName}
-runner</native.image.path>
            <java.util.logging.manager>org.jboss.logmanager
.LogManager</java.util.logging.manager>
            <maven.home>${maven.home}</maven.home>
        </systemPropertyVariables>
    </configuration>
  </execution>
 </executions>
</plugin>
    </plugins>
  </build>
  <properties>
    <quarkus.package.type>native</quarkus.package.type>
  </properties>
</profile>
```

Tells the Quarkus
Maven plugin to
build a native
executable in
addition to the
usual Java JAR
runner

If we generate the project from https://code.quarkus.io, the Account service already includes the `native` profile in the pom.xml.

> **NOTE** Instead of using a new profile, we can create a native executable by passing `-Dquarkus.package.type=native` to `mvn clean install`. However, having a profile is more convenient and enables integration testing with a native executable.

Before creating a native executable, it's necessary to install GraalVM for the JDK version and operating system in use, in this instance, JDK 11. Follow the instructions on the Quarkus website for installing and configuring GraalVM: http://mng.bz/GO18. Prerequisites for GraalVM are available at http://mng.bz/zEog.

Once GraalVM is installed, to build the native executable, run the following:

```
mvn clean install -Pnative
```

The native build process can take a few minutes to complete—much slower than regular Java compilation—depending on the number of classes in the application and the number of external libraries included.

Once complete, a `-runner` executable will be in the /target directory, which is the result of the native executable build process. The native executable will be specific to the operating system it was built on, as GraalVM uses native libraries to implement certain functionality.

> **TIP** To create a native executable that is suitable for use within a Linux container, run `mvn package -Pnative -Dquarkus.native.container-build=true`.

Try running the native executable version of the Account service, shown here:

```
./target/chapter2-account-service-1.0.0-SNAPSHOT-runner
```

As with the earlier startup, listing 2.20 contains the console output when the native executable starts. Notice the startup time for the Account service? In this case it was only 0.023s!

Listing 2.20   Quarkus-native executable startup

```
  __  ____  __  _____   ___  __ ____  _____
 --/ __ \/ / / / _ | / _ \/ //_/ / / / __/
 -/ /_/ / /_/ / __ |/ , _/ ,< / /_/ /\ \
--_____/_/ |_/_/|_/_/|_|\____/___/
INFO  [io.quarkus] (main) chapter2-account-service 1.0.0-SNAPSHOT native
(powered by Quarkus 2.1.3.Final) started in 0.023s. Listening on:
http://0.0.0.0:8080
INFO  [io.quarkus] (main) Profile prod activated.
INFO  [io.quarkus] (main) Installed features: [cdi, resteasy,
resteasy-jsonb, smallrye-context-propagation]
```

> **NOTE** Within a native executable, we still have garbage collection, though it uses different garbage collectors than the JVM. One impact of this is very long-running processes will see better memory performance over time with the JVM instead of the native executable, due to the JVM continually optimizing memory utilization.

In addition to the native executable build, we can now also run native executable tests, as was seen with the generated project earlier. To run the current test with a native executable, create the test as shown in the next code listing.

Listing 2.21   Account

```
@NativeImageTest
public class NativeAccountResourceIT extends AccountResourceTest {
  // Execute the same tests but in native mode.
}
```

`mvn clean install -Pnative` will do the native executable build as before, but also run the earlier tests against that generated executable. If everything works as expected, the native executable will build, and the tests defined in `AccountResource-Test` will execute and all will pass.

2.5   *Running in Kubernetes*

Quarkus focuses on Kubernetes native, so it's time to put that to the test, packaging and deploying the Account service to Kubernetes. We have several options when it comes to deploying Quarkus applications to Kubernetes, and this section covers some of them.

2.5.1   *Generating Kubernetes YAML*

When using Kubernetes, everything is YAML—there's just no way around that. However, Quarkus provides some ways to alleviate the hassle of handcrafting YAML by offering extensions to generate it.

The first thing to do is add a dependency into the Account service pom.xml, as follows:

```
<dependency>
  <groupId>io.quarkus</groupId>
  <artifactId>quarkus-kubernetes</artifactId>
</dependency>
```

This dependency adds the Kubernetes extension for Quarkus, which offers the ability to generate, and customize, the necessary YAML for deploying to Kubernetes.

To see what it produces, run `mvn clean install` on the project, then look at the files produced in /target/kubernetes. By default, it will produce a .yml and a .json version of the required configuration.

An example of what can be seen for the Account service is shown in the next code snippet.

Listing 2.22   kubernetes.yml

```
---
apiVersion: "v1"               ┐ Defines the Kubernetes
kind: "Service"            ◁─── │ service, Account service,
metadata:                      ┘ to be provisioned
  annotations:
    app.quarkus.io/build-timestamp: "...."
    app.quarkus.io/commit-id: "...."
  labels:
    app.kubernetes.io/name: "chapter2-account-service"
    app.kubernetes.io/version: "1.0.0-SNAPSHOT"
  name: "chapter2-account-service"
spec:
  ports:                       ┐ Indicates the service will expose
  - name: "http"           ◁── │ port 80, and the application will
    port: 80                   ┘ be running on 80
    targetPort: 80
  selector:
    app.kubernetes.io/name: "chapter2-account-service"
    app.kubernetes.io/version: "1.0.0-SNAPSHOT"
  type: "ClusterIP"
---
apiVersion: "apps/v1"          ┐ Creates the Kubernetes
kind: "Deployment"        ◁─── │ Deployment of the
metadata:                      ┘ service
  annotations:
    app.quarkus.io/build-timestamp: "...."
    app.quarkus.io/commit-id: "...."
  labels:
    app.kubernetes.io/name: "chapter2-account-service"
```

```
      app.kubernetes.io/version: "1.0.0-SNAPSHOT"
  name: "chapter2-account-service"
spec:
  replicas: 1          ◄──────────────
  selector:
    matchLabels:
      app.kubernetes.io/name: "chapter2-account-service"
      app.kubernetes.io/version: "1.0.0-SNAPSHOT"
  template:
    metadata:
      annotations:
        app.quarkus.io/build-timestamp: "...."
        app.quarkus.io/commit-id: "...."
      labels:
        app.kubernetes.io/name: "chapter2-account-service"
        app.kubernetes.io/version: "1.0.0-SNAPSHOT"
    spec:
      containers:
      - env:
        - name: "KUBERNETES_NAMESPACE"
          valueFrom:
            fieldRef:
              fieldPath: "metadata.namespace"
        image: "{docker-user}/chapter2-account-service:1.0.0-SNAPSHOT"  ◄───┐
        imagePullPolicy: "Always"
        name: "chapter2-account-service"
        ports:
        - containerPort: 80
          name: "http"
          protocol: "TCP"
```

> **Tells Kubernetes to create only one instance; it's possible to set the value higher, but it's not necessary in this situation.**

> **Names the Docker image to use for the Deployment**

With the default kubernetes.yml, the following customizations are worth making:

- Change the name of the service to account-service.
- Use a more meaningful name for the Docker image.

To make these changes, modify application.properties in src/main/resources to include the following:

```
quarkus.container-image.group=quarkus-mp
quarkus.container-image.name=account-service
quarkus.kubernetes.name=account-service
```

After running mvn clean install again and looking at kubernetes.yml in /target/ kubernetes, notice that the name used is now account-service, and the Docker image is quarkus-mp/account-service:1.0.0-SNAPSHOT.

With Minikube as the deployment target, we can generate specific resource files. These resource files are required to expose the Kubernetes services to the local machine. Add the following dependency into the pom.xml:

```
<dependency>
    <groupId>io.quarkus</groupId>
```

```
    <artifactId>quarkus-minikube</artifactId>
</dependency>
```

TIP Full details on how to deploy to Minikube can be found here: https://quarkus.io/guides/deploying-to-kubernetes#deploying-to-minikube.

Running `mvn clean install` will now generate Minikube-specific resources into the target/kubernetes directory. Looking at the files, we see they're virtually identical. The only difference is with the `Service` definition, as shown here:

```
spec:
  ports:
  - name: http
    nodePort: 30704         ◁  For Kubernetes, nodePort is not required, but
    port: 80                   when using Minikube, the nodePort indicates
    targetPort: 80             which port on the local machine will receive
  selector:                    any traffic forwarded from the service.
    app.kubernetes.io/name: account-service
    app.kubernetes.io/version: 1.0.0-SNAPSHOT    With Kubernetes the type is set
type: NodePort             ◁                     to ClusterIP, but for Minikube,
                                                 NodePort is required.
```

IMPORTANT It is not recommended to use Minikube-specific Kubernetes resources when deploying to a Kubernetes environment for production. The examples will use the dependency, because it exposes the services to localhost.

2.5.2 *Packaging an application*

With Quarkus we have the following ways to package an application for deployment to Kubernetes:

- Jib (https://github.com/GoogleContainerTools/jib)
- Docker
- S2I (Source to Image) binary build

Each requires the addition of their respective dependency to the pom.xml, either `quarkus-container-image-jib`, `quarkus-container-image-docker`, or `quarkus-container-image-s2i`.

To minimize the required dependencies for running the examples, Docker is not required. The advantage with Jib is that all requirements for producing container images are part of the dependency itself. Container images with Docker utilize the contents of the src/main/docker directory but require the Docker daemon to be installed.

Add the following dependency into the pom.xml:

```
<dependency>
    <groupId>io.quarkus</groupId>
    <artifactId>quarkus-container-image-jib</artifactId>
</dependency>
```

Then run the following code to create the container image for JVM execution:

```
mvn clean package -Dquarkus.container-image.build=true
```

> **IMPORTANT** If there isn't a Docker daemon running locally, the container image creation will fail. The Docker daemon inside Minikube can be used instead. Run `minikube start`, and then expose the Minikube Docker daemon with `eval $(minikube -p minikube docker-env)`. It's necessary for the `eval` command to be run in each terminal window running the Maven commands to create a container, because the evaluation is specific to each terminal window.

When successful, running `docker images` will show the `quarkus-mp:account-service` image:

```
➔ docker images
REPOSITORY                      TAG             IMAGE ID      CREATED        SIZE
quarkus-mp/account-service      1.0.0-SNAPSHOT  8bca7928d6a9  4 seconds ago 200MB
```

2.5.3 *Deploying and running an application*

It's time to deploy to Minikube! If Minikube isn't already installed and running, install Minikube using the instructions provided in appendix A.

Once installed, open a new terminal window and run the following:

```
minikube start
```

> **WARNING** If it's the first time you've run Minikube, it could take some time to download the necessary container images.

This will start Minikube with the default settings of 4 GB RAM and 20 GB HDD.

> **IMPORTANT** Run `eval $(minikube -p minikube docker-env)` in each terminal window that will be executing commands to build and deploy containers.

Time to deploy! Run the following:

```
mvn clean package -Dquarkus.kubernetes.deploy=true
```

This command generates the necessary container image, using whichever container extension is installed, and deploys to the Kubernetes cluster specified in .kube/config. The Minikube cluster will be present in /[HOME]/.kube/config if `minikube start` was executed.

If successful, the build should finish with messages similar to the following:

```
[INFO] [io.quarkus.kubernetes.deployment.KubernetesDeployer] Deploying to
kubernetes server: https://192.168.64.2:8443/ in namespace: default.
```

```
[INFO] [io.quarkus.kubernetes.deployment.KubernetesDeployer] Applied:
Service account-service.
[INFO] [io.quarkus.kubernetes.deployment.KubernetesDeployer] Applied:
Deployment account-service.
```

> **IMPORTANT** Attempting to redeploy an application already present in Kubernetes with mvn package -Dquarkus.kubernetes.deploy=true will result in an error in Quarkus 2.x. Follow the issue for updates on a resolution. You can work around the problem by removing the application first with kubectl delete -f /target/kubernetes/minikube.yaml.

The log messages indicate the following Kubernetes resources that were deployed and that were present within the kubernetes.yml generated earlier:

- Service
- Deployment

With Account service deployed, run minikube service list to see the details of all services:

```
|-------------|------------------|---------------|---------------------------|
|  NAMESPACE  |      NAME        |  TARGET PORT  |            URL            |
|-------------|------------------|---------------|---------------------------|
|  default    |  account-service |  http/80      | http://192.168.64.2:30704 |
|  default    |  kubernetes      |  No node port |                           |
|  kube-system|  kube-dns        |  No node port |                           |
|-------------|------------------|---------------|---------------------------|
```

For account-service, the URL for use locally is http://192.168.64.2:30704.

> **NOTE** Because Minikube binds to the IP address of the machine, using http://localhost:30704 will not access the service in Minikube.

To see the list of all accounts, open a browser to http://192.168.64.2:30704/accounts. Test out the other endpoints Account service has to make sure they work as expected when deployed to Minikube.

   That is a lot of information to digest. Let's recap the key tasks we covered during the chapter: how to generate a Quarkus project from https://code.quarkus.io/, using live coding to improve development speed, writing tests for a Quarkus microservice, building native executables to reduce image size and improve startup speed, and what's needed to deploy a Quarkus microservice to Kubernetes.

Summary

- You can open up https://code.quarkus.io/ in a browser and select the desired extensions for an application, choosing the name of the application, before generating the project code to download.

- Start a microservice with `mvn quarkus:dev` to begin live coding with Quarkus. Make changes to a JAX-RS resource in the IDE, and see immediate changes to the running application when refreshing the browser.

- Add `@QuarkusTest` on a test class so that Quarkus packages the application for a test in the same manner as the Quarkus Maven plugin. This makes the test as near to an actual build as possible, improving the chances of catching any issues within a test early.

- Generate a native executable of a Quarkus application with `mvn clean install -Pnative`, with the `native` profile in pom.xml. The generated executable can optimize memory usage and startup time in constrained or FaaS- (function as a service) type environments, where services aren't necessarily running for weeks on end.

- Kubernetes needs resource definitions to know what is being deployed. When adding the Kubernetes extension to a Quarkus application, the extension automatically creates the JSON and YAML needed to deploy it to Kubernetes.

- Add `quarkus-container-image-jib` dependency to pom.xml for generating the necessary container images for deployment to Kubernetes. Running `mvn clean package -Dquarkus.container-image.build=true` will generate the image for Kubernetes.

Part 2

Developing microservices

Part 2 delves into developing microservices with MicroProfile and Quarkus. Whether it be reading configuration, using Panache to simplify database development, consuming external microservices, securing microservices, documenting the available HTTP endpoints, implementing resilience within and between microservices, or introducing reactive programming and bridging it into the imperative world, part 2 covers them all in detail.

Configuring microservices

This chapter covers

- Externalized configuration
- MicroProfile Config
- Accessing application configuration
- Configuration sources
- Quarkus configuration features
- Using Kubernetes ConfigMaps and Secrets

Chapter 2 introduced the Account service, which runs both locally and in Kubernetes. It can run in many more than two contexts, as shown next. Each context varies, having external services like a database, messaging system, and backend business microservices. The Account service has to interact with each service in its context, each with configuration requirements.

Figure 3.1 represents how enterprises may use different databases depending on the context. The developer uses a local desktop database during development, like the H2 embedded database. Integration testing uses a low-cost database like PostgreSQL. Production uses a large-scale enterprise-grade database like Oracle, and staging mimics production as closely as possible, so it also uses Oracle. The application needs a way to access and apply a configuration specific to each context

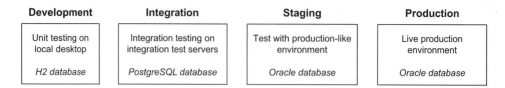

Development	Integration	Staging	Production
Unit testing on local desktop	Integration testing on integration test servers	Test with production-like environment	Live production environment
H2 database	*PostgreSQL database*	*Oracle database*	*Oracle database*

Figure 3.1   Example microservice contexts

without having to recompile, repackage, and redeploy for each context. What is required is *externalized configuration*, where the application accesses the configuration specific to the context in which it is running.

3.1   MicroProfile Config architecture overview

MicroProfile Config enables externalized configuration, where the application can access and apply configuration properties without having to modify the application when a configuration changes. Quarkus also uses MicroProfile Config to configure itself and receives the same context-specific configuration benefits. For example, Quarkus may need to expose a web application on port 8080 locally, whereas in staging and production, Quarkus may need to be configured for port 80 without modifying application code.

Figure 3.2 outlines the MicroProfile Config architecture that enables externalized configuration.

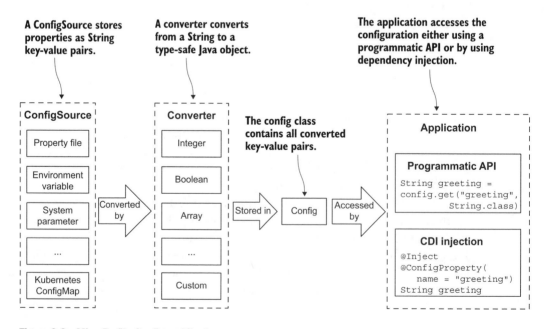

Figure 3.2   MicroProfile Config architecture

Properties are String key-value pairs defined in a configuration source. When the application starts, Quarkus uses MicroProfile Config to load properties from all available configuration sources. As the properties are loaded, they are converted from Strings to a Java data type and stored in a Config object. An application can then access the properties from the Config object using either a programmatic API or an annotation-based CDI injection API.

This section offers an overview of the MicroProfile Config architecture, and the remainder of this chapter details the components of this architecture most often used by developers. MicroProfile Config offers some advanced capabilities like creating converters for custom data types and building custom data sources, but these are beyond the scope of this book.

3.2 Accessing a configuration

Applications access a configuration through the `Config` object. MicroProfile Config includes two API styles for accessing the `Config` object. The following examples show the two API styles by retrieving the value of the `greeting` property from the `Config` object and storing it in a `greeting` variable:

- *Programmatic API*—The programmatic API is available for runtimes that do not have CDI injection available. The following listing shows a brief example.

Listing 3.1 Programmatic API

```
Config config = ConfigProvider.getConfig();

String greeting = config.getValue("myapp.greeting", String.class);
```

Directly looks up the greeting using config.getValue() programmatic API

- *CDI injection*—Available to runtimes that support CDI injection. Because Quarkus supports CDI injection (see the next listing), future examples will focus exclusively on CDI injection.

Listing 3.2 CDI injection API example

```
@Inject
@ConfigProperty(name="myapp.greeting")
String greeting;
```

Injects the value of myapp.greeting into greeting using CDI injection

NOTE When injecting a property with `@ConfigProperty`, the MicroProfile Config specification requires the use of the `@Inject` annotation. Quarkus, with its focus on *developer joy*, makes the use of `@Inject` on `@ConfigProperty` annotations optional to simplify code. The remainder of this chapter will use the CDI approach exclusively.

3.3 The Bank service

With a background in externalized configuration and MicroProfile Config in place, the next step is to apply them. Let's begin by creating a microservice, the Bank service, that uses the configuration APIs. The Bank service is basic, allowing the focus to remain on its configuration. It consists of the following configurable fields that are accessed using MicroProfile Config and exposed through REST endpoints:

- `name`—String field containing the name of the bank
- `mobileBanking`—Boolean indicating support for mobile banking
- `supportConfig`—Java object with multiple configuration values for obtaining bank support

In later chapters, we'll extend the Bank service with additional capabilities, including those that extend across to the Account service, like invoking remote REST endpoints, propagating security tokens, and tracing requests.

3.3.1   Creating the Bank service

In chapter 2, we used `code.quarkus.io` to generate an application. We use the Quarkus maven plugin here as an alternative approach. See the following listing for the Maven command line to create the Bank service Quarkus project.

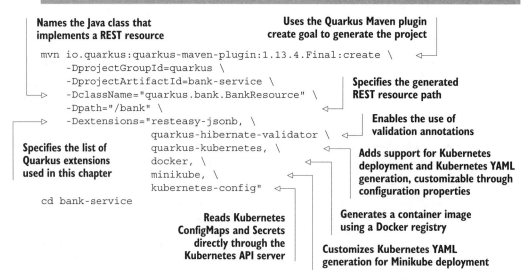

Listing 3.3   Generating `bank-service` using Maven

Extensions can be easily added at any time using the `add-extensions` Maven goal and removed using the `remove-extension` goal. If running in development mode (`mvn quarkus:dev`), Quarkus will automatically reload the application with the extension changes included! (See the Maven Tooling Guide at https://quarkus.io/guides/maven-tooling.) To improve the developer experience, the `-Dextensions` property accepts shortened extension names. The shortened name must be specific enough to select only one extension or the command will fail. The `quarkus-resteasy-jsonb` extension, selected with the shortened "resteasy-jsonb" name, adds JSON-B serialization support to RESTEasy (JAX-RS).

NOTE A Quarkus command line tool to create and manage Quarkus applications is in experimental status at the time of this writing. See the Quarkus command line interface guide (https://quarkus.io/guides/cli-tooling) to learn more.

To prepare for this chapter's examples, execute the following steps:

- Remove the src/test directory and its subdirectories. This example will frequently break the generated tests by intentionally modifying the output.
- To prevent potential port conflicts, stop the Account service started in the previous chapter if it is still running.

With the project created and prerequisite steps taken, start the application in developer mode with the command line shown next.

Listing 3.4 Start Live Coding

```
mvn quarkus:dev
```

With developer mode enabled, it's time to start configuring the Bank service.

3.3.2 Configuring the Bank service name field

Beginning with the bank.name property, add the getName() method in BankResource .java, shown in the next listing.

Listing 3.5 Injecting and using bank name property

```
@ConfigProperty(name="bank.name")          Injects the value of the
String name;                                bank.name property
                                            into name
@GET
@Path("/name")
@Produces(MediaType.TEXT_PLAIN)             The return value will
public String getName() {                   be in text format.
    return name;            Returns the
}                           injected name
```

Load the http://localhost:8080/bank/name endpoint and notice the error page similar to that shown in figure 3.3.

The error identifies a shortcoming in the code, and Quarkus places the source of the error immediately at the top of the page. The code attempts to inject the value of the bank.name property, but bank.name has not been defined. Quarkus, as required by the MicroProfile Config specification, throws a DeploymentException when attempting to inject an undefined property.

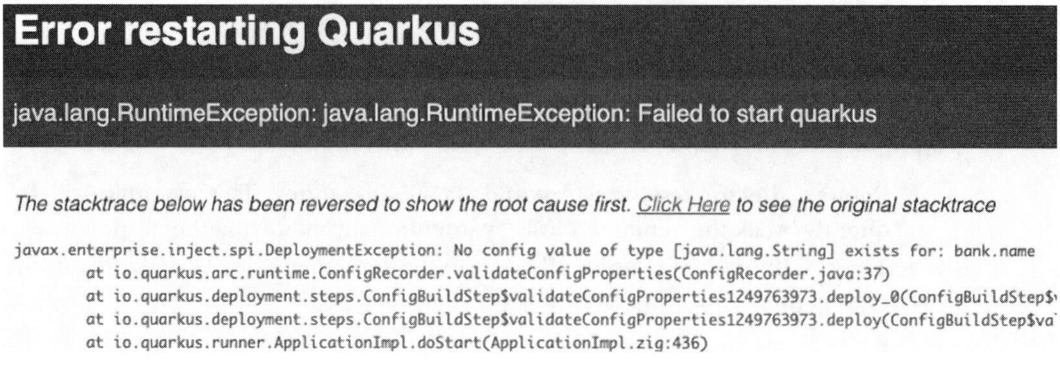

Error restarting Quarkus

java.lang.RuntimeException: java.lang.RuntimeException: Failed to start quarkus

The stacktrace below has been reversed to show the root cause first. <u>Click Here</u> to see the original stacktrace

```
javax.enterprise.inject.spi.DeploymentException: No config value of type [java.lang.String] exists for: bank.name
    at io.quarkus.arc.runtime.ConfigRecorder.validateConfigProperties(ConfigRecorder.java:37)
    at io.quarkus.deployment.steps.ConfigBuildStep$validateConfigProperties1249763973.deploy_0(ConfigBuildStep$
    at io.quarkus.deployment.steps.ConfigBuildStep$validateConfigProperties1249763973.deploy(ConfigBuildStep$va
    at io.quarkus.runner.ApplicationImpl.doStart(ApplicationImpl.zig:436)
```

Figure 3.3　Browser output

We can address missing property values in the following three ways, and all are commonly used depending on the need:

- *Default value*—A fallback value that is general enough to apply in all situations when a property is missing.
- *Supply a value*—Define the property and value within a property source.
- *Java* `Optional`—Use when a missing property value needs to be supplied by custom business logic.

Let's look at the first two in more detail, and the third shortly after that.

Assigning a default value is simple. Update the `@ConfigProperty` code.

Listing 3.6　Assigning a property a default value

```
@ConfigProperty(name="bank.name",
            defaultValue = "Bank of Default")
```

> **Assigns a default value, which is used when bank.name is undefined**

Reloading the URL will show the updated bank name.

Listing 3.7　Output: `Bank of Default`

```
Bank of Default
```

The second option, assigning the property a value, can be easily accomplished by adding the `bank.name` property to the application.properties file.

Listing 3.8　Defining `bank.name` property in application.properties

```
bank.name=Bank of Quarkus
```

Reloading the URL will show the updated bank name, as shown in the next listing.

Listing 3.9 Output: `Bank of Quarkus`

```
Bank of Quarkus
```

3.4 *Configuration sources*

A configuration source is a source of configuration values defined as key-value pairs. application.properties is a configuration source, and Quarkus supports nearly a dozen more. It is common for a microservice to consume its configuration from more than one source. Figure 3.4 shows configuration sources and sample values used throughout this chapter.

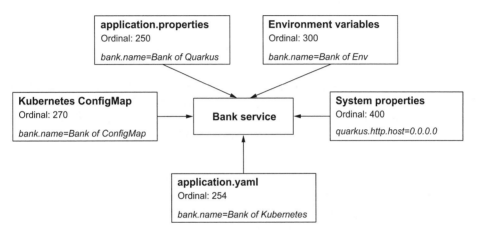

Figure 3.4 Configuration sources

The same property is often intentionally defined in more than one configuration source. If this is the case, which one takes precedence? MicroProfile Config uses a simple but effective approach for property conflict resolution. Each configuration source is assigned an *ordinal*. The properties defined in a configuration source with a higher ordinal take precedence over properties defined in a configuration source with a lower ordinal. MicroProfile Config requires support for three configuration sources, each with its own ordinal. Table 3.1 outlines the required MicroProfile Config configuration sources and additional Quarkus-supported configuration sources used in this chapter and their ordinals.

Table 3.1 Example MicroProfile Config sources

Source	Ordinal	Description
System properties	400	Required by MicroProfile Config. These are JVM properties that override nearly all property sources by using `-Dproperty=value` on the Java command line.

Table 3.1   Example MicroProfile Config sources *(continued)*

Source	Ordinal	Description
Environment variables	300	Required by MicroProfile Config. Overrides most property settings. Linux containers use environment variables as a form of parameter passing.
Kubernetes ConfigMap client	270	Directly access a Kubernetes ConfigMap. Overrides values in application.properties.
application.yaml	254	Store properties in YAML format in files with a .yaml or .yml file extension.
application.properties	250	The default property file used by most Quarkus applications.
microprofile-config.properties	100	Required by MicroProfile Config. Useful for MicroProfile-centric applications that prefer application portability across MicroProfile implementations.

NOTE MicroProfile Config requires support for the META-INF/microprofile-config.properties file for application portability. Quarkus supports microprofile-config.properties but defaults to application.properties. This book uses application.properties, although microprofile-config.properties works equally well.

Let's put the configuration source ordinal values to the test, starting with environment variables. Environment variables are a special case. Property names can contain dots, dashes, and forward slash characters, but some operating systems do not support them in environment variables. For this reason, these characters are mapped to characters that are broadly supported by operating systems.

MicroProfile Config searches for environment variables in the following order (e.g., `bank.mobileBanking`):

1 *Exact match*—Search for `bank.mobileBanking`. If not found, move to the next rule.
2 *Replace each nonalphanumeric with _*—Search for `bank_mobileBanking`. If not found, move to the next rule.
3 *Replace each nonalphanumeric with _ ; convert to uppercase*—Search for `BANK_MOBILEBANKING`.

Define a `BANK_NAME` environment variable as shown in the next code listing.

Listing 3.10   Defining `BANK_NAME` environment variable

```
export BANK_NAME="Bank of Env"
```

Start Quarkus in developer mode (`mvn quarkus:dev`) to verify that the environment variable overrides application.properties. Reloading the http://localhost:8080/bank/name URL will result in the output shown next.

Listing 3.11   Output: Bank of Env

```
Bank of Env
```

Next, start Quarkus as a runnable JAR to test two outcomes at once. The first is to test the system property configuration source, and the second is to test externalized configuration with a different packaging format.

Restart the application with the system property as shown in the following two code samples.

Listing 3.12   Running the Bank service as a runnable .jar file

```
mvn -Dquarkus.package.type=uber-jar package        ◁

java "-Dbank.name=Bank of System" \
    -jar target/bank-service-1.0.0-SNAPSHOT-runner.jar
```

Packages the application into a runnable uber-JAR. Only the JAR file and the JVM are needed to run the application.

Runs the application, specifying bank.name as a system property

Listing 3.13   Startup output

```
 __  ____  __  _____   ___  __ ____  _____
 --/ __ \/ / / / _ | / _ \/ //_/ / / / __/
 -/ /_/ / /_/ / __ |/ , _/ ,< / /_/ /\ \
 --\___\_\\____/_/ |_/_/|_/_/|_|\____/___/
2021-05-10 14:27:25,976 INFO  [io.quarkus] (main) bank-service
1.0.0-SNAPSHOT on JVM (powered by Quarkus 1.13.4.Final) started in 0.587s.   ◁
Listening on: http://0.0.0.0:8080
2021-05-10 14:27:25,993 INFO  [io.quarkus] (main) Profile prod activated.
2021-05-10 14:27:25,994 INFO  [io.quarkus] (main) Installed features: [cdi,
resteasy]
```

Quarkus running as an uber-JAR started in 0.587 seconds!

Reload the http://localhost:8080/bank/name endpoint, with the output shown next.

Listing 3.14   Output: Bank of System

```
Bank of System
```

There are a couple of items to point out in this approach. First, Quarkus applications can run as an uber-JAR file like many popular Java runtimes. Second, it started in just over .5 seconds! Although uber-JARs have become a popular package format in recent years, it is not container friendly. For this reason, Quarkus applications are rarely packaged as uber-JARs. More on this later.

Stop Quarkus and remove the BANK_NAME environment variable as follows.

Listing 3.15   Removing environment variable

```
unset BANK_NAME
```

3.5   *Configuring the mobileBanking field*

To begin coding `mobileBanking` configuration, start Quarkus in developer mode. To avoid exceptions, in this example we use an approach different from the earlier `defaultValue` by introducing the use of the Java `Optional` type. Add the code in from the next listing to BankResource.java.

Listing 3.16   Add `mobileBanking` support to `BankResource`

```
@ConfigProperty(name="app.mobileBanking")
Optional<Boolean>  mobileBanking;

@GET
@Produces(MediaType.TEXT_PLAIN)
@Path("/mobilebanking")
public Boolean getMobileBanking() {
    return mobileBanking.orElse(false);
}
```

Injects the value of
app.mobileBanking into
the mobileBanking field

With Optional types, MicroProfile
Config will not throw an exception
if a property is not defined.

If the mobileBanking field
is undefined, returns false

`mobileBanking` is a Boolean, and properties are stored as strings. The string needs to be converted to a Boolean data type for proper injection. As shown in figure 3.2, converters in the MicroProfile Config architecture convert properties from strings to primitive data types, including Booleans.

NOTE   There is also an API for creating converters for custom data types.

MicroProfile Config supports the Java `Optional` data type for working with undefined properties while avoiding a `DeploymentException`. In the `getMobileBanking()` method, `mobileBanking` returns the configured value if defined, or `false` if left undefined.

To test the code, load the /bank/mobilebanking endpoint to see an HTTP response of `false`, this time without the need for exception handling. The value of `app.mobileBanking` in application.properties, either `true` or `false`, will be the returned value at the endpoint.

3.6   *Grouping properties with @ConfigProperties*

An alternative approach to individually injecting each property is to inject a group of related properties into fields of a single class. Annotating a class with `@Config-Properties`, as shown in the next listing, makes every field in the class a property. Every field will have its value injected from a property source.

Listing 3.17   BankSupportConfig.java: defining `@ConfigProperties`

```
@ConfigProperties(prefix="bank-support")
public class BankSupportConfig {
    private String phone;
```

Annotating a class with
@ConfigProperties makes every
field a configuration property.

A configuration class should
be a plain old Java object
(POJO) with no business logic.

```
    public String email;

    public String getPhone() {
        return phone;
    }

    public void setPhone(String phone) {
        this.phone = phone;
    }
}
```

Fields become properties regardless of access modifiers. For example, BankSupportConfig contains both private and public fields.

The optional `prefix` parameter specifies the property prefix. For example, `bank-support.email` and `bank-support.phone` are the property names in this code snippet. The prefix applies to all properties in the class.

> **TIP** Import `org.eclipse.microprofile.config.inject.ConfigProperties` and not `io.quarkus.arc.config.ConfigProperties`, which is deprecated.

The next listing adds code to BankResource.java to inject the configuration and to return the injected property values at a JAX-RS endpoint.

Listing 3.18 BankResource.java: using `@ConfigProperties`

```
@ConfigProperties(prefix="bank-support")
BankSupportConfig supportConfig;

@GET
@Produces(MediaType.APPLICATION_JSON)
@Path("/support")
public HashMap<String, String> getSupport() {
    HashMap<String,String> map = new HashMap<>();

    map.put("email", supportConfig.email);
    map.put("phone", supportConfig.getPhone());

    return map;
}
```

Injects BankSupportConfig into supportConfig. Quarkus does not require the @Inject annotation as a developer convenience, but it can be used when application portability to other MicroProfile runtimes is desired.

The return value (map) will be converted to a JSON representation.

Adds the properties to the map

`supportConfig.email` can be added directly because `email` is a public field, whereas `supportConfig.phone` is accessed through the `getPhone()` accessor method because `phone` is a private field. A best practice is to choose a consistent approach for better readability.

With the `BankSupportConfig` class and JAX-RS endpoint defined, the last step is defining the properties themselves. The following code snippet specifies the field property values.

Listing 3.19 Defining support properties in application.properties

```
bank-support.email=support@bankofquarkus.com
bank-support.phone=555-555-5555
```

Applies the prefix defined in listing 3.18

When accessing the http://localhost:8080/bank/support REST endpoint, the result should look the same as that shown next.

Listing 3.20   Support endpoint JSON output

```
{"phone":"555-555-5555","email":"support@bankofquarkus.com"}
```

3.7 *Quarkus-specific configuration features*

The focus so far has been on features defined by the MicroProfile Config specification. Quarkus goes beyond the specification by adding Quarkus-specific configuration features.

3.7.1 *Quarkus configuration profiles*

With *profiles*, Quarkus enables us to use multiple configurations within a single configuration source. Quarkus defines the following three built-in profiles:

- dev—Activated when in developer mode (e.g., mvn quarkus:dev)
- test—Activated when running tests
- prod—Activated when not in development or test modes. In chapter 4, we use profiles to differentiate between production and development database configuration properties.

As shown in the next listing, the syntax for specifying a profile is %profile.key=value, so the application.properties file defines the bank.name property three times.

Listing 3.21   Example application.properties with profiles

The default property definition

```
bank.name=Bank of Quarkus
%dev.bank.name=Bank of Development
%prod.bank.name=Bank of Production
```

This property definition is used when running Quarkus in developer mode.

This property definition is used when the application is started with java -jar or when running a natively compiled binary.

When running Quarkus in development mode, like mvn quarkus:dev, the value of bank.name will be *Bank of Development*. When running in production, like java -jar target/quarkus-app/quarkus-run.jar, the value of bank.name will be Bank of Production. bank.name, with no profile prefix, is a fallback value used when a profile value is not defined. For example, when running mvn quarkus:test in this example, the %dev and %prod properties don't apply. A %test.bank.name property is not defined. So, the fallback value of Bank of Quarkus is used.

We can also define custom profiles. Earlier in the chapter, we covered four contexts: development, integration, staging, and production. Because Quarkus inherently supports development and production profiles, let's create a custom staging profile and update application.properties, as shown next.

Listing 3.22 Add a `staging` profile `bank.name` property value

```
%staging.bank.name=Bank of Staging
```

We can activate custom profiles by either setting the name of the quarkus.profile system property (e.g., java -Dquarkus.profile=staging -jar myapp.jar) or by setting the QUARKUS_PROFILE environment variable.

Start Quarkus in developer mode with mvn compile quarkus:dev and access the endpoint at http://localhost:8080/bank/name. The output is shown next.

Listing 3.23 Quarkus developer mode output

```
Bank of Development
```

To see the production profile output, see the following two code listings.

Listing 3.24 Running the application in production mode

```
mvn package
java -jar target/quarkus-app/quarkus-run.jar
```

Listing 3.25 Production mode output from http://localhost:8080/bank/name

```
Bank of Production
```

3.7.2 Property expressions

Quarkus supports property expressions in application.properties, where an expression follows the ${my-expression} format. Quarkus resolves properties as it reads them. Let's modify the next code to use property expressions.

Listing 3.26 Property expression example

```
support.email=support@bankofquarkus.com        ◁─────┐  Adds support.email property
bank-support.email=${support.email}    ◁───────┐     │  for the support email address
bank-support.phone=555-555-5555                 │
                                        Updates bank-support.email
                                        to use a property expression
```

Reload the /bank/support endpoint to validate that the support email address matches the code shown next.

Listing 3.27 Support endpoint JSON output

```
{"phone":"555-555-5555","email":"support@bankofquarkus.com"}
```

Although support.email and bank-support.${support-email} are in the same configuration source in this example, they do not have to be. In chapter 4, we use property expressions for database credentials. We define the databases credentials and the property expression that refers to the credentials in different configuration sources.

3.7.3   *Quarkus ConfigMapping*

Quarkus offers a custom API, @ConfigMapping, that groups properties together like MicroProfile @ConfigProperties but is more flexible and feature-rich. @ConfigMapping is so feature-rich that it could be an entire chapter by itself! This section demonstrates two features: nested groups and property validation. The remainder of the features is documented in the *Quarkus ConfigMapping Guide* (https://quarkus.io/guides/config-mappings).

A @ConfigMapping is defined as a Java interface as shown in the following code.

Listing 3.28   BankSupportConfigMapping.java

```
@ConfigMapping(prefix = "bank-support-mapping")      ◁——   Uses the @ConfigMapping
interface BankSupportConfigMapping {  ◁————                 annotation, and specifies a prefix
    @Size(min=12, max=12)
    String phone();                     ◁——
                                               BankSupportConfigMapping is a Java
    String email();                            interface. Properties are defined as
                                               method names, like phone() and email().

    Business business();     ◁——————
                                               Unlike MicroProfile Config @ConfigProperties,
                                               @ConfigMapping properties can be validated
    interface Business {     ◁——               using Bean Validation constraints.
        @Size(min=12, max=12)
        String phone();               References the Business interface
        String email();               to load business properties
    }
}
```

The nested group business defines a Java interface with properties relevant to the bank's business customers.

With the @ConfigMapping created, the next step is to add the relevant properties to application.properties as shown here.

Listing 3.29   application.properties

The prefix, specified in listing 3.28, is bank-support-mapping.

To access the nested properties, append the interface name to the prefix.

```
bank-support-mapping.email=support@bankofquarkus.com
bank-support-mapping.phone=555-555-5555
bank-support-mapping.business.email=business-support@bankofquarkus.com   ◁——
bank-support-mapping.business.phone=555-555-1234
```

> **TIP**   Nested groups can contain nested groups.

Last, add a new JAX-RS resource to BankResource.java to access the @ConfigMapping.

Listing 3.30   BankResource.java

```
@Inject
BankSupportConfigMapping configMapping;      ◁——   Injects BankSupportConfigMapping
                                                    into configMapping
```

```
@GET
@Produces(MediaType.APPLICATION_JSON)
@Path("/supportmapping")
public Map<String, String> getSupportMapping() {
    HashMap<String,String> map = getSupport();

    map.put("business.email", configMapping.business().email());
    map.put("business.phone", configMapping.business().phone());

    return map;
}
```

Properties are accessible at the /bank/supportmapping endpoint. This method is a near copy of the /bank/support endpoint, extended with the business support properties.

Access the nested group by invoking the interface name as a method. Invoking the business() method returns the values of the properties defined in the Business interface.

Load http://localhost:8080/bank/supportmapping in the browser to verify the properties are displayed. With a successful `@ConfigMapping` endpoint up and running, in the following section we change gears a bit by explaining why Quarkus categorizes properties as either runtime or build-time properties.

3.7.4   Run-time vs. build-time properties

As a MicroProfile Config implementation, Quarkus optimizes configuration for containers in general and Kubernetes in particular. Kubernetes is considered an immutable infrastructure, where it restarts pods with a new application configuration instead of modifying an application's configuration within a running pod.

Let's do a quick Quarkus and traditional Java runtime configuration comparison. Most Java runtimes scan the classpath while an application is starting. The runtime scanning creates a dynamic deployment capability at the cost of increased RAM utilization and increased startup time. It can take a significant amount of resources to conduct a classpath scan to build an in-memory model (metamodel) of what it has found. Also, the application pays this resource penalty every time it starts. In a highly dynamic environment like Kubernetes that encourages frequent incremental application updates, this is quite often!

Quarkus, on the other hand, considers its primary target environment to be containers in general and Kubernetes in particular. Quarkus allows extensions to define two types of properties: build time and run time.

Quarkus prescans and compiles as much code as possible when the application is compiled (built), so it is static in nature when loaded and run. Build-time properties influence compilation and how the metamodel (like annotation processing) is prewired. Changing build-time properties at run time has no effect, like when running `java -jar myapp.jar`. Their values, or the effect of their values, are already compiled into myapp.jar. An example is a JDBC driver because developers typically know ahead of time which drivers will be required.

Run-time properties do not impact how code is prescanned and generated, but they do influence run-time execution. Examples include port numbers like `quarkus.http.port=80` and database connection strings like `quarkus.datasource.jdbc.url=jdbc:postgresql://localhost:5432/mydatabase`.

The result of prescanning at build-time is lower run-time memory utilization—consuming only tens of MB of RAM and faster startup time in tens of milliseconds as a native binary and hundreds of milliseconds on the JVM.

Each Quarkus extension guide (https://quarkus.io/guides) lists its configurable properties. The "Quarkus: All Configuration Options" guide (https://quarkus.io/guides/all-config) lists all configuration properties for all Quarkus extensions. In both cases, a lock icon identifies properties fixed at build time.

Figure 3.5 shows a mix of fixed properties and run-time-configurable properties from the "Quarkus: All Configuration Options" guide.

🔒 Configuration property fixed at build time - All other configuration properties are overridable at runtime

FILTER CONFIGURATION

AWS Lambda	Type	Default
quarkus.lambda.handler The handler name. Handler names are specified on handler classes using the @javax.inject.Named annotation. ⌄ Show more	string	

Agroal - Database connection pool	Type	Default
🔒 quarkus.datasource.jdbc If we create a JDBC datasource for this datasource.	boolean	true
🔒 quarkus.datasource.jdbc.driver The datasource driver class name	string	
🔒 quarkus.datasource.jdbc.transactions Whether we want to use regular JDBC transactions, XA, or disable all transactional capabilities. When enabling XA ⌄ Show more	enabled, xa, disabled	enabled
🔒 quarkus.datasource.jdbc.enable-metrics Enable datasource metrics collection. If unspecified, collecting metrics will be enabled by default if the smallrye- ⌄ Show more	boolean	
quarkus.datasource.jdbc.url The datasource URL	string	

Figure 3.5 Build-time properties identified by the lock icon

For example, the Agroal database connection pooling extension "fixes" the quarkus.datasource.jdbc.driver property at build time, but allows the quarkus.datasource.jdbc.url property to change after compilation.

3.8 *Configuration on Kubernetes*

We have been configuring the Bank service throughout the chapter, and application configuration for a Kubernetes deployment is nearly the same. The primary difference is the available configuration sources and how to utilize them.

3.8.1 *Common Kubernetes configuration sources*

Table 3.1 covers the configuration sources we use in this chapter, but let's look at how they are most commonly used in Kubernetes:

- *System properties*—Container images often start a runtime with predefined parameters. A good example is requiring the use of team or corporate standards. The corporate standard in this case is using the JBoss LogManager, shown next:

```
java -Djava.util.logging.manager=org.jboss.logmanager.LogManager \
    -jar /deployment/app.jar
```

- *Environment variables*—A container is a self-contained runnable software package. Environment variables are a formalized and popular parameter-passing technique to configure an application packaged in a container. For example, the Postgres official container image uses environment variables like POSTGRES_USER to define a database user (https://hub.docker.com/_/postgres). This approach to container parameter passing is popular in Kubernetes as well.
- *Kubernetes ConfigMap*—A ConfigMap is a first-class externalized configuration concept for Kubernetes. A ConfigMap stores nonconfidential data as key-value pairs. Think of a ConfigMap as an interface for accessing key-value pairs, and more than one interface implementation exists. The most common implementation is mounting a ConfigMap as a storage volume within a Pod and is, therefore, accessible to all containers within the Pod. Quarkus uses a different ConfigMap implementation. Instead of mounting the configuration file within the container, the Quarkus ConfigMap extension takes a simpler approach by directly accessing the properties from etcd using the Kubernetes REST-based API server. Figure 3.6 compares the two different approaches.
- *application.properties*—Quarkus applications can still include an application .properties file for sensible default values.
- *Third-party configuration sources*—Quarkus supports popular third-party configuration sources that can run in Kubernetes, like the Spring Cloud Config Server, Vault, and Consul.

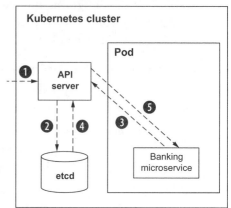

Mounting ConfigMaps

1. **Run** `kubectl create configmap`.
2. **Write** `configmap` **properties to etcd.**
3. **Volume created when Pod created.**
4. **Read** `configmap` **properties from** `etc`.
5. **Mount properties as application.properties.**
6. **Microservice reads properties.**

Direct API server access

1. **Run** `kubectl create configmap`.
2. **Write** `configmap` **properties to etcd.**
3. **Banking microservice requests properties when booted.**
4. **API server requests properties from etcd.**
5. **API server returns properties.**

Figure 3.6   ConfigMaps: mounting vs. API server direct access

3.8.2   Using a ConfigMap for Quarkus applications

Quarkus can recognize ConfigMap files created from application.properties, application.yaml, and application.yml files. Let's create a ConfigMap out of an application.yaml file so as not confuse it with the existing application.properties file. Create the application.yaml in the top-level project directory, as shown in the next listing.

Listing 3.31   Creating application.yaml

```
bank:
  name: Bank of ConfigMap
```

TIP   Make sure to use two spaces before the `name` property because YAML is space sensitive.

Next, create the Kubernetes ConfigMap, as seen in the next code sample.

Listing 3.32   Creating a Kubernetes ConfigMap

```
kubectl create configmap banking \          ⟵ Creates a ConfigMap
        --from-file=application.yaml            named banking
                                            ⟵ Populates the ConfigMap with the
                                              contents of the application.yaml file
```

With the ConfigMap created in Kubernetes, the next step is to configure the banking service to access it, as shown in the application.properties file in the next listing.

Listing 3.33   Configuring Quarkus to use the banking ConfigMap

Enables Kubernetes ConfigMap support. %prod specifies that it applies only when running in production.

The comma-separated list of ConfigMaps to use

```
%prod.quarkus.kubernetes-config.enabled=true
%prod.quarkus.kubernetes-config.config-maps=banking
```

> **TIP**   A ConfigMap can be viewed with `kubectl get cm/banking -oyaml`, edited with `kubectl edit cm/banking`, and deleted with `kubectl delete cm/banking`.

With the ConfigMap created and the banking service configured to use it, deploy the banking service to Kubernetes as shown in the following code listing.

Listing 3.34   Deploying the updated application to Kubernetes

```
mvn clean package -Dquarkus.kubernetes.deploy=true
```

To verify the output, run `minikube service list` to obtain the base URL.

Listing 3.35   Example output of `minikube service list`

```
|-------------|-----------------|--------------|---------------------------|
| NAMESPACE   | NAME            | TARGET PORT  |            URL            |
|-------------|-----------------|--------------|---------------------------|
| default     | banking-service | http/80      | http://192.168.64.8:31763 |
| default     | kubernetes      | No node port |                           |
| kube-system | kube-dns        | No node port |                           |
|-------------|-----------------|--------------|---------------------------|
```

The base URL, although the IP address and port will likely differ from what is shown

Load the URL in the browser, appending /bank/name. The full URL in this example would be http://192.168.64.8:31763/bank/name.

The output should be the contents of bank.name defined in the ConfigMap as shown next.

Listing 3.36   Output obtained from ConfigMap

```
Bank of ConfigMap
```

3.8.3   Editing a ConfigMap

Changing a ConfigMap requires a Pod restart. This boots a new `Bank Service` instance that reloads property values from its configuration sources. The first step, of course, is to edit the ConfigMap. Type `kubectl edit cm/banking`. See the next listing for editing the ConfigMap.

Listing 3.37   ConfigMap contents while editing

```
apiVersion: v1
data:
  application.yaml: |-          ◁──────┘  Contents of
    bank:                                application.yaml
      name: Bank of Quarkus (ConfigMap)  ◁───────  Edit this line to
kind: ConfigMap                                    reflect new value
metadata:                                  ◁──     of bank.name.
  creationTimestamp: "2020-08-04T06:08:56Z"        Ignore all the other content that is
  managedFields:                                   automatically added by Kubernetes
  - apiVersion: v1                                 when creating the ConfigMap. Do not
    fieldsType: FieldsV1                           modify the content outside of the
    fieldsV1:                                      application.yaml because the results
      f:data:                                      will vary depending on the edits.
        .: {}
        f:application.yaml: {}
    manager: kubectl
    operation: Update
    time: "2020-08-04T07:09:30Z"
  name: banking
  namespace: default
  resourceVersion: "863163"
  selfLink: /api/v1/namespaces/default/configmaps/banking
  uid: 3eba39df-336d-4a83-b50f-24ff8b767660
```

Kubernetes offers various ways to restart the Pod; however, the simplest is to redeploy the application as shown in the following code sample.

Listing 3.38   Redeploying the updated application to Kubernetes

```
mvn clean package -Dquarkus.kubernetes.deploy=true
```

> **IMPORTANT**   Attempting to redeploy an application already present in Kubernetes with `mvn package -Dquarkus.kubernetes.deploy=true` will result in an error in Quarkus 2.x. Follow the issue (https://github.com/quarkusio/quarkus/issues/19701) for updates on a resolution. The problem can be worked around by removing the application first with `kubectl delete -f /target/kubernetes/minikube.yaml`.

3.8.4   *Kubernetes Secrets*

ConfigMaps are ideal for general property storage and access. However, some cases, like using usernames, passwords, and OAuth tokens, require working with confidential properties. The Kubernetes solution for storing sensitive information is the *Kubernetes Secret*. By default, Secrets store data in Base 64–encoded format. While this makes sensitive data unreadable to the eye, it can be easily decoded. From an application perspective, Secrets look and feel a lot like ConfigMaps.

> **WARNING**   Like ConfigMaps, Secrets are stored in etcd. Any administrator with access to etcd can decode Base 64–encoded Secrets. Kubernetes can

encrypt secret data at rest as well (https://kubernetes.io/docs/tasks/adminis-ter-cluster/encrypt-data/).

Up to this point, properties have been stored mostly in files including applica-tion.properties and application.yaml. ConfigMaps and Secrets can also store *literals*, meaning key-value pairs, without having to define them within a file. See the next list-ing for the code to create a database username and password using Secrets.

Listing 3.39 Creating Kubernetes Secrets from literals

Creates a Kubernetes Secret named db-credentials

Stores username=admin as a Base 64–encoded property

Stores password=secret as a Base 64–encoded property

```
kubectl create secret generic db-credentials \
        --from-literal=username=admin \
        --from-literal=password=secret \
        --from-literal=db.username=quarkus_banking \
        --from-literal=db.password=quarkus_banking
```

Stores db.username= quarkus_banking as a Base 64–encoded property

Stores db.password=quarkus_banking as a Base 64–encoded property

Next, run the command in the next listing, and view the output in listing 3.41 to check it is encoded.

Listing 3.40 Getting the Secret contents

```
kubectl get secret db-credentials -oyaml
```

Listing 3.41 `kubectl` output

```
- apiVersion: v1
  data:
    db.password: cXVhcmt1c19iYW5raW5n
    db.username: cXVhcmt1c19iYW5raW5n
    password: c2VjcmV0
    username: YWRtaW4=
  kind: Secret
  metadata:
...
```

Encoded database password

Encoded database username

Encoded password

Encoded username

With a Kubernetes Secret containing username and password properties, the next step is to verify that these properties can be injected and used within the application. We will use the database username and password later. Extend BankResource as shown the in next listing.

Listing 3.42 Access Secret from BankResource.java

```
@ConfigProperty(name="username")
String  username;

@ConfigProperty(name="password")
String password;
```

Injects the username and password into the BankResource fields

```
@GET
@Produces(MediaType.APPLICATION_JSON)
@Path("/secrets")
public Map<String, String> getSecrets() {
    HashMap<String,String> map = new HashMap<>();

    map.put("username", username);
    map.put("password", password);

    return map;
}
```

Inserts the username and
password into a HashMap
and returns as a JSON string

Like a ConfigMap, applications need two Quarkus properties defined to access a Secret.
See the next listing.

Listing 3.43   Enabling Secret access in application.properties

Enables access to Secrets. %prod specifies that
it applies only when running in production.

The comma-
separated list of
Secrets to include
for property lookup

```
%prod.quarkus.kubernetes-config.secrets.enabled=true
%prod.quarkus.kubernetes-config.secrets=db-credentials
```

Redeploy the application and open the /bank/secrets endpoint. The output should
look like the next listing.

Listing 3.44   Browser output

```
{"password":"secret","username":"admin"}
```

Summary

This chapter covered a lot of ground. It introduced externalized configuration, Micro-
Profile Config, Quarkus-specific configuration features, and Kubernetes Config-
Maps. The top two takeaways from this chapter are that externalized configuration
is a microservice deployment necessity, and Quarkus uses MicroProfile Config and
custom configuration features to make Kubernetes deployments both practical
and seamless.

Here are the key detailed points:

- Quarkus uses the MicroProfile Config API for application configuration and to
  configure itself.
- MicroProfile Config uses configuration sources to abstract where configuration
  values are stored.
- There is an order of precedence when loading property values from configuration sources.
- Properties can be loaded individually using `@ConfigProperty` or in bulk using
  `@ConfigProperties` or `@ConfigMapping`.

- Quarkus supports configuration profiles for loading context-dependent configuration values, such as for development, test, and production.
- Not all Quarkus properties can be modified at run time.
- Quarkus supports ConfigMaps by reading ConfigMap key-value pairs using the Kubernetes API server.
- Applications can store and access sensitive information in Kubernetes Secrets.

Database access
with Panache

This chapter covers

- What Panache is
- Simplifying JPA development with Panache
- Database testing with Panache and
  `@QuarkusTest`

In chapter 2, we created the Account service to show how to develop JAX-RS end-points with Quarkus. In this chapter, we take that Account service and add database storage for the account data, instead of the data being held only in memory.

Because most microservices will need to store some type of data, or interact with data stored by another microservice, being able to read and store data to a database is a key feature to learn and understand. Though stateless microservices are "a thing," and certainly a goal, if appropriate, for a microservice, there are also times when denying the need to store data leads to unnecessary mental gymnastics, leading to a significantly more complex distributed system.

To simplify the development of microservices requiring storage, Quarkus created *Hibernate ORM with Panache (Panache)*, an opinionated means of storing and retrieving state from a database, heavily inspired by the Play framework, Ruby on Rails, and JPA experience. Panache offers two different paths, depending on developer preference: *active record* and *data repository*. The data repository approach will be familiar to those with experience in Spring Data JPA.

Before getting into how Panache can simplify database development in a microservice, we will alter the Account service to store data with the known JPA approach. Showing how to store data with JPA will make it easier to compare the approaches, both in terms of the amount of code and the different coding styles they facilitate.

4.1 *Data sources*

Before delving into modeling objects for persistence, we need to define a data source for JPA, or Panache, to communicate with the database.

The *Agroal* extension from Quarkus handles data source configuration and setup. However, adding a dependency for the extension is unnecessary when being used for JPA or Panache, because they have a dependency on Agroal. At a minimum, the type of data source and database URL must be specified in configuration, and usually a username and password, as follows:

```
quarkus.datasource.db-kind=postgresql
quarkus.datasource.username=database-user
quarkus.datasource.password=database-pwd
quarkus.datasource.jdbc.url=jdbc:postgresql://localhost:5432/my_database
```

> **NOTE** The username and password values shown here are just examples. What they need to be set to depends on the database being connected to.

In this particular example, the configuration tells Quarkus that the application will be connecting to a PostgreSQL database. The JDBC configuration indicates the URL of the database.

With the previous configuration, no data source name is mentioned. That is because the configuration is defining the *default* data source that should be used by anything needing a JDBC data source. Multiple data sources are created by setting a specific name in the configuration. For instance, the next configuration creates a data source called `orders`:

```
quarkus.datasource.orders.db-kind=postgresql
quarkus.datasource.orders.username=order-user
quarkus.datasource.orders.password=order-pwd
quarkus.datasource.orders.jdbc.url=jdbc:postgresql://localhost:5432/orders_db
```

Data sources can be created for many kinds of databases, but the more popular ones are h2 (mostly for testing), `mysql`, `mariadb`, and `postgresql`.

In addition to defining the data source configuration, a JDBC driver must be present for Quarkus to create the data source and to communicate with the database! For that, use a dependency such as the following:

```
<dependency>
  <groupId>io.quarkus</groupId>
  <artifactId>quarkus-jdbc-postgresql</artifactId>
</dependency>
```

The previous dependency matches the configuration from earlier that specified the database type as postgresql. If a different database is used, the application would require a different dependency, where the artifact is prefixed with quarkus-jdbc- and suffixed with the database type name.

Although it is possible to use the regular JDBC driver dependencies directly with Quarkus, using the Quarkus-provided JBDC driver extensions allows them to be automatically configured with Quarkus but also means they are guaranteed to work as part of a native executable. At present, most JDBC driver dependencies won't work inside a native executable.

Quarkus has a fantastic feature to help with testing when using a database. Adding @QuarkusTestResource(H2DatabaseTestResource.class) onto a test class will start an H2 in-memory database as part of the test startup. Being an in-memory database, H2 is convenient for testing without needing external databases running. It needs the quarkus-test-h2 dependency, and a JDBC driver as well, as shown here:

```
<dependency>
  <groupId>io.quarkus</groupId>
  <artifactId>quarkus-test-h2</artifactId>
  <scope>test</scope>
</dependency>
<dependency>
  <groupId>io.quarkus</groupId>
  <artifactId>quarkus-jdbc-h2</artifactId>
  <scope>test</scope>
</dependency>
```

Most applications don't need to interact with a data source directly: they use another layer on top to simplify the code. Now it's time to modify the Account service from chapter 2 to use JPA to store its data instead of storing it in memory.

4.2 JPA

Before we delve into what a Quarkus microservice that uses JPA looks like, look at figure 4.1, which shows the components involved and their interaction.

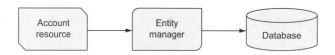

Figure 4.1   Account service: JPA

Though JPA may not be the favored approach to database interactions by many developers, it provides an easy migration path for anyone familiar with Java EE and Jakarta EE development with JPA. In addition, it provides a good basis for comparison with the Panache approaches covered later in the chapter.

As seen in figure 4.1, the `AccountResource` uses an `EntityManager` to interact with the database. Whether it's finding entities, creating new ones, or updating existing ones, it all happens through the `EntityManager` instance.

Let's begin converting the Account service from chapter 2 to use JPA for data storage. To add JPA to the Account service, the following dependencies need to be added:

```
<dependency>
  <groupId>io.quarkus</groupId>
  <artifactId>quarkus-hibernate-orm</artifactId>
</dependency>
<dependency>
  <groupId>io.quarkus</groupId>
  <artifactId>quarkus-jdbc-postgresql</artifactId>
</dependency>
```

`quarkus-hibernate-orm` adds the Hibernate implementation of JPA to the project, and `quarkus-jdbc-postgresql` adds the JDBC driver for PostgreSQL discussed in section 4.1.

The updated code for the Account service from chapter 2 can be found in the chapter4/jpa/ directory of the book source.

Next is to modify the `Account` class to be a JPA entity.

Listing 4.1 Account

Another named query, this one finding accounts that match accountNumber

Indicates the POJO is a JPA entity

Defines a named query to retrieve all accounts, and orders the result by accountNumber

```
@Entity
@NamedQuery(name = "Accounts.findAll",
  query = "SELECT a FROM Account a ORDER BY a.accountNumber")
@NamedQuery(name = "Accounts.findByAccountNumber",
  query = "SELECT a FROM Account a WHERE a.accountNumber = :accountNumber
    ORDER BY a.accountNumber")
public class Account {
  @Id
  @SequenceGenerator(name = "accountsSequence", sequenceName =
    "accounts_id_seq",
    allocationSize = 1, initialValue = 10)
  @GeneratedValue(strategy = GenerationType.SEQUENCE,
    generator = "accountsSequence")
  private Long id;

  private Long accountNumber;
  private Long customerNumber;
  private String customerName;
  private BigDecimal balance;
  private AccountStatus accountStatus = AccountStatus.OPEN;

  ...
}
```

Tells JPA that the id field is the primary key of the database table

Creates a sequence generator for the id field, starting with the number 10. Starting at 10 provides space to import some records on startup for testing.

Uses the sequence generator from the previous line to specify where the generated value comes from for the primary key

When using JPA, the fields can be marked private instead of public.

NOTE Getter and setter methods, general object methods, and equals and hashcode methods from chapter 2 are excluded from the listing for clarity.

All constructors were removed from the Account class, because constructing instances directly is not needed when using JPA.

With the JPA entity defined, it's now possible to use an EntityManager to interact with the database for that entity. The first change to AccountResource is to inject an instance of the EntityManager:

```
@Inject
EntityManager entityManager;
```

Now the entityManager instance can be used for retrieving all the accounts, as shown in the next listing.

Listing 4.2 AccountResource

Tells the entityManager to use the named query "Accounts.findAll" defined on Account in listing 4.1 and that the expected results will be of the Account type

```
@GET
public List<Account> allAccounts() {
  return entityManager
    .createNamedQuery("Accounts.findAll", Account.class)    ◁
    .getResultList();        ◁
}
```

Converts the results from the database into a List of Account instances

There was another named query for finding accounts by their number on Account, shown in the following listing.

Listing 4.3 AccountResource

Passes the parameter into the query, setting the name of the parameter in the query and passing the value

Uses the "Accounts.findBy-AccountNumber" named query

```
public Account getAccount(@PathParam("acctNumber") Long accountNumber) {
  try {
    return entityManager
      .createNamedQuery("Accounts.findByAccountNumber", Account.class)    ◁
      .setParameter("accountNumber", accountNumber)
      .getSingleResult();        ◁
  } catch (NoResultException nre) {
    throw new WebApplicationException("Account with " + accountNumber
      + " does not exist.", 404);
  }
}
```

For a given accountNumber, there should only be one account, so requests the return of a single Account instance.

To retain the exception handling added in chapter 2, catches any NoResultException thrown when there is no account and converts it to a WebApplicationException

Now for a look at how to add a record to the database with an EntityManager, see the next listing.

Listing 4.4 `AccountResource`

Tells Quarkus that a transaction should be created for this operation
A transaction is necessary here because any exception from within
the method needs to result in a "rollback" of any proposed database
changes before they're committed. In this case it's a new Account.

```
@Transactional          ◁
public Response createAccount(Account account) {
    ...
    entityManager.persist(account);          ◁
    return Response.status(201).entity(account).build();
}
```

Calls persist with the Account
instance, adding it to the
persistent context for committing
to the database at the completion
of the transaction, in this case,
createAccount()

Now that we've shown how to use named queries and persist a new entity instance, how do we update an entity that already exists? Calling `entityManager.persist()` throws an exception if it's already persisted, so instead we use the following code.

Listing 4.5 `AccountResource`

Requires a transaction
during method execution

```
@Transactional
public Account withdrawal(@PathParam("accountNumber") Long accountNumber,    ◁
        String amount) {
    Account entity = getAccount(accountNumber);          ◁
    entity.withdrawFunds(new BigDecimal(amount));          ◁
    return entity;
}
```

Retrieves an Account instance
using accountNumber

Withdraws the funds from
the account, modifying the
state of the entity

For those that noticed, in listing 4.5, `entityManager` was not used. It wasn't necessary to call any methods on `entityManager` because retrieving the account instance had already happened. Retrieving the account puts the instance into the persistence context as a *managed* object. Managed objects can be updated at will and persisted in the database when the transaction commits.

If the method had a parameter of `Account`, instead of `accountNumber` and `amount`, the instance would be *unmanaged* because it does not exist in the current persistence context. Updating the balance would require the next code:

```
@Transactional
public Account updateBalance(Account account) {
    entityManager.merge(account);          ◁
    return account;
}
```

Merges the unmanaged
instance into the persistence
context, making it managed

IMPORTANT When using unmanaged instances to update the state in a database, it's necessary to ensure that the state hasn't been updated in the meantime. For example, the earlier method updating the balance requires the account to have been retrieved previously. An update to the balance could have occurred in another request between retrieval of the account and a call to update the balance. We have means to mitigate this problem, such as versioning JPA entities, but the use of `entityManager.merge()` needs to be carefully considered.

With only the code changes done so far, it's possible to run the application with *Dev Services* from Quarkus. With Docker running, run `mvn quarkus:dev`. The application will start a PostgreSQL database first. Dev Services are a recent addition to Quarkus for extensions enabling the automatic creation of necessary containers when configuration is not present for an external service. Details on how it works for data sources can be found at https://quarkus.io/guides/datasource#dev-services.

It's time to write some tests! To be able to test with an H2 database but use PostgreSQL in a production deployment, we need to use configuration profiles. Here's a snippet of the needed `application.properties`:

Overrides the password to empty, because H2 does not require a password

Defines the data source configuration for production, when building the application, and for Live Coding

```
quarkus.datasource.db-kind=postgresql
quarkus.datasource.username=quarkus_banking
quarkus.datasource.password=quarkus_banking
quarkus.datasource.jdbc.url=jdbc:postgresql://localhost/quarkus_banking

%test.quarkus.datasource.db-kind=h2
%test.quarkus.datasource.username=username-default
%test.quarkus.datasource.password=
%test.quarkus.datasource.jdbc.url=jdbc:h2:tcp://localhost/mem:default

quarkus.hibernate-orm.database.generation=drop-and-create
quarkus.hibernate-orm.sql-load-script=import.sql
```

Defines the data source configuration for tests

Indicates the SQL script to import data into the tables upon creation

Lets Quarkus know to drop any existing tables, based on the defined entities, and recreate them on startup

`%test.` is one of the configuration profiles introduced in chapter 3. Using the test profile for H2 configuration enables a separate configuration for production and Live Coding modes.

The next code listing contains a test using the H2 database described in section 4.1.

Listing 4.6   `AccountResourceTest`

```
@QuarkusTest
@QuarkusTestResource(H2DatabaseTestResource.class)
@TestMethodOrder(OrderAnnotation.class)
public class AccountResourceTest {
  @Test
  @Order(1)
  void testRetrieveAll() {
    Response result =
        given()
          .when().get("/accounts")
          .then()
            .statusCode(200)
```

Tells Quarkus to start an H2 database prior to the tests being executed

```
        .body(
            containsString("Debbie Hall"),
            containsString("David Tennant"),
            containsString("Alex Kingston")
        )
        .extract()
        .response();

    List<Account> accounts = result.jsonPath().getList("$");
    assertThat(accounts, not(empty()));
    assertThat(accounts, hasSize(8));
  }
}
```

This test may look familiar from chapter 2. The only difference between the similar test in chapter 2 and this one is that @QuarkusTestResource was added to the test class. Another change is in verifying the customer names. Why are they different? In chapter 2, all the data was in memory only, but now it's within a database.

To add records for testing, define an import.sql in the chapter4/jpa/src/main/-resources directory, as shown here:

```
INSERT INTO account(id, accountNumber, accountStatus, balance, customerName,
  customerNumber) VALUES (1, 123456789, 0, 550.78, 'Debbie Hall', 12345);
INSERT INTO account(id, accountNumber, accountStatus, balance, customerName,
customerNumber) VALUES (2, 111222333, 0, 2389.32, 'David Tennant', 112211);
INSERT INTO account(id, accountNumber, accountStatus, balance, customerName,
customerNumber) VALUES (3, 444666, 0, 3499.12, 'Billie Piper', 332233);
INSERT INTO account(id, accountNumber, accountStatus, balance, customerName,
customerNumber) VALUES (4, 87878787, 0, 890.54, 'Matt Smith', 444434);
INSERT INTO account(id, accountNumber, accountStatus, balance, customerName,
customerNumber) VALUES (5, 990880221, 0, 1298.34, 'Alex Kingston', 778877);
INSERT INTO account(id, accountNumber, accountStatus, balance, customerName,
customerNumber) VALUES (6, 987654321, 0, 781.82, 'Tom Baker', 908990);
INSERT INTO account(id, accountNumber, accountStatus, balance, customerName,
customerNumber) VALUES (7, 5465, 0, 239.33, 'Alex Trebek', 776868);
INSERT INTO account(id, accountNumber, accountStatus, balance, customerName,
customerNumber) VALUES (8, 78790, 0, 439.01, 'Vanna White', 444222);
```

Then inform Quarkus to use it by adding the following code to application.properties:

```
quarkus.hibernate-orm.sql-load-script=import.sql
```

With all that in place, from the chapter4/jpa/ directory, run the following:

```
mvn clean install
```

The test will execute using the H2 database, and if everything went well, the test passes!

In developing the Account service to use JPA, we made no mention of a persistence.xml file. Why is that? Everyone familiar with developing JPA code in Java EE and Jakarta EE knows about creating a persistence.xml file to configure the driver, data source name, and other JPA configuration elements.

With Quarkus, there's no need for a persistence.xml. What is present in that file either is performed automatically based on dependencies, has sensible defaults, or can be customized with application.properties instead. Though it is possible to use a persistence.xml file with Quarkus, we won't demonstrate it.

As an exercise for the reader, add additional test methods for the following:

- Creating an account
- Closing an account
- Withdrawing funds from an account
- Depositing funds into an account

By no means were all aspects of how to use JPA covered in this section—that was not the intention. Although using JPA with Quarkus is an option, the purpose of this section is to outline some key usages of JPA to provide a means of comparing how data access with Panache differs.

4.3   *Simplifying database development*

Using JPA for accessing a database is only one approach of many. Quarkus also includes the ability to choose the active record or data repository approaches to managing state. Both of these approaches are part of the Panache extensions to Quarkus. Panache seeks to make writing entities trivial and fun with Quarkus.

Though we talk about data in the following sections, Panache is emerging as a mini brand within Quarkus for simplification. In addition to simplifying entity development, Panache also has experimental functionality for generating RESTful CRUD endpoints, saving the time it takes to churn out the boilerplate JAX-RS definitions. See https://quarkus.io/guides/rest-data-panache for all the details.

4.3.1   *Active record approach*

Let's take a look at how the active record pattern differs from JPA. As seen in figure 4.2, all interactions occur through the entity itself. As objects usually hold data that needs to be stored, the active record approach puts the data access logic into the domain object directly. The active record approach rose to popularity with Ruby on Rails and the Play framework.

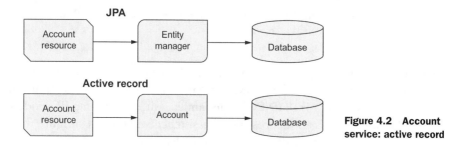

Figure 4.2   Account service: active record

In 2002, Martin Fowler outlined the approach in his book *Patterns of Enterprise Application Architecture* (https://www.martinfowler.com/books/eaa.html). His definition can be found on his site, https://www.martinfowler.com/eaaCatalog/activeRecord.html.

Now to work on the implementation! All the code for this section can be found in the /chapter4/active-record/ directory of the book source code.

Dependencies need to be different, because we need the Panache version, not the regular Hibernate version. For that, add the following dependency:

```
<dependency>
  <groupId>io.quarkus</groupId>
  <artifactId>quarkus-hibernate-orm-panache</artifactId>
</dependency>
```

Because a JDBC driver is needed, the same PostgreSQL dependency used with JPA can be added.

For the entity, that's different because Panache is used, as shown in the next code listing.

Listing 4.7 Account

```
@Entity
public class Account extends PanacheEntity {          ←──    Account extends PanacheEntity,
  public Long accountNumber;            ←──┐                 which provides the data access
  public Long customerNumber;              │ The fields on   helper methods like persist().
  public String customerName;              │ Account need
  public BigDecimal balance;               │ to be public.
  public AccountStatus accountStatus = AccountStatus.OPEN;

  public static long totalAccountsForCustomer(Long customerNumber) {   ←──┐
    return find("customerNumber", customerNumber).count();                │
  }                                                                       │

  public static Account findByAccountNumber(Long accountNumber) {         │
    return find("accountNumber", accountNumber).firstResult();           │
  }                                                                       │
  ...                          Custom static methods can be added to ────┘
}                              enhance those provided with PanacheEntity.
```

> **NOTE** equals() and hashCode() methods are excluded for brevity. The full code can be viewed in the chapter 4 book source code.

Note the following key points in listing 4.7:

- @Entity is still used to indicate the class is a JPA entity.
- Getter and setter methods for the fields are not required. During build time, Panache generates the necessary getter and setter methods, replacing field access in code to use the generated getter and setter methods.
- Definition of id, the primary key, is handled by PanacheEntity. If there was a need to customize the id configuration, we could do it with the usual JPA annotations.

Given the data access methods are present on `Account`, interacting with it must be quite different, as shown next.

Listing 4.8   AccountResource

```
public class AccountResource {

  @GET
  public List<Account> allAccounts() {
    return Account.listAll();
  }

  @GET
  @Path("/{acctNumber}")
  public Account getAccount(@PathParam("acctNumber") Long accountNumber) {
    return Account.findByAccountNumber(accountNumber);
  }

  @POST
  @Transactional
  public Response createAccount(Account account) {
    account.persist();
    return Response.status(201).entity(account).build();
  }

  @PUT
  @Path("{accountNumber}/withdrawal")
  @Transactional
  public Account withdrawal(@PathParam("accountNumber") Long accountNumber,
    String amount) {
    Account entity = Account.findByAccountNumber(accountNumber);
    entity.withdrawFunds(new BigDecimal(amount));
    return entity;
  }
}
```

> Uses the static listAll() from the PanacheEntity superclass of Account to retrieve all the accounts

> Calls the custom static method from listing 4.7, retrieving an Account instance by the accountNumber

> Adds a new Account instance into the persistence context. On transaction commit, the record will be added to the database.

> When modifying an existing instance, it will be persisted on transaction completion.

For testing, `AccountResourceTest` from the JPA example earlier can be copied for use with the active record approach. Because `Account` no longer has methods for retrieving or setting values, the only necessary changes are to provide it direct field usage.

As before, the tests use an in-memory H2 database, and import the data on startup from import.sql. The application-properties doesn't need to change compared with the JPA version.

In the /chapter4/active-record/ directory, run the next code:

```
mvn clean install
```

If all went well, all the tests pass.

To briefly recap, the active record approach with Panache integrates all data access into the JPA entity, while taking care of boilerplate tasks such as defining the primary key. `PanacheEntity` provides simplified methods that don't require deep SQL knowledge to construct queries, enabling developers to focus on the necessary business logic.

4.3.2 Data repository approach

Now on to the last approach, data repository.

Figure 4.3 uses `AccountRepository` as the intermediary for data access methods. There are some similarities with `EntityManager` from JPA, but also key differences. The Spring Framework popularized the data repository approach over the last decade or more.

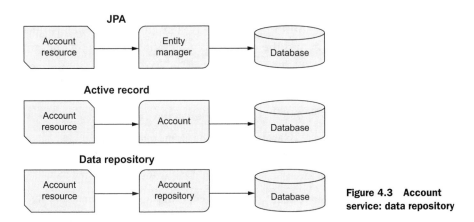

Figure 4.3   Account service: data repository

Martin Fowler also outlined this approach, with active record, in *Patterns of Enterprise Application Architecture* (https://www.martinfowler.com/books/eaa.html). On his website, Fowler explains the approach: https://martinfowler.com/eaaCatalog/repository.html.

So what's needed to implement the data repository approach? Exactly what was needed for the active record approach, as shown here:

```
<dependency>
  <groupId>io.quarkus</groupId>
  <artifactId>quarkus-hibernate-orm-panache</artifactId>
</dependency>
```

One benefit of both approaches being in the same dependency is it's quick to switch between them, or even use each approach in different situations in the same application.

The `Account` entity for the data repository approach is shown in the following listing.

Listing 4.9   Account

```
@Entity
public class Account {
  @Id
  @GeneratedValue
  private Long id;

  private Long accountNumber;
  private Long customerNumber;
```

```
private String customerName;
private BigDecimal balance;
private AccountStatus accountStatus = AccountStatus.OPEN;

...
}
```

NOTE Getter and setter methods, general object methods, and equals and hashcode methods are excluded from the listing for brevity.

Listing 4.9 is very similar to listing 4.1 for JPA. The main difference is there are no @NamedQuery annotations, and the default ID-generation process for the primary key is not the same.

Take a look at the repository class, shown in the following code listing.

Listing 4.10   `AccountRepository`

> **@ApplicationScoped tells the container that only one instance should exist.**

```
@ApplicationScoped   ⊲──┘
public class AccountRepository implements PanacheRepository<Account> {   ⊲──
  public Account findByAccountNumber(Long accountNumber) {
    return find("accountNumber = ?1", accountNumber).firstResult();
  }
}
```

Defines a custom data access method

> **Implements PanacheRepository for all the data access methods**

As with the active record approach, a parent class includes the convenience methods for finding and retrieving instances.

But how different is the JAX-RS resource? See the next example.

Listing 4.11   `AccountResource`

```
public class AccountResource {

  @Inject
  AccountRepository accountRepository;   ⊲──

  @GET
  public List<Account> allAccounts() {
    return accountRepository.listAll();   ⊲──
  }

  @GET
  @Path("/{acctNumber}")
  public Account getAccount(@PathParam("acctNumber") Long accountNumber) {
    Account account = accountRepository.findByAccountNumber(accountNumber);   ⊲──
    return account;
  }

  @POST
  @Transactional
  public Response createAccount(Account account) {
    accountRepository.persist(account);   ⊲──
```

> **Injects an AccountRepository instance for data access operations**

> **Retrieves all the accounts with listAll()**

> **Uses the custom data access method on AccountRepository**

> **Persists a new Account instance into the database**

```
      return Response.status(201).entity(account).build();
  }

  @PUT
  @Path("{accountNumber}/withdrawal")
  @Transactional
  public Account withdrawal(@PathParam("accountNumber") Long accountNumber,
     String amount) {
    Account entity = accountRepository.findByAccountNumber(accountNumber);
    entity.withdrawFunds(new BigDecimal(amount));        ◁──────────
    return entity;
  }
}
```

> **Updates the balance on the account without
> needing to call accountRepository.persist(); it's
> done automatically when the transaction completes.**

The `AccountResourceTest` class can be copied from the JPA example, because both
approaches use entities that have getters and setters.

The tests can be run from the /chapter4/data-repository/ directory with the following line:

```
mvn clean install
```

4.3.3 Which approach to use?

Through the previous sections, we have outlined different approaches for JPA, active
record, and data repository. Which one is the best?

As with most things dealing with software, it depends. The key points of each
approach follow:

- JPA
  - Easy migration for existing Java EE and Jakarta EE applications.
  - Requires creation of primary key field; not provided by default.
  - `@NamedQuery` annotations must be placed on an entity or super class.
  - Queries require actual SQL, as opposed to shortcut versions that are used in
    active record or data repository.
  - Non-primary key search requires SQL or `@NamedQuery`.
- Active record
  - Doesn't require getters and setters for all fields.
  - Coupling the data access layer into an object makes testing it without a data-
    base difficult. The flip side is that testing with a database is a lot easier than
    in the past.
  - Another aspect of coupling, it breaks the *single responsibility principle* and *sepa-
    ration of concerns.*
- Data repository
  - Requires creation of a primary key field; not provided by default.
  - Clearly separates data access and business logic, enabling them to be tested
    independently.
  - Without custom methods, it's an empty class. For some, this can seem unusual.

These are some key differences shown through the previous sections; there are likely many more. When it comes down to it, the chosen approach will depend on the requirements of an application and personal choice of the developer, based on their previous experience.

It's worth noting that no one approach is wrong, or right—it all depends on personal perspective and preference.

4.4 Deployment to Kubernetes

Now that the Account service has a database, it's time to deploy it to Kubernetes to see it in action. First, though, we must deploy a PostgreSQL instance that can be used by it.

4.4.1 Deploying PostgreSQL

We need to deploy the following pieces to Kubernetes for setting up a PostgreSQL database:

1   A Kubernetes Secret with encoded username and password. This secret will be used in creating the PostgreSQL database and in the data source configuration in Quarkus.
2   PostgreSQL database deployment.

First, verify Minikube is already running, and if it isn't, run the following:

```
minikube start
```

> **IMPORTANT**   As mentioned in previous chapters, ensure that `eval $(minikube -p minikube docker-env)` is run in each terminal window that will be pushing a deployment to Minikube, because it uses Docker inside Minikube for building the image.

Once Minikube is running, create the Secret as shown next:

```
kubectl create secret generic db-credentials \
--from-literal=username=quarkus_banking \
--from-literal=password=quarkus_banking
```

Creates a new Secret with the name db-credentials

Adds username with the plain text value of quarkus_banking. The value will be encoded as part of creating the Secret.

Also sets a password in the Secret

> **NOTE**   If the Minikube instance being used is the same as in chapter 3, you willl need to execute `kubectl delete secret generic db-credentials` first.

With the Secret created, the PostgreSQL database instance can be started. Doing that requires a Kubernetes Deployment and Service.

Change to the directory /chapter4/ and run the next code:

```
kubectl apply -f postgresql_kubernetes.yml
```

If successful, the terminal contains messages stating the Deployment and Service were created. With a PostgreSQL database running, it's time to package and deploy a service to use it.

4.4.2 Package and deploy

Any of the examples from the chapter could be used to show it working in Kubernetes, but in this instance, we use the active record example.

Before packaging the application, we need to make a few changes because it will be reading Kubernetes Secrets for database configuration. Add a new dependency in pom.xml as follows:

```
<dependency>
  <groupId>io.quarkus</groupId>
  <artifactId>quarkus-kubernetes-config</artifactId>
</dependency>
```

This dependency enables an application to read Kubernetes ConfigMaps and Secrets. For it to know where the information is to read, the following additional properties are needed:

```
%prod.quarkus.kubernetes-config.enabled=true          ⟵  Enables the extension
%prod.quarkus.kubernetes-config.secrets.enabled=true  ⟵  Tells the extension that
%prod.quarkus.kubernetes-config.secrets=db-credentials    Secrets will be read
```

Lists the Secrets to be read; in this case it's just db-credentials.

> **NOTE** The `%prod.` prefix ensures the settings are not used during development and testing.

As well as the previous additions to application.properties, we need to modify the datasource information for Kubernetes, as shown here:

```
%prod.quarkus.datasource.username=${username}   ⟵  Uses variables for the username
%prod.quarkus.datasource.password=${password}       and password because they will
%prod.quarkus.datasource.jdbc.url=jdbc:postgresql://postgres.default:5432/   be retrieved from the Secret
    quarkus_banking   ⟵
```

Updates the URL to be in the format of "<servicename>.<namespace>:<port>/<database>". In this example, postgres is the service name, and the namespace is default.

These are the only changes needed to have the database credentials read from a Secret and the PostgreSQL database used within Kubernetes. With the changes made, it's time to build the image and deploy it to Kubernetes as follows:

```
mvn clean package -Dquarkus.kubernetes.deploy=true
```

With the Account service deployed, run `minikube service list` to see the details of all services, as shown here:

```
|-------------|------------------|----------------|------------------------------|
| NAMESPACE   |       NAME       |  TARGET PORT   |              URL             |
|-------------|------------------|----------------|------------------------------|
| default     | account-service  | http/80        | http://192.168.64.2:30704    |
| default     | kubernetes       | No node port   |                              |
| default     | postgres         | http/5432      | http://192.168.64.2:31615    |
| kube-system | kube-dns         | No node port   |                              |
|-------------|------------------|----------------|------------------------------|
```

Accessing http://192.168.64.2:30704/accounts in a browser will now retrieve all the accounts in the PostgreSQL database running in Kubernetes.

Throughout the chapter, each example has shown the different approaches we can take for writing database code with Quarkus, beginning with JPA for easy migration to Quarkus, before progressing to cover the enhancements to Hibernate ORM that Panache brings through use of active record or data repository approaches.

Summary

- By adding the data source properties for `db-kind`, `username`, `password`, and `jdbc.url`, along with the `quarkus-jdbc-postgresql` dependency, a Quarkus application can connect with a PostgreSQL database.
- Use `@NamedQuery` on a JPA entity class to define custom queries for use with the `EntityManager`.
- Hibernate ORM with Panache offers simplified approaches to JPA with either the active record or data repository approaches.
- Add the `quarkus-hibernate-orm-panache` dependency, and use `Panache-Entity` as a super class for JPA entity classes to use the active record approach. The active record approach provides common methods for use when interacting with a database, simplifying the data access layer in an application.
- When using the data repository approach, create a repository class that implements `PanacheRepository` to hold custom data access methods, such as queries equivalent to `@NamedQuery` on JPA entities.
- Define a PostgreSQL deployment and service in Kubernetes, and create the resources in a Kubernetes environment using Minikube.

Clients for consuming other microservices

5

This chapter covers

- MicroProfile REST Client specification
- Using type-safe interfaces to consume external microservices
- Customizing the content of headers on the request

Although many microservices require only a database or alternative data services, or process a request within their own process, sometimes a microservice needs to communicate with other microservices to fulfill a request. When shifting from monoliths to microservices, the tendency is toward smaller and leaner microservices, which necessitates more of them. More importantly, many of those smaller microservices will need to communicate with each other to complete a task previously achieved with a single method calling other services inside a monolith. All those previously "in-process" method calls are now external microservice invocations.

This chapter introduces the MicroProfile REST Client and describes how Quarkus implements the specification to provide a type-safe means of interacting with external services. Many possible approaches exist, including Java's networking library or third-party libraries like OkHttp and Apache HttpClient. Quarkus abstracts away the underlying HTTP transport construction from the developer, enabling them to focus on the task of defining the external service and interacting with the service as if it were a local method invocation.

Figure 5.1 represents a microservice calling another microservice, but it is also the basis for the examples used throughout the chapter. The examples for this chapter follow from the previous banking domain examples. The Transaction service calls the Account service to retrieve the current balance to ensure the requested transaction doesn't result in an overdrawn account.

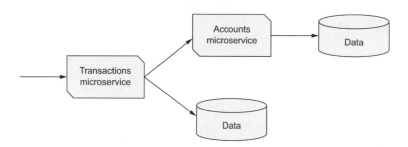

Figure 5.1 Banking microservice consumption

The Account service in this chapter is not the same as the version seen in earlier chapters. Because this chapter's focus is on the calling microservice, and not the called microservice, the Account service API will expose methods only to retrieve the current balance and update it.

> **NOTE** We won't show the Account service for this chapter because it's a derivative of that in earlier chapters. Take a look at the code for chapter 5, in the /chapter5/account-service/ directory, to see how it was implemented.

5.1 What is MicroProfile REST Client?

MicroProfile REST Client is one of the specifications from Eclipse MicroProfile (https://microprofile.io/). The specification defines how a representation of an external service with Java interfaces ensures interactions with that service occur in a type-safe manner. What that means is we use the Java language and compilation process to ensure the code that interacts with an external service is free from obvious errors.

When interacting with services utilizing one of the many HTTP libraries or the JAX-RS client library, it's necessary to perform a lot of casting between objects, transformations from JSON to POJOs, and many other steps that don't rely on the Java language to ensure correctness. Though workable, this leaves code susceptible to failures due to problems being discovered not during compilation but only through testing or even production usage. Using a type-safe approach with MicroProfile REST Client enables us to discover these types of problems during compilation and not much later during execution.

For many years the RESTEasy project (https://resteasy.github.io/) had a custom means of defining external services with Java interfaces. However, because it was included within only one JAX-RS implementation, other JAX-RS implementations didn't have such a feature. Building on the RESTEasy project's work, the Thorntail project (https://thorntail.io/) added a CDI layer on top of the programmatic builder from RESTEasy.

MicroProfile REST Client defines a specification to combine the ideas from RESTEasy and Thorntail for the Eclipse MicroProfile platform. Many aspects within the specification align it with how JAX-RS defines RESTful endpoints.

Some of the more important features of the specification include the following:

- Including additional client headers onto any external request
- Following responses redirecting to another URL
- Calling external services through an HTTP proxy
- Registering custom providers for filtering, message body manipulation, interceptors, and exception mappers
- Automatic registration of JSON-P and JSON-B providers
- Configuring SSL for REST client endpoints

Having covered the origins of the specification and its purpose, it's now time to begin using it with Quarkus.

5.2 Service interface definition

For the Transaction service to be able to communicate with the Account service, it needs to know what methods are available, their parameters, and their return types. Without that information, the Transaction service doesn't know the API contract of the Account service.

Many libraries are available that support communicating with other services via HTTP and other protocols, including classes within the JDK itself. However, taking such an approach requires more complex code to handle setting the appropriate content type, setting any headers, and handling response codes for different situations. Let's take a look at a service definition for `AccountService` in the next code listing.

Listing 5.1 AccountService

Defines the path of the service, excluding the base URL portion

Indicates that the interface should have a CDI bean created that can be injected into classes

```java
@Path("/accounts")
@RegisterRestClient
@Produces(MediaType.APPLICATION_JSON)
public interface AccountService {
  @GET
  @Path("/{acctNumber}/balance")
  BigDecimal getBalance(@PathParam("acctNumber") Long accountNumber);

  @POST
  @Path("{accountNumber}/transaction")
```

Sets all methods of the service to return JSON

Method for retrieving the account balance, with HTTP method and Path annotations

```
    void transact(@PathParam("accountNumber") Long accountNumber,
        BigDecimal amount);
}
```
⟵ **Method for transacting on an account, with HTTP method and Path annotations**

Looking at the interface definition, it likely seems very familiar, and there's a good reason for that. The way in which a Java interface defines the service deliberately uses the well-known JAX-RS annotations for a class and its methods. Using the same JAX-RS annotations on a Java interface to define a remote service as is used for creating a JAX-RS resource class means developers are already familiar with all the annotations used. If defining a service with a Java interface used completely different annotations, or an entirely different way to define the service, developers would find it much more difficult to learn and use.

The only difference in the Java interface compared to what a JAX-RS resource would contain is the @RegisterRestClient annotation. This annotation tells Quarkus that a CDI bean that contains the methods on the interface needs to be created. Quarkus wires up the CDI bean such that calls to the interface methods result in HTTP calls to the external service.

Listing 5.1 utilizes synchronous response types. Asynchronous types such as CompletionStage, Future, and CompletableFuture will be discussed in 5.3.

Let's take a look at how the execution flow works. In figure 5.2, the dotted boxes represent separate process boundaries. It doesn't matter whether it is a physical machine or Kubernetes Pod.

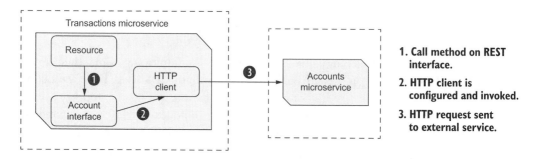

Figure 5.2   Account transaction service: REST client call

The flow of execution when calling the Account service in figure 5.2 follows:

- The JAX-RS resource calls a method on the AccountService interface, which executes the call on the CDI bean that implements the interface.
- The CDI bean, representing the AccountService interface, configures the HTTP client with the URL, HTTP method type, content types, headers, or anything else needing to be set on the HTTP request.
- The HTTP client issues the HTTP request to the external Account service and handles the response that's returned.

One thing that has not been mentioned so far is how to define the URL where the external service exists. As with many things, we can do this in several ways.

When `@RegisterRestClient` is present, we can set the URL directly on the annotation with the `baseUri` parameter. Though this is not a great way to set it for production, because URLs can change, it's an easy way to configure it to get started. With the `baseUri` parameter set on the annotation, it's still possible to override the value with configuration. The configuration key for setting the URL is {packageName}.{interfaceName}/mp-rest/url, which can be added to the application.properties file with the URL of the external service.

For listing 5.1, the configuration key is io.quarkus.transactions.Account-Service/mp-rest/url. Such a long key can be difficult to remember and is open to mistakes. To simplify the configuration key, set the `configKey` parameter of `@Register-RestClient`. For instance, define the `configKey` on the interface as follows:

```
@RegisterRestClient(configKey = "account-service")
public interface AccountService {
}
```

This method makes the configuration key account-service/mp-rest/url, making it less prone to errors.

Having covered how to create a service definition for any external service, let's actually use it in the Transaction service.

5.2.1 *CDI REST client*

The previous section discussed how Quarkus automatically creates a CDI bean from the Java interface when `@RegisterRestClient` is present. See the next listing to see how it's used.

Listing 5.2 `TransactionResource`

To inject the CDI bean for the interface, it is necessary to explicitly use @Inject. Though it's not required for other situations, it is when injecting a REST client interface.

```
public class TransactionResource {
  @Inject
  @RestClient
  AccountService accountService;              ◁──  The REST client
                                                   interface representing
                                                   the external service
  @POST
  @Path("/{acctNumber}")
  public Response newTransaction(@PathParam("acctNumber") Long accountNumber,
      BigDecimal amount) {
    accountService.transact(accountNumber, amount);   ◁──  Calls the external
    return Response.ok().build();                           service method
  }
}
```

CDI qualifier telling Quarkus to inject a type-safe
REST client bean matching the interface

Being able to call an external service with a single method call, as if it was a local service, is extremely powerful and simplifies making HTTP calls in the code. For developers familiar with Java EE, this looks very similar to remote EJBs. In many respects, it is very similar, except that instead of communicating with Remote Method Invocation (RMI), it uses HTTP.

With the interface defined, and a JAX-RS resource method that uses it, now it's time to test the REST Client.

MOCKING THE EXTERNAL SERVICE

When unit testing, setting up and running the service to be called is far from ideal. To verify some basic operation of the Transaction service, it's necessary to use a server to mock the responses that would be received from the Account service. One option is to create a server that handles a request and provides an appropriate response, but thankfully there's a handy library that offers that exact functionality, WireMock.

The first step is to add the required dependency, as follows:

```xml
<dependency>
  <groupId>com.github.tomakehurst</groupId>
  <artifactId>wiremock-jre8</artifactId>
  <scope>test</scope>
</dependency>
```

To assist in setting up an environment for testing, Quarkus provides Quarkus-TestResourceLifecycleManager. Implementing QuarkusTestResourceLifecycle-Manager enables us to customize what happens during start() and stop() during the life cycle of a test. Any implementation is applied to a test with @Quarkus-TestResource. One is needed to interact with the WireMock server, as shown in the next listing.

Listing 5.3 `WiremockAccountService`

Implements QuarkusTestResourceLifecycleManager
to respond to the start and stop events of the test

```java
public class WiremockAccountService implements
    QuarkusTestResourceLifecycleManager {
  private WireMockServer wireMockServer;

  @Override
  public Map<String, String> start() {
    wireMockServer = new WireMockServer();
    wireMockServer.start();

    stubFor(get(urlEqualTo("/accounts/121212/balance"))
        .willReturn(aResponse()
            .withHeader("Content-Type", "application/json")
            .withBody("435.76")
        ));
```

Stores the WireMockServer instance to enable stopping it during test shutdown

Creates the WireMockServer, and starts it

Provides a stub for responding to the HTTP GET method for retrieving an account balance. Because it's a mock server, the account number the server responds to needs to be hardcoded and used in the request from a test.

```
    stubFor(post(urlEqualTo("/accounts/121212/transaction"))
        .willReturn(noContent())
    );

    return Collections.singletonMap(
        "io.quarkus.transactions.AccountService/mp-rest/url",
        wireMockServer.baseUrl());
}

@Override
public void stop() {
    if (null != wireMockServer) {
        wireMockServer.stop();
    }
}
}
```

Creates another stub for responding to the HTTP POST method to create a transaction

Sets an environment variable named io.quarkus.transactions.AccountService/ mp-rest/url to the URL of the WireMock server. The variable name matches the expected name of the configuration key for defining the URL.

Stops the WireMock server during test-shutdown processing

Lastly, we need to write the test shown in the following code sample to use the Transaction service, which will call the mock server.

Listing 5.4 TransactionServiceTest

```
@QuarkusTest
@QuarkusTestResource(WiremockAccountService.class)
public class TransactionServiceTest {
  @Test
  void testTransaction() {
      given()
          .body("142.12")
          .contentType(ContentType.JSON)
          .when().post("/transactions/{accountNumber}", 121212)
          .then()
          .statusCode(200);
  }
}
```

Adds the life cycle manager for WireMock to the test

Issues an HTTP POST request using the account number defined in the WireMock stub

Verifies a response code of 200 is returned

With the test written, open the /chapter5/transaction-service/ directory and run the following:

```
mvn clean install
```

NOTE Be sure to have Docker running for the database.

The test should pass without issue.

Running the test using a mock server doesn't provide much confidence it's correct, so let's deploy all the services to Kubernetes to verify that the code works with a real service.

DEPLOYING TO KUBERNETES

If Minikube is already running, great. If it isn't, run the next line of code:

```
minikube start
```

With Minikube running, we can start the PostgreSQL database instance. To do that, install the Kubernetes Deployment and Service for PostgreSQL.

Change into the /chapter5/ directory and run the following:

```
kubectl apply -f postgresql_kubernetes.yml
```

> **WARNING** This PostgreSQL instance doesn't use Secrets for the username and password, unlike in chapter 4. For this reason, this setup is not recommended for production usage.

Change into the /chapter5/account-service/ directory to build and deploy the Account service to Kubernetes, as shown here:

```
mvn clean package -Dquarkus.kubernetes.deploy=true
```

> **NOTE** Run eval $(minikube -p minikube docker-env) before this command to ensure the container image build uses Docker inside Minikube.

Verify the service has started properly by running `kubectl get pods` as follows:

```
NAME                               READY   STATUS    RESTARTS   AGE
account-service-6d6d7655cf-ktmhv   1/1     Running   0          6m55s
postgres-775d4d9dd5-b9v42          1/1     Running   0          13m
```

If there are errors, indicated by the STATUS column containing Error, run `kubectl logs account-service-6d6d7655cf-ktmhv`, using the actual Pod name, to show the logs of the container for diagnosing the error.

Find the URL of the Account service by running `minikube service list`, and then verify it's working by running the next code:

```
curl http://192.168.64.4:30704/accounts/444666/balance
```

The terminal will show the balance returned, which should be `3499.12` if everything worked.

With the Account service deployed and working, it's time to do the same for the Transaction service. Remember, the URL needs to be set so that the Account service can be found. Do that by modifying application.properties to include the next code:

```
%prod.io.quarkus.transactions.AccountService/mp-rest/url=
    http://account-service:80
```

It uses the production profile (%prod) as the URL, which applies only when deployed to Kubernetes, and it's using the Kubernetes service name for the Account service that is returned from `minikube service list`.

Change to the /chapter5/transaction-service/ directory and deploy the next service:

```
mvn clean package -Dquarkus.kubernetes.deploy=true
```

Verify the service has started without error and issue a request to withdraw funds from an account as follows:

```
curl -H "Content-Type: application/json" -X POST -d "-143.43"
    http://192.168.64.4:31692/transactions/444666
```

If it completes with no errors and messages, run the `curl` command from earlier to check the account balance. If everything worked as intended, the balance returned should now be 3355.69! Have some fun exploring by depositing and withdrawing different amounts from various accounts, and see how the balance changes after each request.

Though we haven't used them so far, many other configuration options are available when using a REST client with CDI. With listing 5.1 as an interface, here is a list of different configurations that could be used:

Timeout for connecting to the remote endpoint in milliseconds

By default, the scope of a CDI bean for a REST client is @Dependent. This would change it to be @Singleton instead.

Comma-separated list of JAX-RS providers that should be used with the client

The URL where the external service is available, as seen in examples earlier

```
io.quarkus.transactions.AccountService/mp-rest/url=http://localhost:8080
io.quarkus.transactions.AccountService/mp-rest/scope=javax.inject.Singleton
io.quarkus.transactions.AccountService/mp-rest/providers=
        io.quarkus.transactions.MyProvider
io.quarkus.transactions.AccountService/mp-rest/connectTimeout=400
io.quarkus.transactions.AccountService/mp-rest/readTimeout=1000
io.quarkus.transactions.AccountService/mp-rest/followRedirects=true
io.quarkus.transactions.AccountService/mp-rest/proxyAddress=http://myproxy:9100
```

Determines if HTTP redirect responses are followed or an error is returned

HTTP proxy to be used for all HTTP requests from the client

How long to wait for a response from a remote endpoint in milliseconds

This configuration can also be achieved with the programmatic API, which we cover in the next section. If `configKey` on `@RegisterRestClient` had been used, all the previous configuration keys could replace `io.quarkus.transactions.AccountService/mp-rest/` with `account-service/mp-rest/`.

Using CDI isn't the only way to use a REST client for connecting to external services. Let's take a look at doing the same as earlier with the programmatic API.

5.2.2 *Programmatic REST client*

In addition to utilizing CDI for injecting and calling REST client beans for external interfaces, we can use a programmatic builder API instead. This API provides more control over the various settings of the REST client without needing to manipulate configuration values. See the next code listing.

Listing 5.5 AccountService

```
@Path("/accounts")
@Produces(MediaType.APPLICATION_JSON)
public interface AccountServiceProgrammatic {
  @GET
  @Path("/{acctNumber}/balance")
  BigDecimal getBalance(@PathParam("acctNumber") Long accountNumber);

  @POST
  @Path("{accountNumber}/transaction")
  void transact(@PathParam("accountNumber") Long accountNumber,
      BigDecimal amount);
}
```

The only difference between this interface and listing 5.1 is the removal of @Register-RestClient. Though the same interface can be used for CDI and programmatic API usage, it's important to show that @RegisterRestClient is not required for programmatic API usage, as shown next.

Listing 5.6 TransactionResource

Uses RestClientBuilder to create a builder instance for setting features programmatically

Sets the URL for any requests with the REST client, which is equivalent to baseUrl on @RegisterRestClient. Uses the configuration value of account.service to create a new URL.

```
@Path("/transactions")
public class TransactionResource {
  @ConfigProperty(name = "account.service", defaultValue =
      "http://localhost:8080")
  String accountServiceUrl;

  ...

  @POST
  @Path("/api/{acctNumber}")
  public Response newTransactionWithApi(@PathParam("acctNumber") Long
      accountNumber, BigDecimal amount) throws MalformedURLException {
    AccountServiceProgrammatic acctService =
        RestClientBuilder.newBuilder()
            .baseUrl(new URL(accountServiceUrl))
            .connectTimeout(500, TimeUnit.MILLISECONDS)
            .readTimeout(1200, TimeUnit.MILLISECONDS)
            .build(AccountServiceProgrammatic.class);

    acctService.transact(accountNumber, amount);
    return Response.ok().build();
  }
}
```

Injects a value for the configuration key account.service, defaulting it to http://localhost:8080 if it's not found

Adds the new programmatic API to the /transactions/api/ URL path

How long to wait for a response before triggering an exception

The maximum amount of wait time allowed when connecting to an external service

Builds a proxy of the AccountServiceProgrammatic interface for calling the external service

Calls the service in the same way as done previously with a CDI bean

Add the following configuration into application.properties:

```
%prod.account.service=http://account-service:80
```

Now build the Transaction service, and redeploy it to Kubernetes as shown next:

```
mvn clean package -Dquarkus.kubernetes.deploy=true
```

Verify the service has started without error, and issue a request to deposit funds into an account as follows:

```
curl -H "Content-Type: application/json" -X POST -d "2.03"
     http://192.168.64.4:31692/transactions/api/444666
```

Running `curl http://192.168.64.4:30704/accounts/444666/balance` will return a balance that should be $2.03 more than it was previously. Try out different combinations of depositing and withdrawing funds from accounts with the programmatic API. Both the CDI bean and programmatic API endpoints shouldn't result in any different outcomes.

Using the programmatic API with `RestClientBuilder` provides greater control over the configuration of the client. Whether specifying the URL of the external service, registering JAX-RS providers, setting connection and read timeouts, or any other setting, we can do it all with the `RestClientBuilder`.

5.2.3 *Choosing between CDI and a programmatic API*

There is no right or wrong answer here—it all comes down to preference.

Some developers are more comfortable dealing with CDI beans, whereas others prefer using programmatic APIs to fully control the process. There is one caveat when using CDI beans for a REST client—it does require more configuration in application .properties compared to the programmatic API approach. However, whether that is a problem very much depends on what aspects the developer wants control over. If they require more control, then it's likely easier to do that with the programmatic API and not configuration properties.

Whichever approach we choose, it doesn't impact the type-safe guarantees of the REST client. It impacts only the interaction with the interface.

In addition, both approaches provide a thread-safe means of communicating with external resources. In listing 5.6, the `acctService` could be stored in a variable on the class. In this case, it wasn't, to simplify the code.

5.2.4 *Asynchronous response types*

In recent years, there's more desire to write reactive code, ideally not blocking threads while waiting. Because calling an external service could be a slow operation, depending on network latency, network load, and many other factors, it would be a good idea to utilize asynchronous types when using the REST client.

The first thing to do is to update the `AccountService` and `AccountService-Programmatic` interfaces with the following method:

```
@POST
@Path("{accountNumber}/transaction")
CompletionStage<Void> transactAsync(@PathParam("accountNumber") Long
    accountNumber, BigDecimal amount);
```

The only change from the original `transact()` method on the interface is the return type. Instead of returning `void`, the method now returns `CompletionStage<Void>`. In essence, the method is still returning a void response, but wrapping it in a `CompletionStage` allows the method to complete, and handling the response from the HTTP request will happen later once received. Although the response has not been received, the method execution completes and processing of the response waits. Doing so frees up the thread that was processing the request to handle other requests while waiting for an asynchronous response.

With the interfaces updated, how different are the JAX-RS resource methods? See the next code listing.

Listing 5.7   `TransactionResource`

```
                                        Uses a different URL path for the
@POST                                   asynchronous version. Return type is now
@Path("/async/{acctNumber}")    ◁——     CompletionStage<Void> instead of Response.
public CompletionStage<Void> newTransactionAsync(@PathParam("acctNumber")
    Long accountNumber, BigDecimal amount) {
  return accountService.transactAsync(accountNumber, amount);   ◁——┐
}
                                                Method body modified
                                                  to return the result
@POST                                              of REST client call
@Path("/api/async/{acctNumber}")
public CompletionStage<Void>
    newTransactionWithApiAsync(@PathParam("acctNumber") Long accountNumber,
    BigDecimal amount) throws MalformedURLException {       As with the newTransaction-
  AccountServiceProgrammatic acctService =                  Async method, instead of
      RestClientBuilder.newBuilder()                     returning a Response to indicate
          .baseUrl(new URL(accountServiceUrl))           everything is OK, returns the
          .build(AccountServiceProgrammatic.class);      CompletionStage returned from
                                                          the REST client call instead
  return acctService.transactAsync(accountNumber, amount);   ◁——
}
```

With the Transaction service updated, redeploy the changes with the following:

```
mvn clean package -Dquarkus.kubernetes.deploy=true
```

After verifying that the service started successfully with `kubectl get pods`, retrieve an account balance and then deposit an amount using the new asynchronous API URL as follows:

```
curl http://192.168.64.4:30704/accounts/444666/balance
curl -H "Content-Type: application/json" -X POST -d "5.63"
    http://192.168.64.4:31692/transactions/async/444666
```

Though the new methods use asynchronous return types, they achieve the same outcome as the synchronous ones. Take some time to experiment with the asynchronous methods—see what the upper limit of the number of parallel requests might be.

5.3 Customizing REST clients

So far, the examples have focused on normal usage: defining an interface and then executing methods on that interface to execute HTTP requests. REST clients offer many other features, some of which will be covered in the following sections.

5.3.1 Client request headers

All requests that are received or sent from applications contain many headers within them—some that everyone is familiar with, such as `Content-Type` and `Authorization`, but many headers are passed down a call chain. With REST client, it's possible to add custom request headers into the outgoing client request or ensure that headers from an incoming JAX-RS request propagate to a subsequent client request.

To see the headers received in the Account service, modify `AccountResource` to return them from the request. Another option is to print the header contents to the console with log statements inside the service, as shown next.

Listing 5.8 `AccountResource`

```
public class AccountResource {
    @POST
    @Path("{accountNumber}/transaction")
    @Transactional
    public Map<String, List<String>> transact(@Context HttpHeaders headers,
        @PathParam("accountNumber") Long accountNumber, BigDecimal amount) {
        ...

        return headers.getRequestHeaders();
    }
}
```

> Injects the HttpHeaders of the HTTP request into the method. @Context is specific to JAX-RS but acts in a manner similar to @Inject with CDI.

> Returns the Map containing the HTTP request headers

With the Account service modified, it's also necessary to modify the `AccountService` interface the Transaction service uses, as shown in the following listing.

Listing 5.9 `AccountService`

> Indicates the default ClientHeadersFactory should be used. The default factory will propagate any headers from an inbound JAX-RS request onto the outbound client request, where the headers are added as a comma-separated list into the configuration key named org.eclipse.microprofile.rest.client.propagateHeaders.

> Adds class-level-param to the outgoing HTTP request header. Adding it on the interface means all methods will have the header added.

```
@Path("/accounts")
@RegisterRestClient
@ClientHeaderParam(name = "class-level-param", value = "AccountService
    interface")
@RegisterClientHeaders
```

```
@Produces(MediaType.APPLICATION_JSON)
public interface AccountService {
    ...
    @POST
    @Path("{accountNumber}/transaction")
    Map<String, List<String>> transact(@PathParam("accountNumber") Long
        accountNumber, BigDecimal amount);

    @POST
    @Path("{accountNumber}/transaction")
    @ClientHeaderParam(name = "method-level-param", value = "{generateValue}")
    CompletionStage<Map<String, List<String>>>
        transactAsync(@PathParam("accountNumber") Long accountNumber,
            BigDecimal amount);
    default String generateValue() {
        return "Value generated in method for async call";
    }
}
```

Modifies the return type to be a Map of the headers

As with the transact method, returns a CompletionStage of the Map of headers

Default method on the interface used to create a value for the header on transactAsync

Similar to the usage of @ClientHeaderParam on the type, it adds the method-level-param header to the outbound HTTP request.

There are new features included in listing 5.9 to cover in detail.

@ClientHeaderParam is a convenient way to add request headers onto the HTTP request that is sent to the external service. As seen previously, the annotation can define a value that is a constant string, or it can use a method, either on the interface itself or in another class, by using curly braces to surround the name of the method. Calling a method to add a header is useful for setting an authentication token on the request, which would be necessary to call secured services, and a token isn't present on the incoming request.

Is there an advantage to using @ClientHeaderParam? Another option is adding header parameters using @HeaderParam on a method parameter. The problem with the @HeaderParam approach is it requires additional parameters on any interface method. Maybe when adding one or two parameters, it's not too bad, but what about three, four, or even six parameters! Not only does it clutter up the method definition in the interface, whenever making a call to the method, we need to pass all those parameters as well. This is where @ClientHeaderParam is helpful, keeping the interface methods uncluttered and simplifying the method invocation.

@RegisterClientHeaders is similar to @ClientHeaderParam, but for propagating headers and not adding new ones. The default behavior when there's an incoming JAX-RS request is for no headers to be passed onto any subsequent REST client call. Using @RegisterClientHeaders allows specific headers to be propagated from an incoming JAX-RS request.

Which headers should be propagated is specified in the configuration with the org.eclipse.microprofile.rest.client.propagateHeaders key, where the value is a comma-separated list of header names to propagate. This feature is especially useful for propagating authentication headers from incoming requests onto REST client calls, but do make sure it makes sense for them to be passed. Sometimes passing authentication headers from incoming to outgoing can have unintended consequences, such as performing operations on a service with an unexpected user identity.

If the default header propagation isn't sufficient—maybe it's needed to modify the content of a particular header—`@RegisterClientHeaders` allows the use of a custom implementation. For example, `@RegisterClientHeaders(MyHeaderClass.class)` says to use a custom implementation, where `MyHeaderClass` extends `ClientHeaders-Factory`. The only method on `ClientHeadersFactory` to implement is `update()`, which has method arguments for the `MultiMap` containing the headers from the incoming JAX-RS request and a `MultiMap` with the headers to be used on the outgoing REST client call. Updating the headers on the outgoing headers will alter what is set on the HTTP request to the external service.

The change to be made in the `TransactionResource` is modifying the return types of `newTransaction` and `newTransactionAsync` to use a `Map` for the headers.

The last thing needed is to specify which headers need to be automatically propagated. Without doing that, `@RegisterClientHeaders` will not propagate anything. Add the following to application.properties of the Transaction service:

```
org.eclipse.microprofile.rest.client.propagateHeaders=SpecialHeader
```

The header name to be propagated is SpecialHeader.

With all those changes made, deploy the updated Account service and Transaction service to Kubernetes as shown here:

```
/chapter5/account-service > mvn clean package
    -Dquarkus.kubernetes.deploy=true
/chapter5/transaction-service > mvn clean package
    -Dquarkus.kubernetes.deploy=true
```

With both services updated, it's time to see the headers being passed. Let's run the synchronous transaction method first, which should have only the class-level header added, as follows:

```
curl -H "Content-Type: application/json" -X POST -d "7.89"
    http://192.168.64.4:31692/transactions/444666
```

The terminal output should contain the next code:

```
{
  "class-level-param":["AccountService-interface"],
  "Accept":["application/json"],
  "Connection":["Keep-Alive"],
  "User-Agent":["Apache-HttpClient/4.5.12 (Java/11.0.5)"],
  "Host":["account-service:80"],
```

Header passed via @ClientHeaderParam on AccountService

```
    "Content-Length":["4"],
    "Content-Type":["application/json"]
}
```

Now let's do the same with the asynchronous transaction. This time both the class level and method level headers should be present, as shown next:

```
curl -H "Content-Type: application/json" -X POST -d "6.12"
    http://192.168.64.4:31692/transactions/async/444666
```

The output should now include the following:

```
{
    "class-level-param":["AccountService-interface"],    ◄──    Class-level header
                                                                from AccountService
    "method-level-param":["Value generated in method for async call"],    ◄──
    "Accept":["application/json"],
    "Connection":["Keep-Alive"],
    "User-Agent":["Apache-HttpClient/4.5.12 (Java/11.0.5)"],
    "Host":["account-service:80"],
    "Content-Length":["4"],                    Header passed via @ClientHeaderParam
    "Content-Type":["application/json"]              on the transactAsync method of
}                                                                AccountService
```

How about the propagation of headers? For that, it's necessary to pass a header with `curl` as follows:

```
curl -H "Special-Header: specialValue" -H "Content-Type: application/json" -X
    POST -d "10.32" http://192.168.64.4:31692/transactions/444666
curl -H "Special-Header: specialValue" -H "Content-Type: application/json" -X
    POST -d "9.21" http://192.168.64.4:31692/transactions/async/444666
```

If it works as expected, the terminal output will contain the headers for each of the previous examples, in addition to the `Special-Header` that was passed into the initial call.

Exercise for the reader

Modify the programmatic API versions in `AccountServiceProgrammatic` and `TransactionResource`, and try out the /api endpoints to see the headers.

In this section, we covered the different approaches to including additional headers on the client request. `@ClientHeaderParam` can be added to a REST client interface for applying to all methods, or added to specific methods only. `@ClientHeaderParam` allows setting a static value as the header, or calling a method to retrieve a necessary value for the header.

5.3.2   *Declaring providers*

Many JAX-RS providers can be written to adjust a request or response, such as `Client-RequestFilter`, `ClientResponseFilter`, `MessageBodyReader`, `MessageBodyWriter`, `ParamConverter`, `ReaderInterceptor`, and `WriterInterceptor`. Each provider type enables developers to customize an aspect of the HTTP request or response processing. Because the providers are part of JAX-RS, example usage will cover only some of them. There is also the `ResponseExceptionMapper` from the REST client.

Figure 5.3 highlights the sequence of JAX-RS and REST client provider execution in preparing the HTTP request and handling the HTTP response.

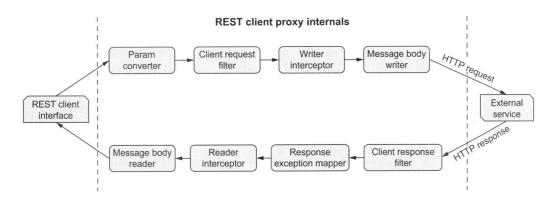

Figure 5.3   Provider processing sequence of REST client proxy

Any provider classes that implement the previous interfaces can register them for use in the following ways:

- Add `@Provider` onto the class itself. This is the least flexible method because it means any JAX-RS interaction will include the provider, irrespective of whether it's an incoming JAX-RS request or an outgoing REST client call.
- Associate a provider class with a specific REST client interface by adding `@RegisterProvider(MyProvider.class)` to the interface.
- When using the programmatic API, call `builder.register(MyProvider.class)` to use the provider with a particular REST client call.
- Implement either `RestClientBuilderListener` or `RestClientListener`, and register the provider directly onto the `RestClientBuilder`.

The following sections cover in detail how to use client filters and exception mappers.

CLIENT REQUEST FILTER

This section shows how to write and apply a `ClientRequestFilter` to REST client calls. A `ClientRequestFilter` can be used to modify the HTTP request before it is sent. Modifications can include anything from modifying header attributes and their values, to modifying the content of the HTTP request. There's not much to writing a request filter, so let's write one to add a new header onto the request containing the name of the invoked method, as shown in the next code listing.

Listing 5.10   `AccountRequestFilter`

Overrides the filter method to perform whatever filtering is needed. The method has access to the ClientRequestContext to amend what is sent in the request.

The class needs to implement ClientRequestFilter.

```
public class AccountRequestFilter implements ClientRequestFilter {
    @Override
    public void filter(ClientRequestContext requestContext) throws IOException {
        String invokedMethod =
            (String) requestContext.getProperty("
                org.eclipse.microprofile.rest.client.invokedMethod");
        requestContext.getHeaders().add("Invoked-Client-Method", invokedMethod);
    }
}
```

The REST client adds a property named org.eclipse.microprofile.rest.client.invokedMethod with the value of the interface method that is being invoked. In this case it is retrieved.

Adds a new request header named Invoked-Client-Method with the value from the previous line

For the previous filter to be used during invocation of a client request, register it as a provider onto `AccountService` as follows:

```
@RegisterProvider(AccountRequestFilter.class)
public interface AccountService { ... }
```

Time to redeploy the updated Transaction service to Kubernetes, like so:

```
mvn clean package -Dquarkus.kubernetes.deploy=true
```

With the service updated, let's see the additional header added to the request by the filter, as shown in the following code. Verification can be done with either the synchronous or asynchronous version of the method. Because it's applied directly on the interface, it works on both executions.

```
curl -H "Content-Type: application/json" -X POST -d "15.64"
    http://192.168.64.4:31692/transactions/444666
```

With the returned headers, the following code should be present in the terminal:

```
{
  "class-level-param":["AccountService-interface"],
  "method-level-param":["Value generated in method for async call"],
  "Accept":["application/json"],
  "Invoked-Client-Method":["transact"],
  "Connection":["Keep-Alive"],
  "User-Agent":["Apache-HttpClient/4.5.12 (Java/11.0.5)"],
  "Host":["account-service:80"],
```

Header added by the AccountRequestFilter showing the transact method of AccountService was called

```
  "Content-Length":["4"],
  "Content-Type":["application/json"]
}
```

The returned results should be the same as the CDI bean version seen earlier.

This section covered how to register a `ClientRequestFilter`, or `ClientResponse-Filter`, for a REST client by adding `@RegisterProvider` with the name of the class.

MAPPING EXCEPTIONS

Another JAX-RS provider type that can be implemented is the `ResponseException-Mapper`. This provider is specific to the REST client and will not work with JAX-RS endpoints. The purpose of the mapper is to convert the `Response` that is received from an external service into a `Throwable` that can be more easily handled.

> **IMPORTANT** The exception type of the mapper must be present on the `throws` clause of the method on the interface for it to work.

As with other JAX-RS providers, we can set a specific `@Priority` to indicate the precedence of an exception mapper compared to others. The lower a priority number, the higher, or earlier, in the ordering it is executed.

Implementations of the REST client provide a default exception mapper designed to handle any `Response` where the status code is greater than or equal to 400. With such a response, the default mapper returns a `WebApplicationException`. The priority of the default exception mapper is the maximum value for an `Integer`, so it can be bypassed with a lower priority.

If the default exception mapper isn't wanted at all, it can be disabled by setting the `microprofile.rest.client.disable.default.mapper` configuration property to `true`.

Let's write the following exception mapper to handle any errors related to an account not being found. For that, there needs to be an exception thrown from the mapper.

```
public class AccountNotFoundException extends Exception {
  public AccountNotFoundException(String message) {
    super(message);
  }
}
```

There's nothing special about the exception, because the string parameter constructor is sufficient.

Now to write the mapper, as shown in the next listing.

Listing 5.11 `AccountRequestFilter`

Implements ResponseExceptionMapper for the AccountNotFoundException type

toThrowable takes the Response and converts it the appropriate exception type, in this case, AccountNotFoundException.

```
public class AccountExceptionMapper implements
    ResponseExceptionMapper<AccountNotFoundException> {
  @Override
  public AccountNotFoundException toThrowable(Response response) {
    return new AccountNotFoundException("Failed to retrieve account");
  }

  @Override
  public boolean handles(int status, MultivaluedMap<String, Object> headers)
    {
    return status == 404;
  }
}
```

Handles a Response only when the status code is 404

Creates an instance of AccountNotFoundException

The handles method provides a way to say whether the mapper is responsible for producing a Throwable based on the Response, or whether it shouldn't be called for it.

Without adding `@Priority` onto `AccountExceptionMapper`, the default priority of `5000` is used.

To see the effect of the exception mapper, modify `TransactionResource` to capture the exception from the REST client call as shown next.

Listing 5.12 `TransactionResource`

```
public class TransactionResource {
  ...
  @POST
  @Path("/{acctNumber}")
  public Map<String, List<String>> newTransaction(@PathParam("acctNumber")
    Long accountNumber, BigDecimal amount) {
    try {
      return accountService.transact(accountNumber, amount);
    } catch (Throwable t) {
      t.printStackTrace();
      Map<String, List<String>> response = new HashMap<>();
      response.put("EXCEPTION - " + t.getClass(),
        Collections.singletonList(t.getMessage()));
      return response;
    }
  }
}
```

Wraps the REST client call in a try-catch

Creates a Map with information about the received exception to return as the response. This is to show the captured exception only; a production service should handle the exception in a more appropriate manner.

Rebuild and deploy the Transaction service to Kubernetes as follows:

```
mvn clean package -Dquarkus.kubernetes.deploy=true
```

Now call the service with an account number that doesn't exist, as shown here:

```
curl -H "Content-Type: application/json" -X POST -d "15.64"
    http://192.168.64.4:31692/transactions/11
```

The headers returned should provide details of the exception, as follows:

```
{
  "EXCEPTION - class javax.ws.rs.WebApplicationException":["Unknown error,
     status code 404"]
}
```

By default, the exception type received from the REST client call is WebApplicationException. This is a result of the default exception mapper being active.

Let's modify `AccountService` to register the custom exception mapper, as shown in the next listing.

Listing 5.13 `AccountService`

```
@RegisterProvider(AccountExceptionMapper.class)
public interface AccountService {
  ...

  @POST
  @Path("{accountNumber}/transaction")
  Map<String, List<String>> transact(@PathParam("accountNumber")
     Long accountNumber,
      BigDecimal amount) throws AccountNotFoundException;
}
```

Registers the AccountExceptionMapper for handling exceptions

transact indicates it can return an AccountNotFoundException, enabling the exception mapper to work.

Time to see how the exception changes with the mapper registered. Redeploy the Transaction service like so:

```
mvn clean package -Dquarkus.kubernetes.deploy=true
```

Now run the same request again as follows:

```
curl -H "Content-Type: application/json" -X POST -d "15.64"
     http://192.168.64.4:31692/transactions/11
```

The terminal should contain the following response:

```
{
  "EXCEPTION - class
     io.quarkus.transactions.AccountNotFoundException":["Failed to retrieve
     account"]
}
```

The exception type received is now AccountNotFoundException.

Exercise for the reader

Try out the different methods on `TransactionResource` to see when the exception mapper is, and is not, applied. Another exercise is to store the transactions into a local database for auditing.

Summary

- By adding `@RegisterRestClient` onto an interface that defines an external service, a CDI bean representing the interface is available for injection with `@RestClient` to execute REST client calls.
- Customization of interface behavior can be achieved with configuration keys that start with `[packageName].[className]/mp-rest/`. The URL of the external service, which CDI bean scope to use, what JAX-RS providers to register, and the connection or read timeouts are all items available for customization.
- When executing REST client calls with services that may require time to execute, it is worth switching the return types to `CompletionStage` to enable asynchronous execution.
- Adding `@RegisterProvider`, with a JAX-RS provider class name as the value, onto an interface of an external service indicates the provider should be used with any REST client calls that involve the interface.
- Implementing `ResponseExceptionMapper` to handle specific HTTP status codes and return a custom exception makes executing REST client calls more like local method execution.

Application health

6

This chapter covers

- Application health, or lack thereof, in a traditional, three-tier, Java monolithic application architecture
- MicroProfile Health and exposing application health
- Exposing Account service and Transaction service application health
- Using Kubernetes probes to address application health issues

The combination of Kubernetes and the microservices architecture have caused a fundamental shift in how developers create applications. What used to be dozens of large monolithic applications are now becoming hundreds (or thousands) of smaller, more nimble microservice instances. The more application instances running, the larger the odds of an individual application instance failing. The increased odds of failure could be a significant challenge in production if application health is not a first-class concern in Kubernetes.

Let's begin with a quick review of how monolithic applications running in application servers react to unhealthy applications.

6.1   *The growing role of developers in application health*

Many enterprise Java developers have experience with Java application servers, dating back to the late 1990s. During most of that time, developers created monolithic, three-tier applications with little awareness of exposing an application's health. From a developer's perspective, monitoring an application's health was the responsibility of system administrators whose job descriptions are to keep applications up and running in production.

Figure 6.1 shows the typical high-availability architecture of monolithic applications running in a traditional, horizontally scaled application server configuration.

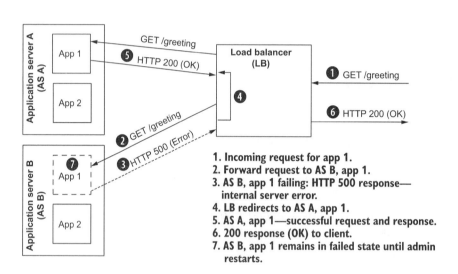

Figure 6.1   Traditional application server, high availability architecture

There are some notable points to make about this architecture:

- *Load balancer*—The load balancer's primary role is to balance load across multiple application instances for application scalability and availability. The load balancer redirects traffic from a failing instance to a properly running instance. It is the responsibility of an administrator to ensure proper load balancer configuration.

- *Handling failed applications*—Addressing failed applications is commonly dealt with manually. Because dealing with a failing application is a manual process, administrators prefer to conduct a root cause analysis to find the cause and address it, so they do not have to spend time on it again at a later date.

Regardless, it is the administrator's responsibility to restart the failed application, which takes time and resources.

- *Roles and responsibilities*—In this scenario, developers have little to no direct role in application health in production. The developer's role is typically limited to helping diagnose issues to determine whether the application is the root cause.
- *Minimal automation*—The only automation in this process is the load balancer recognizing the HTTP 500 error and pausing HTTP traffic to the failing application. Load balancers also recover by occasionally sending traffic to detect a recovered server and resume traffic. Because there is no formal "health" contract among the application, the load balancer, and the application server, no automated way exists to determine if an application is failing.

Given the scale of microservice deployments, with hundreds to thousands of application instances, administrators cannot manually manage individual application instances at this scale. Developers can play a key role in significantly improving the overall health and efficiency of a production environment by reducing the need for manual intervention. More specifically, developers can proactively expose application health to Kubernetes. Kubernetes uses *probes* to check the exposed health and take corrective action if necessary. In the next section, we cover MicroProfile Health as an API to expose application heath and follow that by covering how Kubernetes liveness and readiness probes can take corrective action.

6.2 *MicroProfile Health*

The MicroProfile community recognizes that modern Java microservices run on single-application stacks, which in turn often run in containers. There is also recognition that modern container platforms have defined a formal health contract between the containerized application and the platform. With a formal contract in place, the platform can restart failing application containers and pause traffic to an containerized application that is not ready to accept traffic. The MicroProfile Health specification supports such a contract by defining the following:

- *Health endpoints*—Application health is accessible at the MicroProfile-specified `/health/live` and `/health/ready` endpoints. Quarkus will redirect these to `/q/health/live` and `/q/health/ready` endpoints, respectively.
- *HTTP status code*—The HTTP status code reflects the health status.
- *HTTP response payload*—The JSON payload also provides status, along with additional health metadata and context.
- *Application liveness*—Specifies whether an application is up and running properly.
- *Application readiness*—Specifies whether an application is ready to accept traffic.
- *Application health API*—Exposes application readiness and liveness based on custom application logic.

6.2.1   *Liveness vs. readiness*

Although it may not be apparent, a clear separation of concerns exists between liveness and readiness. The underlying platform makes an HTTP request to the /q/health/live endpoint to determine whether it should restart the application container. For example, an application running out of memory can cause unpredictable behavior that may require a restart.

   The underlying platform makes an HTTP request to the /q/health/ready endpoint to determine whether an application instance is ready to accept traffic. If it is not ready, then the underlying platform will not send traffic to the application instance. An application can be "live" but not be "ready." For example, it may take time to prepopulate an in-memory cache or connect to an external service. During this time, the application is live and running properly but may not be ready to receive external traffic because a service it depends on may not be running properly.

> **NOTE**   Sending an HTTP request to the /health endpoint returns the combined liveness and readiness status. MicroProfile Health has deprecated this endpoint in favor of separate /health/live and /health/ready endpoints. Quarkus prefers using /q/health/live and /q/health/ready endpoints directly to avoid an HTTP redirect.

6.2.2   *Determining liveness and readiness status*

The underlying platform has two means to determine status: it can check the HTTP status code or parse the JSON payload to obtain the status (UP, DOWN). Table 6.1 shows the correlation between the HTTP status code and JSON payload.

Table 6.1   Health endpoints, status codes, and JSON payload status

Health check endpoints	HTTP status	JSON payload status
/q/health/live and /q/health/ready	200	UP
/q/health/live and /q/health/ready	503	DOWN
/q/health/live and /q/health/ready	500	Undetermined *

* Request processing failed.

Figure 6.2 shows the flow of probe traffic on the left-hand side and the flow of application traffic on the right-hand side, in time sequence from top to bottom. The figure shows that after a period of unsuccessful attempts, the container will be restarted, and normal application traffic will resume until the probe detects the next health issue.

HTTP liveness check

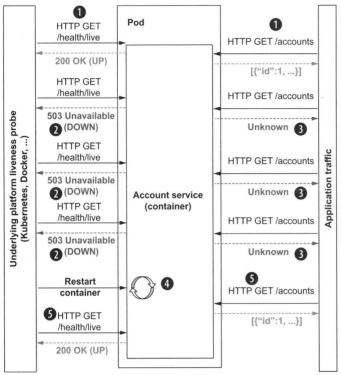

1. **The liveness check and application traffic are executing normally.**
2. **The application liveness check fails.**
3. **The Account service is down; the HTTP response depends on the error.**
4. **After three unsuccessful attempts, the container is restarted. Traffic is redirected to another instance during restart.**
5. **The liveness check and application traffic are executing normally.**

Figure 6.2   **Liveness check and application traffic flow**

Figure 6.3 shows a flow similar to figure 6.2, but instead represents a readiness health check. The figure shows that when a database connection is lost, the readiness check fails. The failure causes Kubernetes to redirect flow to another application instance until the database connection resumes.

A couple of notes about these figures: First, we will address these use cases shortly in code examples. Second, the probes are configurable, and we will also cover them shortly.

In fact, let's start coding now!

6.3   *Getting started with MicroProfile Health*

This chapter extends the Account service and Transaction service with application health logic. This logic provides Kubernetes enough metadata to take corrective action if necessary.

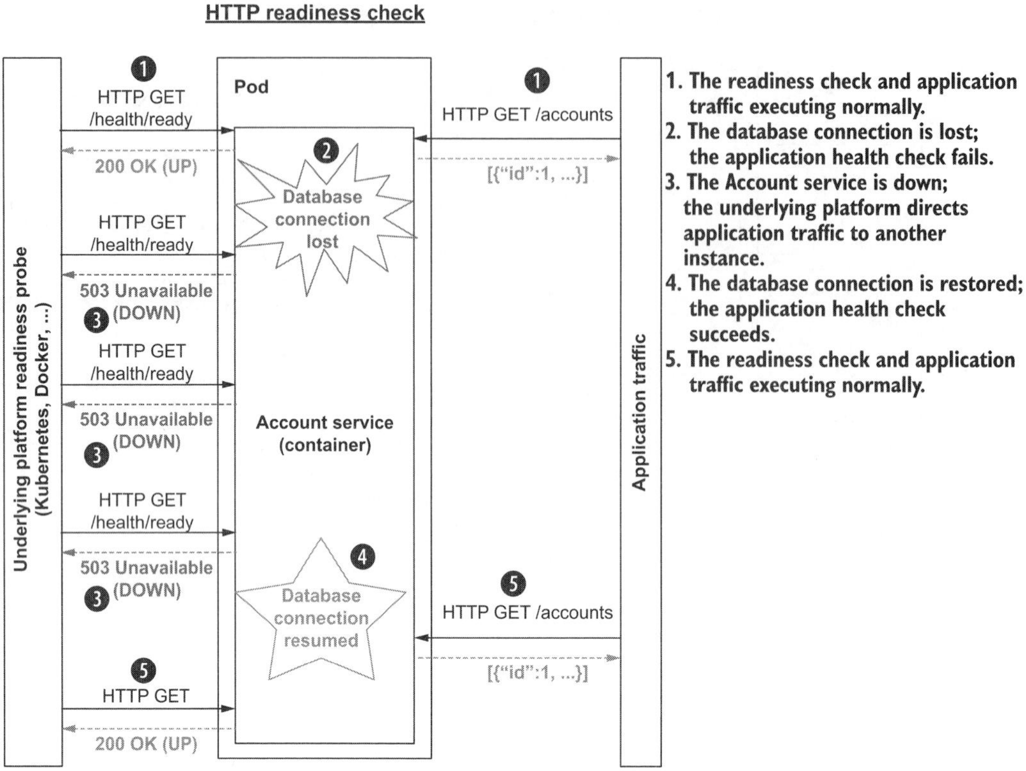

HTTP readiness check

1. The readiness check and application traffic executing normally.
2. The database connection is lost; the application health check fails.
3. The Account service is down; the underlying platform directs application traffic to another instance.
4. The database connection is restored; the application health check succeeds.
5. The readiness check and application traffic executing normally.

Figure 6.3   Readiness check and application traffic flow

The Account service uses a PostgreSQL database, which must be up and ready to accept requests. We can do this using the following steps:

1 Check if PostgreSQL is running in the Kubernetes cluster by running `kubectl get pods`. If the output does not contain text similar to `postgres-58db5b6954-27796`, then the database is not running.

2 If the database is not running, deploy the database by running `kubectl deploy -f postgresql_kubernetes.yml` from the top-level `chapter06` directory.

3 Once the database is running, forward local database traffic to the PostgreSQL Pod in the Kubernetes cluster. To do this, run the command in the next code listing.

Listing 6.1   PostgreSQL port forwarding

```
# This will forward traffic until CTRL-C is pressed
kubectl port-forward service/postgres 5432:5432
```

Forwards traffic on localhost port 5432 to the Kubernetes Pod port 5432. During development, the Account service uses localhost port 5432, which forwards traffic to the PostgreSQL Pod.

With the database running, the next step is to start the Account service. Install the parent pom.xml, and then start the Account service.

Listing 6.2 Installing parent pom and build artifacts

```
mvn clean install -DskipTests    ◁──┤ Installs the
cd account-service                     parent pom.xml
mvn quarkus:dev    ◁───┐
                       └── Starts the account-service
                           in developer mode
```

Check the health endpoint to determine the Account service health status using the command shown next.

Listing 6.3 Checking health endpoint availability

```
curl -i localhost:8080/q/health/live
```

The resulting output in listing 6.4 shows that Quarkus does not include a liveness health check endpoint by default.

Listing 6.4 Quarkus health endpoint unavailable

```
HTTP/1.1 404 Not Found
Content-Length: 0
Content-Type: application/json
```

Account service requires an additional Quarkus extension for MicroProfile Health support. Using the code in the following snippet, add the `quarkus-smallrye-health` extension.

Listing 6.5 Add MicroProfile Health support using the `smallrye-health` extension

```
mvn quarkus:add-extension -Dextensions="quarkus-smallrye-health"
```

Because Quarkus is running in developer mode, the extension will be loaded automatically.

6.3.1 *Account service MicroProfile Health liveness*

With MicroProfile Health support loaded, check the endpoint again with `curl -i localhost:8080/q/health/live`. This time, as seen in the next code listing, the result is very different.

Listing 6.6 Liveness health check output

```
HTTP/1.1 200 OK                                    ◁──┤ An HTTP response code of
content-type: application/json; charset=UTF-8        │ 2XX means the service is up
content-length: 46                                   │ and running as expected.
              ┌── The HTTP response is a       The overall status of the service is
{          ◁──┤  JSON-formatted payload.       UP. An HTTP response code of 2XX
    "status": "UP",    ◁──────────────────     will always result in an UP status.
```

```
        "checks": [
        ]
}
```

The checks JSON array contains named health checks and their status. The array is empty, meaning there are currently no custom liveness health checks.

Although the output is relatively simple, we do have some useful context to cover. First, without writing a custom health check, MicroProfile Health requires a default status of UP.

Second, the HTTP status maps to the JSON payload status. A 200 HTTP status maps to UP, and a 5XX HTTP status maps to DOWN. The underlying platform has the option of considering the remainder of the JSON payload for additional context before taking corrective action.

Last, the MicroProfile Health specification requires that the JSON payload returns two items. First, it must return a status of UP or DOWN. Second, it must return an array of checks that aggregate all liveness health checks. If one or more liveness health checks are DOWN, then the overall status for the health check is DOWN.

Having seen a liveness health check, it's time to create a custom liveness health check.

6.3.2   *Creating an Account service liveness health check*

To learn the API, let's start by creating a liveness health check that always returns UP, as seen in the following code.

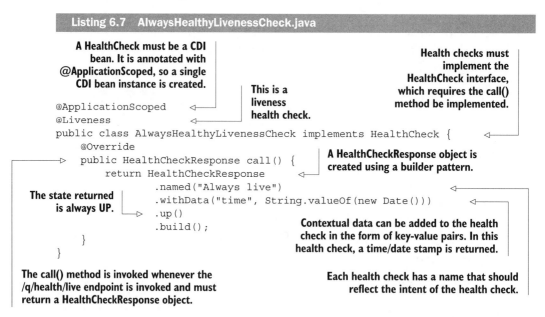

Listing 6.7   AlwaysHealthyLivenessCheck.java

A HealthCheck must be a CDI bean. It is annotated with @ApplicationScoped, so a single CDI bean instance is created.

This is a liveness health check.

Health checks must implement the HealthCheck interface, which requires the call() method be implemented.

```
@ApplicationScoped
@Liveness
public class AlwaysHealthyLivenessCheck implements HealthCheck {
    @Override
    public HealthCheckResponse call() {
        return HealthCheckResponse
            .named("Always live")
            .withData("time", String.valueOf(new Date()))
            .up()
            .build();
    }
}
```

A HealthCheckResponse object is created using a builder pattern.

The state returned is always UP.

Contextual data can be added to the health check in the form of key-value pairs. In this health check, a time/date stamp is returned.

The call() method is invoked whenever the /q/health/live endpoint is invoked and must return a HealthCheckResponse object.

Each health check has a name that should reflect the intent of the health check.

To test the liveness health check, run curl localhost:8080/q/health/live. The results should match the next listing.

Listing 6.8   Liveness health check output

```
HTTP/1.1 200 OK                                    ◁─┐   The HTTP status returns
content-type: application/json; charset=UTF-8          OK because the application
content-length: 220                                    status is UP.

                              The JSON health status
                              UP matches the HTTP
{                             response status.
    "status": "UP",      ◁────┘
    "checks": [
                         ┌─ ▷  {                 The AlwaysHealthyLivenessCheck status is UP.
The remainder of         │                       Therefore, the overall status is also UP. If any
the JSON reflects the    │         "name": "Always live",   individual health check status is DOWN, then
values defined in the    │         "status": "UP",    ◁──┘   the overall status is DOWN.
HealthCheckResponse      │         "data": {
object.                            "time": "Mon Sep 28 23:56:38 PDT 2020"
                                 }
                           }
    ]
}
```

Next, let's get a firmer understanding of application readiness.

6.3.3   Account service MicroProfile Health readiness

With a sound understanding of application liveness, the next step is to check application readiness using `curl -i http://localhost:8080/q/health/ready`. Interestingly, the output shown next may be a bit unexpected.

Listing 6.9   Account service is ready to accept traffic

```
HTTP/1.1 200 OK
content-type: application/json; charset=UTF-8
content-length: 150

{                              ┌─ The database
    "status": "UP",           │   connection is
    "checks": [        ◁───────┘   operating properly.
        {
            "name": "Database connections health check",
            "status": "UP"
        }
    ]
}
```

The output includes a preconfigured database readiness health check. If the database becomes unavailable, then the Account service will return an HTTP 503 status code, and Kubernetes will not forward traffic to the service. What is providing the database readiness health check? The Hibernate ORM with Panache extension automatically adds the Agroal data source extension as an application dependency. The Agroal datasource extension provides the readiness health check. All relational databases supported by Quarkus will benefit from a readiness check.

> **NOTE** As a general rule of thumb, Quarkus extensions that provide client connectivity to backend services have built-in readiness health checks, including relational and nonrelational databases, messaging systems like Kafka and JMS, Amazon services like S3 and DynamoDB, and more.

6.3.4   *Disabling vendor readiness health checks*

Sometimes it is preferable to disable vendor readiness health checks like the Agroal readiness health check. For example, instead of pausing traffic to an application, the application can continue with fallback logic if the backend service is unreachable. We can disable vendor readiness health checks in two ways.

First, by setting the MicroProfile Health `mp.health.disable-default-procedures` to `true`, all vendor health checks are disabled. Disabling all vendor readiness health checks is a coarse-grained approach.

Second, Quarkus readiness health checks can be disabled on an extension-by-extension basis. To disable a Quarkus extension's readiness health check, use `quarkus.<client>.health.enabled=false`, where `<client>` is the extension to disable. For example, to disable the data source health check provided by the Agroal extension, use `quarkus.datasource.health.enabled=false`. The Quarkus extension guides document the relevant property name.

6.3.5   *Creating a readiness health check*

Creating a readiness health check is nearly identical to creating the liveness health check. The only differences are using the `@Readiness` annotation instead of the `@Liveness` annotation and the business logic to determine readiness. Because the Account service already has a built-in database readiness health check, let's create a readiness health check on the Transaction service that checks the Account service readiness. If it is not ready, then the Transaction service will return `DOWN` as well. First, we'll need to add the health extension to the Transaction service as shown in the following listing.

Listing 6.10   Adding the health extension to the Transaction service

```
cd transaction-service
mvn quarkus:add-extension -Dextensions="quarkus-smallrye-health"
```

With the health extension added, create the `AccountHealthReadinessCheck` class shown in the next code listing.

Listing 6.11   AccountHealthReadinessCheck.java

A readiness
health check
⌐▷ @Readiness

Quarkus automatically makes this a @Singleton CDI bean when no scope is provided. Although not a portable feature, this does tidy up the code a bit and delivers some Quarkus developer joy.

```
public class AccountHealthReadinessCheck implements HealthCheck {
    @Inject
```

```
    @RestClient
    AccountService accountService;          ⊲───┐  Injects an instance of the
                                                 │  AccountService REST client, which will
                                                 │  be used to invoke the Account service
    BigDecimal balance;

                                            Tests Account service availability by invoking
    @Override                                an endpoint and getting the balance of a
    public HealthCheckResponse call() {          special "Health Check" account
        try {
            balance = accountService.getBalance(999999999L);      ⊲──────────┘
        } catch (WebApplicationException ex) {
            // This class is a singleton, so clear last request's balance
            balance = new BigDecimal(Integer.MIN_VALUE);

            if (ex.getResponse().getStatus() >= 500) {
                return HealthCheckResponse
                       .named("AccountServiceCheck")
                       .withData("exception", ex.toString())
                       .down()
                       .build();
            }
        }                                          Returns an UP
    }                                              status along with
                                                   the balance
        return HealthCheckResponse          ⊲───┘
               .named("AccountServiceCheck")
               .withData("balance", balance.toString())
               .up()
               .build();
    }
}
```

Returns a DOWN status only if there is a 5XX HTTP status code, meaning the service was unable to respond to a valid HTTP request. All other status codes imply that the service is responding to requests.

Add a readiness health check account to the accounts table as shown next.

Listing 6.12   Adding test account to src/main/resources/import.sql

```
INSERT INTO account(id, accountNumber, accountStatus, balance, customerName,
➥ customerNumber) VALUES (9, 999999999, 0, 999999999.01, 'Readiness
    HealthCheck', 99999999999);
```

Update application.properties with the properties in the following listing.

Listing 6.13   Additional Transaction service properties

The account service is already listening on port 8080, so the Transaction service will listen on port 8088 to avoid a port conflict when running in developer mode.

```
%dev.quarkus.http.port=8088      ⊲──┘
%dev.io.quarkus.transactions.AccountService/mp-rest/url=http://localhost:8080
```

Because the Account service is also running locally on port 8080, the REST client must access the Account service on localhost when running in developer mode.

Within a new terminal window, start the Transaction service as shown next.

```
mvn compile quarkus:dev \
    -Ddebug=5006              ◄──
```
Quarkus defaults the debug port to 5005, which is the debug port for the Account service that is already running. Set the Transaction service debug port to 5006.

To test `AccountHealthReadinessCheck`, run `curl -i localhost:8088/q/health/ready` to see the output shown here.

```
HTTP/1.1 200 OK
content-type: application/json; charset=UTF-8    ◄──
content-length: 234
```
The overall HTTP status is 200, meaning the service is ready to accept traffic.

```
{
    "status": "UP",
    "checks": [
        {
            "name": "AccountServiceCheck",    ◄──
            "status": "UP",
            "data": {
                "balance": "999999999.01"
            }
        }
    ]
}
```
The Account service is ready to accept traffic.

Currently, three services are up and running: PostgreSQL, the Account service, and the Transaction service. Figure 6.4 shows the service health readiness status of these services.

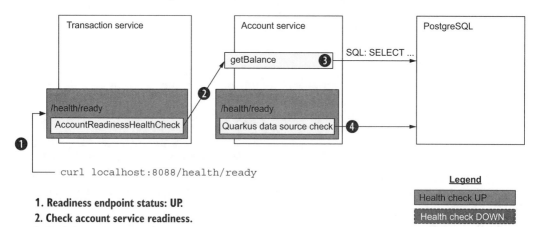

1. Readiness endpoint status: UP.
2. Check account service readiness.
3. Get balance from database.
4. Quarkus data source readiness check: UP.

Figure 6.4   Service readiness health check status

Next, stop the port forwarding started in 6.1 by pressing CTRL-C in the terminal running the `kubectl port-forward …` command. Check the readiness endpoint again by running `curl -i localhost:8088/q/health/ready`. The result, shown next, illustrates that the transaction service is DOWN and not ready.

> **Listing 6.16 `AccountHealthReadinessCheck` is DOWN and not ready**

```
HTTP/1.1 503 Service Unavailable                     ◁──    The Transaction
content-type: application/json; charset=UTF-8               service is not
content-length: 276                                         ready.

{
    "status": "DOWN",
    "checks": [
        {
            "name": "AccountServiceCheck",              Invoking the Account service results in
            "status": "DOWN",                           an exception, causing the Transaction
            "data": {                            ◁──    service to be down.
                "exception": "javax.ws.rs.WebApplicationException: Unknown
     error, status code 500"
            }
        }
    ]
}
```

As a result of the database being down, there is a cascading failure of the Account service not being ready, followed by the Transaction service not being ready. This is outlined in figure 6.5.

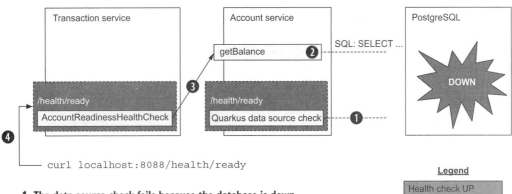

curl localhost:8088/health/ready

1. **The data source check fails because the database is down.**
2. **HTTP 500 error—JDBCConnectionException.**
3. **HTTP 500 error—WebApplicationException; the readiness check fails.**
4. **HTTP 503—AccountReadinessHealthCheck: DOWN.**

Figure 6.5 Service readiness cascading failure

NOTE In the next chapter, section 7.3 discusses how to avoid cascading failures.

The next couple of sections will cover Quarkus-specific health features, and then we deploy the services to Kubernetes.

6.3.6   *Quarkus health groups*

Quarkus extends the MicroProfile Health feature set by adding *health groups*. A health group allows for custom grouping of health checks. Health groups are useful for monitoring health checks that do not impact container access (readiness) and container life cycle (liveness) because they exist at separate REST endpoints. These endpoints are likely not monitored directly by Kubernetes liveness or readiness probes but instead by third-party or custom tooling. For example, external tooling can probe a health group's endpoint to monitor informational, noncritical health checks.

To create a health group, use `@HealthGroup("group-name")`. The next code listing shows an example of a health check group.

Listing 6.17   CustomGroupLivenessCheckHealth.java health check group example

```java
@ApplicationScoped                    Specifies the custom
@HealthGroup("custom")         ◁──    health group
public class CustomGroupLivenessCheck implements HealthCheck {

    @Override
    public HealthCheckResponse call() {
        return HealthCheckResponse.up("custom liveness");    ◁──────
    }
}                        Similar to the AlwaysHealthyReadinessCheck, the CustomGroupLivenessCheck
                            always returns UP. In a real-world scenario, this health group check
                            would use business logic to determine the health status.
```

All health groups can be accessed at `/q/health/group`, and a specific health check group can be accessed at `/q/health/group/<group>`, where `group` is the health group name. See the following code listing for example output when running `curl -i http://localhost:8088/q/health/group/custom` to access the `custom` health group.

Listing 6.18   Health check group output

```
HTTP/1.1 200 OK
content-type: application/json; charset=UTF-8
content-length: 132


{
    "status": "UP",
    "checks": [
        {
            "name": "custom liveness",
            "status": "UP"
        }
    ]
}
```

Having just covered a Quarkus-specific feature, let's cover one more Quarkus-specific application health feature, the Quarkus health UI, before moving on to Kubernetes deployments.

6.3.7 *Displaying the Quarkus Health UI*

As an option to viewing the JSON output, Quarkus includes a helpful Health UI for viewing health status while developing an application, though it is not intended to be a production tool. To enable the UI, as seen in figure 6.6, add `quarkus.smallrye-health.ui.enable=true` to the application.properties file. The Health UI can also be autorefreshed at regular intervals by clicking the gear icon in the Health UI title bar and setting the refresh interval. This example shows the Health UI (available at `http://localhost:8080/q/health-ui`) enabled on the Account service without access to the PostgreSQL database.

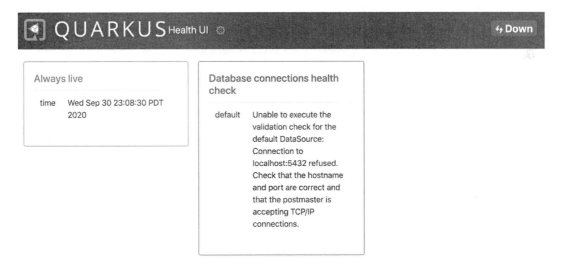

Figure 6.6   Health UI enabled on Account service

The UI can also be included in production builds, like native binaries and JAR deployments, by adding the property `quarkus.smallrye-health.ui.always-include=true` to application.properties.

It is time to put all of this newfound health check knowledge to work by adding Kubernetes health check probes and deploying to Kubernetes.

6.4 *Kubernetes liveness and readiness probes*

Kubernetes is one of the underlying platforms that offer liveness and readiness health check probes as a built-in capability. However, they need to be enabled and configured. Table 6.2 describes Kubernetes health check probe configuration parameters. The parameters are configured with Quarkus properties in application.properties.

Table 6.2   Kubernetes health check probe configuration parameters

Kubernetes probe parameter	Quarkus property	Description and Quarkus defaults
`initialDelaySeconds`	<ul><li>quarkus.kubernetes.liveness-probe.initial-delay</li><li>quarkus.kubernetes.readiness-probe.initial-delay</li></ul>	The amount of time to wait before starting to probe. Defaults to 0 seconds.
`periodSeconds`	<ul><li>quarkus.kubernetes.liveness-probe.period</li><li>quarkus.kubernetes.readiness-probe.period</li></ul>	Probe interval. Defaults to 30 seconds.
`timeout`	<ul><li>quarkus.kubernetes.liveness-probe.timeout</li><li>quarkus.kubernetes.readiness-probe.timeout</li></ul>	Amount of time to wait for probe to complete. Defaults to 10 seconds.
`successThreshold`	<ul><li>quarkus.kubernetes.liveness-probe.success-threshold</li><li>quarkus.kubernetes.readiness-probe.success-threshold</li></ul>	Minimum consecutive successful probes to be considered successful after having failed. Defaults to 1. Must be 1 for liveness.
`failureThreshold`	<ul><li>quarkus.kubernetes.liveness-probe.failure-threshold</li><li>quarkus.kubernetes.readiness-probe.failure-threshold</li></ul>	Retry `failureThreshold` times before giving up. Giving up on a liveness probe will restart container. Giving up on a readiness probe will pause traffic to container. Defaults to 3.

NOTE   See the Quarkus Kubernetes and OpenShift Extension documentation (https://quarkus.io/guides) for additional liveness and readiness probe properties.

The Quarkus health extension generates the Kubernetes probe YAML automatically. A snippet of the liveness probe YAML that was generated automatically in `target/kubernetes/minikube.yaml` follows.

Listing 6.19   Generated liveness probe YAML

```
# ...
        livenessProbe:
          failureThreshold: 3
          httpGet:                       ◁──── Probe health endpoint using HTTP GET
            path: /q/health/live          ◁──── Health path to probe
            port: 80                      ◁──── Port to probe
            scheme: HTTP                  ◁──── Probe using HTTP (vs. HTTPS)
          initialDelaySeconds: 0
          periodSeconds: 30
          successThreshold: 1
          timeoutSeconds: 10
# ...
```

> **NOTE** Pods can have more than one container. Liveness and readiness probes are defined per container. Therefore probes restart and pause traffic to individual containers within the Pod and not the Pod as a whole.

6.4.1 Customizing health check properties

The probe parameters listed in table 6.2 specify reasonable defaults. Health check probes can be customized to reflect the specific needs of the business and the application. For example, from a business perspective, probes can check business-critical applications at a more frequent interval to more rapidly detect and resolve potential issues. On the other hand, some applications take longer to start and should have a higher `initialDelay-Seconds` setting. Determining proper probe settings may take a bit of trial-and-error testing, but accepting the default probe property values is a good place to start.

To make developing probes easier, add the properties shown in the next code listing to application.properties of both the Account service and the Transaction service. The intent is to encounter liveness and readiness issues sooner to make the round-trip coding faster. Do not use these values in production if they do not meet the needs of the application.

Listing 6.20 Overriding probe defaults for quicker round-trip development and testing

```
# Health Probe configuration                          ◁┐  The properties generate
quarkus.kubernetes.liveness-probe.initial-delay=10     │  YAML files similar to those
quarkus.kubernetes.liveness-probe.period=2             │  in listing 6.19 but with the
quarkus.kubernetes.liveness-probe.timeout=5            │  specified values.

quarkus.kubernetes.readiness-probe.initial-delay=10
quarkus.kubernetes.readiness-probe.period=2
quarkus.kubernetes.readiness-probe.timeout=5
```

With updated health check properties in place, the next step is to deploy the updated services to Kubernetes and see liveness probes (container restarts) and readiness probes (traffic pauses) in action.

6.4.2 Deploying to Kubernetes

Before deploying to Kubernetes, set the Docker registry to the instance running in Minikube. Generated container images will now be pushed directly into the Kubernetes Docker registry. With the Docker registry set, deploy to Kubernetes and then track the deployment. See the following listing for the steps.

Listing 6.21 Deploying the Account service to Kubernetes

Uses the Docker registry running in Minikube. Alternatively, run minikube docker-env, and set the environment variables manually.

Deploys the Account service and Transaction service to Kubernetes

```
eval $(minikube -p minikube docker-env)     ◁┘

# Run this command in the chapter top-level directory
mvn clean package -DskipTests -Dquarkus.kubernetes.deploy=true     ◁┘
```

```
# Run next command in a separate terminal window, and leave running
kubectl get pods -w          ◁───┐  Follows the deployment by
                                 │  watching Pod life cycles
```

IMPORTANT   Attempting to redeploy an application already present in Kubernetes with `mvn package -Dquarkus.kubernetes.deploy=true` will result in an error in Quarkus 2.x. Follow https://github.com/quarkusio/quarkus/issues/ 19701 for updates on a resolution. The problem can be worked around by removing the application first with `kubectl delete -f /target/kubernetes/ minikube.yaml`.

See the following listing for the output of the `kubectl get pods -w` command.

Listing 6.22   Pod status terminal window output

The Pod and its containers are scheduled to be created on a node in the cluster.

The READY column identifies the number of containers in the Pod ready to accept traffic. 0/1 means zero of one container is ready. 1/1 means one of one container is ready. The RESTARTS column is incremented each time a container restarts.

```
      NAME                                  READY   STATUS             RESTARTS   AGE     ◁─
      ...
┌──▷  account-service-68f7c4779c-jpggz      0/1     Pending            0          0s
├──▷  account-service-68f7c4779c-jpggz      0/1     ContainerCreating  0          0s
├──▷  account-service-68f7c4779c-jpggz      0/1     Running            0          3s
│     transaction-service-5fb7f69496-d86sg  0/1     Pending            0          0s
│     transaction-service-5fb7f69496-d86sg  0/1     ContainerCreating  0          0s
│     transaction-service-5fb7f69496-d86sg  0/1     Running            0          2s
│     account-service-68f7c4779c-jpggz      1/1     Running            0          13s    ◁──┐
│     transaction-service-5fb7f69496-d86sg  1/1     Running            0          15s    ◁──┤
```

The container has been created, is starting, but is not yet ready to accept traffic.

Kubernetes is creating the Pod and its containers. This includes downloading the container image from an image registry like Docker Hub.

There are equivalent steps for the Transaction service. Both services should start successfully.

The container is running and ready to accept traffic.

IMPORTANT   There may be container restarts during the deployment. Deploying multiple services with minimal CPU cores allocated Minikube may result in a service starting to surpass the `initial-delay` setting. One or two restarts are possible until the deployment assumes a steady state. If the number of restarts for a Pod surpasses four or five, then it will be time to troubleshoot with commands like `kubectl logs <POD_NAME>`.

To simplify accessing the Transaction service URL, store the service URL in an environment variable using the command shown in the next code listing.

Listing 6.23   Getting the transaction service URL

```
export TRANSACTION_URL=$(minikube service --url transaction-service)   ◁──┐
```

Stores the transaction-service URL in the TRANSACTION_URL environment variable

Next, verify the Transaction service is healthy by running `curl -i $TRANSACTION_URL/q/health/live`, with the resulting HTTP status shown here.

Listing 6.24　Output of `curl -i $TRANSACTION_URL/q/health/live`

```
HTTP/1.1 200 OK                                      ◁─┐ Only the HTTP status
content-type: application/json; charset=UTF-8          │ code is shown in this
content-length: 411                                    │ listing.
...
```

Last, test that the Transaction service is ready with `curl -i $TRANSACTION_URL/q/health/ready`. The output should be identical to listing 6.15, returning an HTTP status of 200 and a JSON payload status of UP. Figure 6.7 shows the flow of readiness checks between services.

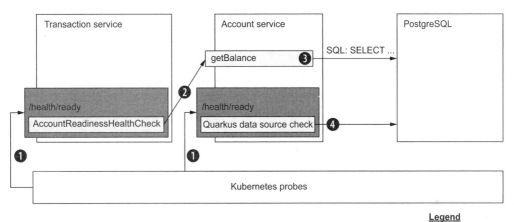

1. Kubernetes checks readiness endpoint(s).
2. Check account service readiness.
3. Get balance from database.
4. Quarkus data source readiness check: UP.

Figure 6.7　Service readiness health check status in Kubernetes

6.4.3　*Testing the readiness health check in Kubernetes*

With the healthy services up and running, let's introduce a readiness failure. An easy way of doing this is to scale down the number of PostgreSQL instances to zero, so the data source health check fails. It is helpful to have the Pod status terminal window created in listing 6.21 easily viewable when running the commands in this chapter to track the Pod life cycle.

Run the command in the next code listing to scale down the number of PostgreSQL instances to zero.

Listing 6.25   Scaling the database to zero instances (replicas)

```
kubectl scale --replicas=0 deployment/postgres
```

The pod status terminal window, shown next, will update to show the Pods terminating.

Listing 6.26   Output of `kubectl get pods -w` when scaling to zero Pods

The postgres Pod is no longer ready and is terminating or has been terminated.

The postgres Pod is ready but is terminating.

```
NAME                                    READY   STATUS        RESTARTS   AGE
...
postgres-58db5b6954-2pg7x               1/1     Terminating   0          13m    ◁
postgres-58db5b6954-2pg7x               0/1     Terminating   0          13m
account-service-68f7c4779c-jpggz        0/1     Running       0          7m59s
transaction-service-5fb7f69496-d86sg    0/1     Running       0          7m50s  ◁
```

The Account service Pod is no longer ready (0/1). Its readiness health check status is DOWN because the database is DOWN. The Pod is still running but is not accepting traffic.

The Transaction service Pod is no longer ready (0/1). Its readiness health check status is DOWN because the Account service is not accepting traffic. The Pod is still running but is not accepting traffic.

Access the Transaction service readiness endpoint with `curl -i $TRANSACTION_URL/q/health/ready`, and notice there is a Connection Refused message. By scaling down the number of PostgreSQL instances to zero, the probe causes a pause to the Account service container traffic, which paused traffic to the Transaction service, including its `/q/health/ready` endpoint. Figure 6.8 shows the cascading service failure in Kubernetes.

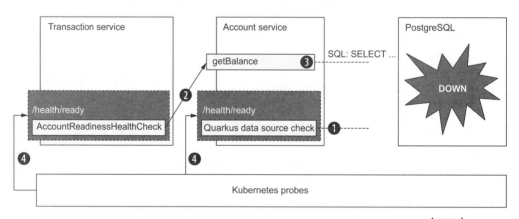

1. Quarkus data source readiness check: DOWN.
2. HTTP 500 error; AccountReadinessHealthCheck fails.
3. getBalance() fails; cannot connect to database.
4. Kubernetes checks both readiness endpoints. Checks fail. Kubernetes pauses traffic to containers.

Figure 6.8   Service readiness health check cascading failure in Kubernetes

To resume back to a healthy status, restart the database by running the command shown in the following listing.

Listing 6.27   Scaling the database to one instance

```
kubectl scale --replicas=1 deployment/postgres
```

By scaling the database down to zero instances and then scaling it back up to one instance, the database contents are lost because the database schemas and data are ephemeral in the current configuration. The easiest way to correct this is to create a new `account-service` instance to regenerate the tables and repopulate the database. Real-world production deployments would not regenerate tables and repopulate databases every time a Pod is created. However, it is helpful as a learning aid in this case. To add another `account-service` instance, run the following command. Note the output in the Pod status terminal window in the following code listing.

Listing 6.28   Scaling the `account-service` to two instances

```
kubectl scale --replicas=2 deployment/account-service
```

Listing 6.29   Pod status output when scaling to two instances

The Pod container is running but is not yet ready.

The Pod is being created.

Kubernetes is scheduling the Pod creation.

```
NAME                                  READY   STATUS              RESTARTS   AGE
...
account-service-68f7c4779c-bf458      0/1     Pending             0          1s
account-service-68f7c4779c-bf458      0/1     ContainerCreating   0          1s
account-service-68f7c4779c-bf458      0/1     Running             0          2s
account-service-68f7c4779c-bf458      1/1     Running             0          12s
transaction-service-5fb7f69496-d86sg  1/1     Running             0          23m
```

The Pod is ready to service traffic.

The new account-service instance connects to the database and inserts the special "Health Check" account. This results in the Transaction service readiness health check state changing to UP and ready to accept traffic.

Of course, a real production scenario would include a database with persistent configuration and data, so this step to create two instances would typically be unnecessary.

Verify the UP status by running `curl -i $TRANSACTION_URL/q/health/ready`.

Summary

- Traditional application servers require manual intervention to react to failure. Manual intervention does not scale well in an environment with hundreds to thousands of containers.
- Combining the automation of Kubernetes health check probes with developer health checks can provide a more responsive and efficient Kubernetes cluster and microservices architecture.

- Kubernetes can pause traffic to a container that is unable or not yet ready to accept traffic and resume traffic when ready, based on developer guidance through health checks.
- Kubernetes can restart a failing or failed container, based on developer guidance through health checks.
- Developers can create readiness and liveness health checks to provide more accurate application-specific health status reports.

Resilience strategies 7

This chapter covers

- The importance of building resilient applications
- MicroProfile Fault Tolerance strategies
- When and how to apply each fault tolerance strategy
- How to configure and disable fault tolerance annotations using properties

Application robustness is critically important in a microservices architecture, which can have many service interdependencies. A service susceptible to failure can negatively impact other services. This chapter covers using resilience patterns to improve application robustness to maintain overall health.

7.1 Resilience strategies overview

Services eventually experience downtime, whether planned or unplanned. A service can reduce its downtime using resilience strategies when the services it depends on are unreliable or unavailable.

Quarkus offers its resilience strategies using the MicroProfile Fault Tolerance APIs. These annotation-based APIs are applied to classes or methods, standalone or in combination. Table 7.1 lists the available Fault Tolerance annotations.

Table 7.1   MicroProfile Fault Tolerance annotations

Annotation	Description
@Asynchronous	Executes a method using a separate thread
@Bulkhead	Limits the number of concurrent requests
@CircuitBreaker	Avoids repeated failures
@Fallback	Uses alternative logic when a method completes exceptionally (throws an exception)
@Retry	Retries a method call when the method completes exceptionally
@Timeout	Prevents a method from executing for longer than a specified amount of time

7.2   Executing a method under a separate thread with @Asynchronous

A service may have to call a slow-responding remote service. Instead of blocking a worker thread by waiting for a response, the @Asynchronous annotation uses a separate thread to invoke the remote service to increase concurrency and throughput. See the next code listing for an example.

Listing 7.1   @Asynchronous example

```
@Asynchronous
public String invokeLongRunningOperation() {
  callLongRunningRemoteService();
}
```

Uses a thread from a separate thread pool to execute a blocking operation

This book does not advocate using the @Asynchronous annotation with Quarkus and will not cover the annotation in detail. The @Asynchronous annotation is for runtimes that make heavy use of threads and thread pools to achieve higher concurrency and throughput, like Jakarta EE runtimes. Quarkus uses a nonblocking network stack and event loop execution model based on Netty and Eclipse Vert.x. It can achieve higher concurrency and throughput using its inherent asynchronous and reactive APIs while using less RAM and CPU overhead.

For example, the Quarkus *RESTEasy Reactive* extension enables the use of JAX-RS annotations and handles requests directly on the IO thread. Developers can use the APIs they already know while benefiting from the throughput typically reserved for asynchronous runtimes like Vert.x.

7.3   Constraining concurrency with bulkheads

The bulkhead concept comes from shipbuilding, which constrains a compromised section of a ship's hull by closing bulkhead doors to isolate the incoming water. The bulkhead architectural pattern applies this concept to prevent a failure in one service from cascading to another service by limiting the number of concurrent method invocations.

For example, a service may make remote calls to a slow-executing backend service. In thread-per-request runtimes like traditional Java EE and Spring, each remote invocation to a slow service consumes memory resources and threads from a thread pool in the calling service, eventually overcoming available resources. As with the @Asynchronous annotation, this is less of an issue with Quarkus RESTEasy Reactive due to its efficient threading model.

Bulkheads are also useful when a remote service is memory- or CPU-constrained, and too many concurrent requests will overload it and cause it to fail. For example, a microservice may invoke a business-critical legacy system that is too costly or difficult to upgrade its software or hardware. The legacy system can benefit from a high-traffic microservice using a bulkhead to limit concurrent access.

MicroProfile Fault Tolerance specifies bulkheads using the @Bulkhead annotation, which can be applied to either a method or a class. See the next listing for an example.

Listing 7.2 Bulkhead example

```
@Bulkhead(10)
public String invokeLegacySystem() {
...
}
```

⊲ invokeLegacySystem() is limited to 10 concurrent invocations. Attempting to exceed 10 will result in a BulkheadException.

The @Bulkhead annotation accepts the parameters defined in table 7.2.

Table 7.2 `@Bulkhead` parameters

Parameter	Default	Description
value	10	The maximum number of concurrent invocations.
waitingTaskQueue	10	When @Bulkhead is used with @Asynchronous, this parameter specifies the size of the request thread queue.

value uses a semaphore, allowing only the specified number of concurrent invocations. When annotating the same method with @Bulkhead and @Asynchronous, value defines the number of concurrent threads allowed to invoke a method concurrently.

The @Bulkhead annotation can be used together with @Asynchronous, @Circuit-Breaker, @Fallback, @Retry, and @Timeout.

Figure 7.1 demonstrates a bulkhead limiting the number of concurrent invocations to two. Now that we have a firm understanding of bulkheads, the next step is to apply the @Bulkhead annotation using a service.

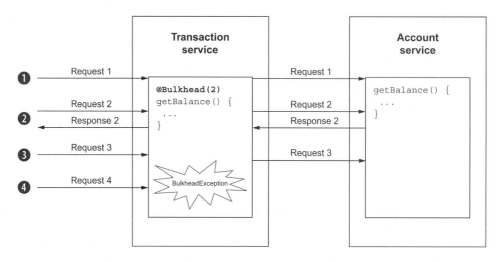

1. TransactionService receives request 1, invokes `AccountService.getBalance()`, and is waiting for a response. Semaphore count: 1.
2. TransactionService receives request 2 and invokes `AccountService.getBalance()`. Semaphore count (during request): 2. Semaphore count (after response): 1.
3. TransactionService receives request 3, invokes `AccountService.getBalance()`, and is waiting for a response. Semaphore count: 2.
4. TransactionService receives request 3. Semaphore count already at limit of 2. `BulkheadException` is thrown.

Figure 7.1   Bulkhead sequence diagram

7.4   *Updating a TransactionService with a bulkhead*

To use MicroProfile Fault Tolerance APIs with Quarkus, install the `quarkus-smallrye-fault-tolerance` extension as shown next.

Listing 7.3   Install Quarkus MicroProfile Fault Tolerance extension

```
cd transaction-service
mvn quarkus:add-extension -Dextensions="quarkus-smallrye-fault-tolerance"
```

Update the `newTransactionWithApi()` method to use a bulkhead. To keep testing simple, the bulkhead will allow one concurrent invocation.

Listing 7.4   Add `@Bulkhead` to the `newTransactionWithAPI()` method

```
@POST
@Path("/api/{acctNumber}")
@Bulkhead(1)
public Response newTransactionWithApi(
    @PathParam("acctNumber") Long accountNumber,
    BigDecimal amount)
```

If more than one concurrent operation is attempted, a BulkheadException will be thrown.

```
throws MalformedURLException {
    ...
}
```

As with prior chapters, start the PostgreSQL database and start port forwarding using the commands shown here.

Listing 7.5 Starting PostgreSQL and port forwarding

```
# From chapter7 top-level directory
kubectl apply -f ./postgresql_kubernetes.yml

# It may take some time for PostgreSQL to start
kubectl port-forward service/postgres 5432:5432
```

Start the `AccountService` in terminal 1 using `mvn quarkus:dev`. In terminal 2, start `TransactionService` using `mvn quarkus:dev -Ddebug=5006`. This instance of Quarkus has to specify a debug port that does not conflict with the default debug port (5005) used by `AccountService`.

Open two more terminals, terminal 3 and terminal 4. Each terminal will run simple `curl` commands to avoid installing any special tools. Run the code from the next listing in both terminals at the same time.

Listing 7.6 Terminal 3 and terminal 4

```
count=0
while (( count++ <= 100 )); do
    curl -i \
        -H "Content-Type: application/json" \
        -X POST \
        -d "2.03" \
        http://localhost:8088/transactions/api/444666
    echo
done
```

In each terminal, the output should show a random mix of `HTTP/1.0 200 OK` responses and `BulkheadException` output as shown next.

Listing 7.7 Sample terminal 3 and terminal 4 output

```
HTTP/1.1 200 OK
Content-Length: 0

HTTP/1.1 500 Internal Server Error
content-type: text/html; charset=utf-8
content-length: 13993
...
...
org.eclipse.microprofile.faulttolerance.exceptions.BulkheadException
...
```

```
. . .

HTTP/1.1 200 OK
Content-Length: 0
```

The bulkhead is successfully limiting the method to a single concurrent invocation. However, a 500 Internal Server Error is not an ideal HTTP response to return to the caller!

The next section introduces the @Fallback annotation to execute alternative logic to handle a bulkhead exception properly.

7.5   *Exception handling with fallbacks*

The @Fallback annotation facilitates exception handling by specifying a fallback method containing alternative logic when the annotated method completes exceptionally. @Fallback can be triggered by any Java exception, including those thrown by other Fault Tolerance resilience strategies.

@Fallback accepts the parameters defined in table 7.3.

Table 7.3   @Fallback parameters

Parameter	Description
applyOn	List of exceptions that trigger a fallback
fallbackMethod	Method to invoke when the annotated method throws an exception. fallbackMethod must have the same method signature (parameter types and return type) as the annotated method. Use either this parameter or the value parameter.
skipOn	List of exceptions that should *not* trigger fallbackMethod. This list takes precedence over the types listed in the applyOn parameter.
value	FallbackHandler class. Use either this parameter or the fallbackMethod parameter.

This example uses a fallbackMethod to replace the 500 Internal Server Error_ HTTP status code caused by the BulkheadException with a meaningful HTTP status code. Add the @Fallback annotation to newTransactionWithApi() and a fallbackMethod as shown in the following code sample.

Listing 7.8   Adding @Fallback to the newTransactionWithAPI() method

```
@POST
@Path("/api/{acctNumber}")
@Bulkhead(1)
@Fallback(fallbackMethod = "bulkheadFallbackGetBalance",    ⬅
              applyOn = { BulkheadException.class })         ⬅
public Response newTransactionWithApi(
     @PathParam("acctNumber") Long accountNumber,
     BigDecimal amount)
```

Invokes the bulkheadFallbackGetBalance() method on an exception

More specifically, invokes the fallbackMethod on a BulkheadException. Any other exceptions will be handled in a default manner.

```
throws MalformedURLException {
   ...
}

public Response bulkheadFallbackGetBalance(Long accountNumber,
                                 BigDecimal amount) {
  return Response.status(Response.Status.TOO_MANY_REQUESTS).build();
}
```

The fallback method has the same method signature (parameter types and return type) as newTransactionWithApi().

Returns a more context-appropriate 429 TOO_MANY_REQUESTS HTTP status code

Rerun the shell script outlined in listing 7.6 in terminal 3 and terminal 4 at the same time. The output should look similar to the following code listing.

Listing 7.9 Output after adding a `fallbackMethod`

```
HTTP/1.1 200 OK
Content-Length: 0

HTTP/1.1 429 Too Many Requests        ◄───
Content-Length: 0

HTTP/1.1 200 OK
Content-Length: 0
```

The 500 Internal Server Exception HTTP status code and Java exception output is now a 429 Too Many Requests HTTP status code with an empty response body.

A fallback can be combined with other MicroProfile Fault Tolerance annotations. In the next section, we will use @Fallback with the @Timeout annotation.

7.6   *Defining execution timeouts*

Method invocations intermittently take a long time to execute. When a thread is blocked, waiting for method completion, it is not handling other incoming requests. Additionally, the service may also have response time requirements to meet business objectives impacted by latency. Use @Timeout to limit the amount of time a thread can use to execute a method.

@Timeout accepts the parameters defined in table 7.4.

Table 7.4 @Timeout parameters

Parameter	Default	Description
value	1000	A TimeoutException will be thrown if method execution time exceeds this value.
unit	ChronoUnit.MILLIS	Time unit of the value parameter.

The @Timeout annotation can be used together with @Asynchronous, @Bulkhead, @CircuitBreaker, @Fallback, and @Retry.

Add a method to the `TransactionService` to get the account balance from the `AccountService`. It has a timeout of 100 ms and will call a fallback method on a `TimeoutException`. Add the code as shown in the next listing.

Listing 7.10   Adding a `getBalance()` method to TransactionResource.java

```
@GET
@Path("/{acctnumber}/balance")
@Timeout(100)                                          ◄─── Throws a TimeoutException
@Fallback(fallbackMethod = "timeoutFallbackGetBalance")     if getBalance() takes longer
@Produces(MediaType.APPLICATION_JSON)                       than 100 ms to execute
public Response getBalance(
        @PathParam("acctnumber") Long accountNumber) {
    String balance = accountService.getBalance(accountNumber).toString();

    return Response.ok(balance).build();
}


public Response timeoutFallbackGetBalance(Long accountNumber) {
    return Response.status(Response.Status.GATEWAY_TIMEOUT).build();   ◄───
}
```

Throws a TimeoutException if getBalance() takes longer than 100 ms to execute

Calls timeoutFallbackGetBalance() if any exception is thrown

Invokes accountService.getBalance() and returns the account balance. AccountService.getBalance() will need to complete in less than 100 ms or a TimeoutException will be thrown.

Returns a reasonably context-appropriate HTTP GATEWAY_TIMEOUT status code.

The `@Timeout` annotation will be tested using WireMock and JUnit tests.

Update the WireMock `AccountService` to include calls to the new `getBalance()` method as shown in the next listing. This class will also include a small amount of refactoring.

Listing 7.11   Updating `WireMockAccountService` to test `@Timeout`

```
public class WiremockAccountService implements
        QuarkusTestResourceLifecycleManager {
    private WireMockServer wireMockServer;

    @Override
    public Map<String, String> start() {
        wireMockServer = new WireMockServer();
        wireMockServer.start();

        mockAccountService();     ◄─── Refactors mockAccountService()
        mockTimeout();                 into its own method

        return
          Collections.singletonMap("io.quarkus.transactions.AccountService/mp-
          rest/url", wireMockServer.baseUrl());
    }

    protected void mockAccountService() {     ◄─── Refactored mockAccountService() method
        stubFor(get(urlEqualTo("/accounts/121212/balance"))
            .willReturn(aResponse().withHeader("Content-Type",
          "application/json").withBody("435.76")));
```

```
    stubFor(post(urlEqualTo("/accounts/121212/transaction")).willReturn(
      aResponse()
        // noContent() needed to be changed once the external service
      returned a Map
        .withHeader("Content-Type",
      "application/json").withStatus(200).withBody("{}")));
  }

  protected void mockTimeout() {
    stubFor(get(urlEqualTo("/accounts/123456/balance"))
        .willReturn(aResponse()
        .withHeader("Content-Type","application/json")
        .withStatus(200)
        .withFixedDelay(200)
        .withBody("435.76")));

    stubFor(get(urlEqualTo("/accounts/456789/balance"))
        .willReturn(aResponse()
        .withHeader("Content-Type", "application/json")
        .withStatus(200) .withBody("435.76")));
        .withBody("435.76")));
  }

  @Override
  public void stop() {
    if (null != wireMockServer) {
      wireMockServer.stop();
    }
  }
}
```

Any invocation of the /accounts/123456/balance endpoint will invoke this stub.

Returns a 200 HTTP OK status code

Adds a 200 ms delay, which will force a TimeoutException on any remote call with a timeout less than 200 ms

Any invocation of the /accounts/456789/balance endpoint will invoke this stub, which will not force a TimeoutException.

With the `AccountService` endpoint mocked, create the JUnit test to test the `@Timeout` annotation, as shown in the next code listing.

Listing 7.12 Creating a `FaultyAccountServiceTest` class

```
@QuarkusTest
@QuarkusTestResource(WiremockAccountService.class)
public class FaultyAccountServiceTest {
  @Test
  void testTimeout() {
    given()
      .contentType(ContentType.JSON)
    .get("/transactions/123456/balance").then().statusCode(504);

    given()
      .contentType(ContentType.JSON)
    .get("/transactions/456789/balance").then().statusCode(200);
  }
}
```

Binds the WiremockAccountService to the life cycle of QuarkusTest

The mocked /transactions/456789/balance endpoint returns a 200 (OK) HTTP status code.

The mocked /transactions/1234546/balance endpoint defines a 200 ms delay. The getBalance() method defines a 100 ms timeout, forcing a TimeoutException. The timeout results in a call to the fallback method with a return of a 504 GATEWAY TIMEOUT HTTP status code.

Before running the test, stop the `AccountService` to avoid port conflicts between the `AccountService` and the WireMock server. Test the application using `mvn test`, with the sample output shown here.

Listing 7.13 Sample `mvn test` output

```
[INFO] Results:
[INFO]
[INFO] Tests run: 2, Failures: 0, Errors: 0, Skipped: 0
[INFO]
[INFO] ------------------------------------------------------------------------
[INFO] BUILD SUCCESS
[INFO] ------------------------------------------------------------------------
```

The next section introduces the `@Retry` resilience strategy and how it can be combined with other resilience strategies like `@Timeout` to improve the overall resilience of `TransactionService`.

7.7 Recovering from temporary failure with @Retry

In cases where failure is rare, for example, where a remote system has an occasional unstable connection, it may be appropriate to retry a method call a few times before handling the failure in this context.

The `@Retry` annotation retries method invocations a configurable number of times if the method completes exceptionally. The annotation accepts the parameters defined in table 7.5.

Table 7.5 `@Retry` parameters

Parameter	Default	Description
abortOn	None	A list of exceptions that do not trigger a retry.
delay	0	A delay between each retry.
delayUnit	ChronoUnit.MILLIS	The time unit of the delay parameter.
jitter	0	Adds or subtracts a random amount of time between each retry. For example, a delay of 100 ms with a jitter of 20 ms results in a delay between 80 ms and 120 ms.
jitterDelayUnit	ChronoUnit.MILLIS	The time unit of the value parameter.
maxDuration	1800000	The maximum duration for all retries.
durationUnit	ChronoUnit.MILLIS	The time unit of the `maxDuration` parameter.
maxRetries	3	The maximum number of retry attempts.
retryOn	Any exception	A list of exceptions that trigger a retry.

WARNING Use the `@Retry` resilience strategy with caution. Retrying a remote call on an overloaded backend service with a small delay exacerbates the problem.

The `@Retry` annotation can be used together with `@Asynchronous`, `@Bulkhead`, `@CircuitBreaker`, `@Fallback`, and `@Timeout`.

Add the following `@Retry` code to `transactionService.getBalance()`.

Listing 7.14 Adding the `@Retry` annotation

```
@GET
@Path("/{acctnumber}/balance")
@Timeout(100)
@Retry(delay = 100,
       jitter = 25,
       maxRetries = 3,
       retryOn = TimeoutException.class)
@Fallback(fallbackMethod = "timeoutFallbackGetBalance")
@Produces(MediaType.APPLICATION_JSON)
public Response getBalance(
      @PathParam("acctnumber") Long accountNumber) {
  String balance = accountService.getBalance(accountNumber).toString();

    return Response.ok(balance).build();
}
```

Waits 100 ms between retries

Adds or subtract 25 ms from the retry delay. The delay between retries will be a random value between 75 ms and 125 ms.

Retries up to 3 times

Retries on a TimeoutException only. Other exceptions will be handled normally.

Test the `@Retry` annotation by running `mvn test`. The output will not change from listing 7.13. The mock always returns a `504 GATEWAY TIMEOUT`. As a result, the `@Retry` annotation consumes three timeout exceptions, and the final result remains a `504 GATEWAY TIMEOUT`.

The `@Retry` resilience strategy attempts to recover from a failure. The next section discusses the `@CircuitBreaker` resilience strategy as another popular approach to handling a failure.

7.8 Avoiding repeated failure with circuit breakers

A circuit breaker avoids operations that are likely to fail. It is a resilience pattern popularized by the Netflix Hystrix framework and is also the most complex resilience pattern to understand. A circuit breaker consists of the following three steps:

1 Detect repeated failure, typically of expensive operations like a remote service invocation.
2 "Fail fast" by immediately throwing an exception instead of conducting an expensive operation.
3 Attempt to recover by occasionally allowing the expensive operation. If successful, resume normal operations.

All three steps are configurable to meet contextual needs.

7.8.1 *MicroProfile Fault Tolerance: @CircuitBreaker*

The MicroProfile Fault Tolerance specification defines the @CircuitBreaker annotation and its behavior. The annotation accepts the parameters defined in table 7.6.

Table 7.6 `@CircuitBreaker` parameters

Parameter	Default	Description
requestVolumeThreshold	20	The size of the rolling window (number of requests) used to calculate the opening of a circuit.
failureRatio	.5	Opens the circuit if the ratio of failed requests within the requestVolume-Threshold window exceeds this number. For example, if the requestVolume-Threshold is 4, then two failed requests of the last four will open the circuit.
delay	5000	The amount of time the circuit remains open before allowing a request.
delayUnit	ChronoUnit.MILLIS	The time unit of the delay parameter.
successThreshold	1	The number of successful trial requests to close the circuit.
failOn	Any exception	The list of exceptions that should be considered failures.
skipOn	None	The list of exceptions that should *not* open the circuit. This list takes precedence over the types listed in the failOn parameter.

The @CircuitBreaker annotation can be used together with @Timeout, @Fallback, @Asynchronous, @Bulkhead, and @Retry.

7.8.2 *How a circuit breaker works*

Figure 7.2 shows a visual time sequence of a circuit breaker, followed by a description of each labeled step:

1 *Successful request*—The requestVolumeThreshold is 3. The last three requests have been successful, identified by the three checkmarks.
2 *Unsuccessful request*—AccountService is down. The MicroProfile REST Client throws an HttpHostConnectException. One third (33%) of the requests have failed, identified by the X and two checkmarks.
3 *Unsuccessful request*—AccountService is down. An HttpHostConnectException is thrown. The failure rate is two-thirds (66%), as shown by two Xs. Two-thirds meets the failureRatio, and the next failure will result in a CircuitBreaker-Exception. All requests for the next delay seconds (set to 5 seconds) will automatically result in a CircuitBreakerOpenException.

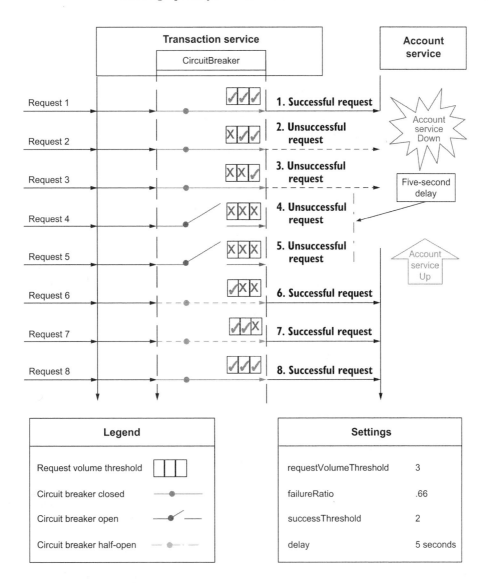

Figure 7.2   A circuit breaker in action

4 *Unsuccessful request*—The last three requests have failed. Note, the circuit opens at the end of the step 3 circuit. This step represents all requests that occur during the 5-second delay.

5 *Unsuccessful request*—Although AccountService is back up and running, the circuit breaker will not allow any requests until 5 seconds have passed.

6 *Successful request*—After a 5-second delay, the circuit is in a half-open state until successThreshold requests (set at 2) have successfully completed. This is the first successful request with the circuit in the half-open state.

7 *Successful request*—The second successful request. After the request, the success-Threshold increments to 2, and the circuit will close.

8 *Successful request*—Normal request processing resumes.

7.8.3 *Updating the TransactionService to use @CircuitBreaker*

Instead of creating another fallback method to handle a CircuitBreakerException, all fallback handling is moved into a separate FallbackHandler class with convenient console output. Add the code shown next.

The FallbackHandler must implement the handle() method.
The ExecutionContext parameter gives contextual information
such as the annotated method that generated the fallback
and the exception that generated.

```
public
  class TransactionServiceFallbackHandler
        implements FallbackHandler<Response> {         ◁── A FallbackHandler class must implement the FallbackHandler interface.

    Logger LOG = Logger.getLogger(TransactionServiceFallbackHandler.class);

    @Override
    public Response handle(ExecutionContext context) {
        Response response;                             The fallback handler
        String name;                                   logic keys on the
                                                       exception name.

        if (context.getFailure().getCause() == null) {
            name = context.getFailure() .getClass().getSimpleName();    ◁──
        } else {
            name =
    context.getFailure().getCause().getClass().getSimpleName();
        }

        switch (name) {                        A BulkheadException will return
            case "BulkheadException":          a TOO_MANY_REQUESTS HTTP
                response = Response             status code with an empty body.
                        .status(Response.Status.TOO_MANY_REQUESTS)   ◁──
                        .build();
                break;                         A TimeoutException will return a
                                               GATEWAY_TIMEOUT HTTP status
            case "TimeoutException":           code with an empty body.
                response = Response
                        .status(Response.Status.GATEWAY_TIMEOUT)    ◁──
                        .build();
                break;

            case "CircuitBreakerOpenException":
                response = Response
                        .status(Response.Status.SERVICE_UNAVAILABLE)   ◁──
                        .build();
                break;                         A CircuitBreakerException will return
                                               a SERVICE_UNAVAILABLE HTTP status
                                               code with an empty body.
```

```
            case "WebApplicationException":
            case "HttpHostConnectException":
                response = Response
                            .status(Response.Status.BAD_GATEWAY)
                            .build();
                break;
        default:
            response = Response
                        .status(Response.Status.NOT_IMPLEMENTED)
                        .build();

        }

        LOG.info("******** "
            + context.getMethod().getName()
            + ": " + name
            + " ********");

        return response;
    }
}
```

The MicroProfile REST Client generates an HttpHostConnectException when it cannot connect to the backend REST service, and the circuit breaker circuit is in the open state.

The `@Fallback` annotations need the `fallbackMethod` replaced with the Fallback-Handler. Add the `@CircuitBreaker` annotation to the `newTransactionWithApi()` method as shown in the next code listing.

Listing 7.16 Add `@CircuitBreaker` to `newTransactionWithApi()`

```
@POST
@Path("/api/{acctNumber}")
@Bulkhead(1)
@CircuitBreaker(
    requestVolumeThreshold=3,
    failureRatio=.66,
    delay = 5,
    delayUnit = ChronoUnit.SECONDS,
    successThreshold=2
)
@Fallback(value = TransactionServiceFallbackHandler.class)
  public Response newTransactionWithApi(
      @PathParam("acctNumber") Long accountNumber, BigDecimal amount) {
  ...
}

...

@GET
@Path("/bulkhead/{acctnumber}/balance")
@Timeout(100)
@Fallback(value = TransactionServiceFallbackHandler.class)
@Produces(MediaType.APPLICATION_JSON)
```

Sets a delay of 5 seconds

Sets the delay time unit to seconds

To make testing the circuit breaker simpler, sets the requestVolumeThreshold to the low value of 3

Sets a failure ratio of .66 (two-thirds). If two of the most recent three requests fail, the circuit breaker will open.

A circuit breaker in the half-open state will close with 2 continuous successful requests.

Updates newTransactionWithAPI to invoke the TransactionServiceFallbackHandler instead of the fallbackMethod

Updates getbalance() to invoke the TransactionServiceFallbackHandler instead of the fallbackMethod

```
public Response getBalance(
    @PathParam("acctnumber") Long accountNumber) {
  ...
}
```

7.8.4   *Testing the circuit breaker*

To test the circuit breaker, extend the `WiremockAccountService` with the following:

```
public class WiremockAccountService implements
      QuarkusTestResourceLifecycleManager {
  private WireMockServer wireMockServer;

  private static final String SERVER_ERROR_1 = "CB Fail 1";
  private static final String SERVER_ERROR_2 = "CB Fail 2";
  private static final String CB_OPEN_1 = "CB Open 1";
  private static final String CB_OPEN_2 = "CB Open 2";
  private static final String CB_OPEN_3 = "CB Open 3";
  private static final String CB_SUCCESS_1 = "CB Success 1";
  private static final String CB_SUCCESS_2 = "CB Success 2";

  ...

  @Override
  public Map<String, String> start() {
    wireMockServer = new WireMockServer();
    wireMockServer.start();

    mockAccountService();
    mockTimeout();
    mockCircuitBreaker();

    ..
  }

  void mockCircuitBreaker() {
    // Define wiremock scenario to support the required by a circuitbreaker
      state machine

    createCircuitBreakerStub(Scenario.STARTED, SERVER_ERROR_1, "100.00", 200);
    createCircuitBreakerStub(SERVER_ERROR_1, SERVER_ERROR_2, "200.00", 502);
    createCircuitBreakerStub(SERVER_ERROR_2, CB_OPEN_1, "300.00", 502);
    createCircuitBreakerStub(CB_OPEN_1, CB_OPEN_2, "400.00", 200);
    createCircuitBreakerStub(CB_OPEN_2, CB_OPEN_3, "400.00", 200);
    createCircuitBreakerStub(CB_OPEN_3, CB_SUCCESS_1, "500.00", 200);
    createCircuitBreakerStub(CB_SUCCESS_1, CB_SUCCESS_2, "600.00", 200);
  }
```

The states defined for the circuitbreaker WireMock "scenario." Each field defines a circuit breaker state in order.

Creates the circuit breaker mock

The circuit breaker is open. Even though the request returns 200, simulating service availability, the circuit breaker is in its delay period.

Returns a 502, the second error the circuit breaker receives. This second error will open the circuit breaker.

Returns a 502, the first error the circuit breaker receives

Creates a WireMock circuit breaker stub for each scenario state transition. This first stub defines the initial request in the requestVolumeThreshold.

The second successful call closes the circuit.

The first successful call after the delay period

```
void createCircuitBreakerStub(String currentState, String nextState,   ◁─────
                             String response, int status) {

    stubFor(post(urlEqualTo("/accounts/444666/transaction")).inScenario("cir
    cuitbreaker")

    .whenScenarioStateIs(currentState).willSetStateTo(nextState).willRetur
    n(
            aResponse().withStatus(status).withHeader("Content-Type",
    MediaType.TEXT_PLAIN).withBody(response)));
}
```

> **Any call to the /accounts/444666/transaction endpoint invokes a stub. Each call to the endpoint will advance the state in the circuitbreaker scenario. The body of the response is the account balance.**

```
...
```

With the `WiremockAccountService` updated to support a circuit breaker, the next step is to update `FaultyAccountService` to test the circuit breaker, as follows.

Listing 7.17 Circuit breaker JUnit test

This successful request defines the initial request in the requestVolumeThreshold window.

The circuit breaker is still open.

The circuit breaker is open.

Expects a 502, the second error the circuit breaker receives. This request will open the circuit breaker.

Expects a 502, the first error the circuit breaker receives

```
@Test
void testCircuitBreaker() {
  RequestSpecification request =
    given()
      .body("142.12")
      .contentType(ContentType.JSON);

  request.post("/transactions/api/444666").then().statusCode(200);
  request.post("/transactions/api/444666").then().statusCode(502);   ◁───
  request.post("/transactions/api/444666").then().statusCode(502);   ◁──
  request.post("/transactions/api/444666").then().statusCode(503);   ◁─
  request.post("/transactions/api/444666").then().statusCode(503);   ◁

  try {
    TimeUnit.MILLISECONDS.sleep(1000);   ◁──  Sleeps long enough
  } catch (InterruptedException e) {              to get past the
  }                                               circuitbreaker delay

  request.post("/transactions/api/444666").then().statusCode(200);
  request.post("/transactions/api/444666").then().statusCode(200);   ◁──
}
```

The first successful call after the delay period

The second successful call closes the circuit. The circuit is now closed, and further invocations will continue normally.

NOTE Early Quarkus releases used the Hystrix framework as the underlying implementation. Hystrix has been deprecated, so later Quarkus releases use a custom implementation. Because developers develop to the MicroProfile Fault Tolerance specification, their application source code did not change. This demonstrates the real-world value of developing to specifications instead of implementations.

7.9 Overriding annotation parameter values using properties

MicroProfile Fault Tolerance can globally enable or disable fault tolerance annotations or modify annotation parameters at runtime using properties. This feature recognizes that operational needs change as the deployment environment changes. By overriding annotation parameters using properties, non-Java developers responsible for a reliable production environment can adjust fault tolerance parameters to address production needs.

Service meshes, which give the operations team more control and visibility into a microservices deployment, are becoming more common. A service mesh can shape network traffic and apply its own fault tolerance features to maintain a more reliable Kubernetes cluster. By externalizing fault tolerance annotation parameters using properties, the operations team can ensure that application @Timeout or @Retry annotations do not conflict with the equivalent service mesh settings.

Four ways to enable/disable fault tolerance annotations using properties follow:

1. `MP_Fault_Tolerance_NonFallback_Enabled=true`—Disables all fault tolerance annotations, except for @Fallback annotations.

2. `<annotation>/enabled=false`—Disables all fault tolerance annotations of a specific type used within the application. For example, `Bulkhead/enabled=false` disables all bulkheads in the application.

3. `<class>/<annotation>/enabled=false`—Disables the specified annotation on the specified class. For example, `io.quarkus.transactions.Transaction-Resource/Timeout/enabled=false` disables all @Timeout annotations defined on the `TransactionResource` class and any of its methods.

4. `<class>/<method>/<annotation>/enabled=false`—Disables the specified annotation on a specified method in the specified class. For example, `io.quarkus.transactions.TransactionResource/getBalance/Timeout/enabled=false` disables the @Timeout annotation on the `TransactionResource.getBalance()` method, and all other @Timeout annotations in `TransactionResource` are unaffected.

As shown in the next listing, add the following to application.properties to disable all timeouts in the `TransactionResource` class.

Listing 7.18 application.properties

```
# Modify the MicroProfile Fault Tolerance settings
io.quarkus.transactions.TransactionResource/Timeout/enabled=false
```

Run mvn test. As shown in the following listing, the test fails because the expected timeout no longer occurs. Although failing a test is not ideal, this does show that the @Timeout annotation has been disabled.

Listing 7.19 `mvn test` failure: expected timeout does not occur

```
[INFO]
[INFO] Results:
[INFO]
[ERROR] Failures:
[ERROR]    FaultyAccountServiceTest.testTimeout:21 1 expectation failed.
Expected status code <504> but was <502>.

[INFO]
[ERROR] Tests run: 3, Failures: 1, Errors: 0, Skipped: 0
```

To change an annotation parameter, the property format is `<class>/<method>/<annotation>/<parameter>=value`. Define the following property as shown next.

Listing 7.20 application.properties

Comments out the property
disabling timeouts

```
# io.quarkus.transactions.TransactionResource/Timeout/enabled=false   ⊲─┘
io.quarkus.transactions.TransactionResource/getBalance/Timeout/value=150   ⊲─┐
```

Changes the timeout value from 100 to 150.
This remains under the WireMock stub delay of
200 ms, which will force a TimeoutException.

Run `mvn test`. All tests should pass. With everything working locally, the next step is to deploy the services to Kubernetes.

7.10 *Deploying to Kubernetes*

Deploy the updated `TransactionService` to Kubernetes as shown in the following listing. Run the same commands for the `AccountService` to ensure they are both up and running.

Listing 7.21 Terminal 2

```
# Use the Minikube Docker daemon to build the image
eval $(/usr/local/bin/minikube docker-env)

# Deploy to Kubernetes. Run this for both the AccountService
# and the TransactionService
mvn package -Dquarkus.kubernetes.deploy=true
```

> **IMPORTANT** Attempting to redeploy an application already present in Kubernetes with `mvn package -Dquarkus.kubernetes.deploy=true` results in an error in Quarkus 2.x. Follow https://github.com/quarkusio/quarkus/issues/19701 for updates on a resolution. The problem can be worked around by removing the application first with `kubectl delete -f /target/kubernetes/minikube.yaml`.

Test the bulkhead logic while running in Kubernetes. The approach and code are nearly identical to that of listing 7.6. In terminal 1 and terminal 2, simultaneously run the code shown in the next listing.

Listing 7.22   Terminal 1

```
TRANSACTION_URL=`minikube service transaction-service --url`
count=0
while (( count++ <= 100 )); do
   curl -i \
        -H "Content-Type: application/json" \
        -X POST \
        -d "2.03" \
        $TRANSACTION_URL/transactions/api/444666
   echo
done
```

Next, run the command in each terminal simultaneously. The output will look similar to the following listing.

Listing 7.23   Terminal 1 output

```
HTTP/1.1 200 OK        ◁─── Successful request
Content-Length: 0
                                          The response returned when a
                                          CircuitBreakerException is thrown.
HTTP/1.1 200 OK        ◁─── Successful request
Content-Length: 0                         Between terminal 1 and terminal 2
                                          requests, at least two of the most
                                          recent three requests resulted in a
HTTP/1.1 503 Service Unavailable  ◁────── BulkheadException.
Content-Length: 0


HTTP/1.1 503 Service Unavailable  ◁──┐
Content-Length: 0                     The circuit breaker remains open. The
                                      circuit breaker will likely not close until the
                                      script is run from one terminal at a time.
```

NOTE   To test the bulkhead and receive the `429 TOO_MANY_REQUESTS` HTTP status code, the circuit breaker must skip `BulkheadExceptions`. Either set the `@CircuitBreakerskipOn` parameter to `BulkheadException.class`, or set it using application.properties with `io.quarkus.transactions.Transaction-Resource/newTransactionWithApi/CircuitBreaker/skipOn=org.eclipse.mic-roprofile.faulttolerance.exceptions.BulkheadException`. We leave this as an exercise for the reader.

Summary

- Resilience strategies improve application robustness.
- MicroProfile Fault Tolerance supports six resilience strategies: `@Asynchronous`, `@Bulkhead`, `@CircuitBreaker`, `@Fallback`, `@Retry`, and `@Timeout`.
- `@Asynchronous` executes threads on a separate thread.
- `@Bulkhead` limits the number of concurrent requests to avoid cascading failures.

- `@CircuitBreaker` prevents repeated failures by recognizing a failure and avoids executing logic for a period of time.
- `@Fallback` executes alternative logic when an exception is thrown.
- `@Retry` retries a method call when an exception is thrown.
- `@Timeout` prevents a method from waiting longer than a specified amount of time.
- The Quarkus RESTEasy Reactive extension eliminates the need for the `@Asynchronous` annotation.
- MicroProfile Fault Tolerance annotations can be enabled, disabled, and customized using properties.

Reactive in an imperative world

A Microservice being *responsive* refers to its ability to complete the task required of it within a given time. The complexity of the task will impact the time a microservice takes to complete its work. Different microservices performing their tasks can require different amounts of time to complete them, yet both be considered responsive. Developing responsive microservices is key in a modern age where users—the customers—are expecting near instantaneous loading of web pages and answers to their queries. Microservices that are not responsive enough will fail when subjected to intensive high load. In an age of "going viral," it is critical that an application remain responsive while sustaining high load.

Although being reactive represents different aspects, in this chapter we focus on using *Reactive Streams* to create an execution pipeline within an application and between applications. After covering Reactive Streams, we introduce the MicroProfile Reactive Messaging specification and how it's used to build responsive microservices, including how to interact with Apache Kafka or other messaging systems. In the last section of the chapter, we explain how developers can bridge their imperative and reactive code within a single application or microservice.

8.1 Reactive example

Figure 8.1 details how each of the banking microservices interact with a messaging system, Apache Kafka, to implement message passing between them. Two separate message flows are created between the various services.

The first flow send an event from the Account service when overdrawn. The event will be added to a Kafka topic and then consumed by the Overdraft service. The

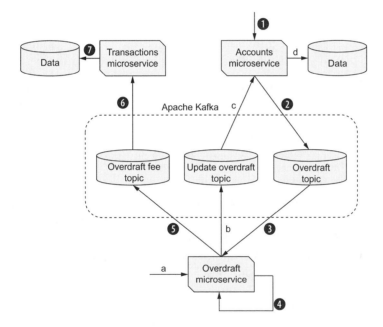

Flow 1: Account overdrawn event

1. Request to withdraw funds.
2. If account is now overdrawn, emit a message to a Kafka topic.
3. Process the message from Kafka.
4. Put the message onto the internal memory channel.
5. Emit a message to a Kafka topic with overdraft fee details.
6. Process the message from Kafka.
7. Write the transaction for the overdraft fee to the database.

Flow 2: Overdraft limit adjustment

a. Admin user adjusts the account overdraft limit.
b. Emit a message to a Kafka topic.
c. Process the message from Kafka.
d. Update the account in the database with the new overdraft limit.

Figure 8.1   Microservices utilizing Reactive Messaging

Overdraft service determines the appropriate fee for being overdrawn and sends a new event to a different Kafka topic to process the fee as an account transaction.

What is a Kafka topic?

Topics contain events, or messages, durably stored for retrieval. Every topic can receive events from zero, one, or many producers and have zero, one, or many consumers subscribing to those events. Unlike traditional messaging systems, events in a topic are not deleted after they're consumed. For better performance while scaling with load, a topic is partitioned between many broker instances. Any event written to a topic is only appended, ensuring the entire series of events can be replayed from the beginning, if desired, to reach the same end state of the data.

The second flow enables an admin user to adjust the overdraft limit for specific accounts, based on high-value customers, for instance. An event containing the new overdraft limit is sent to a Kafka topic for processing by the Account service.

> **NOTE** Throughout the chapter, the terms *event* and *message* are used interchangeably. In the worlds of reactive messaging and event-driven architectures, the two terms are synonymous. Which is preferred can often depend on the community using it, or whether it's being used in reference to a related term, such as *reactive messaging* or *event-driven architecture*.

8.2   *What is Reactive Streams?*

Reactive Streams is an asynchronous streaming specification for interactions between different libraries and/or technologies. In JDK 9, it's implemented as `java.util` `.concurrent.Flow`. However, Reactive Streams is not intended for direct usage by developers. It needs to underpin the libraries and technologies that developers use, and which they need to be aware about, but they are not concerned with its usage.

Reactive streams are necessary for the construction of *reactive systems*; see https://www.reactivemanifesto.org/ for further details. Reactive systems are an architectural style for designing responsive systems. The key characteristics of reactive systems are resiliency, elasticity, and asynchronous message passing.

A developer *does* need to understand the following fundamental building blocks of Reactive Streams: Publisher, Subscriber, and Processor (see figure 8.2).

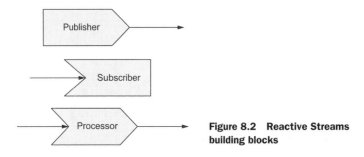

Figure 8.2   **Reactive Streams building blocks**

8.2.1   Publisher, Subscriber, and Processor

A *Publisher* is the first stage of a Reactive Stream, or pipeline; there is nothing before it. Any pipeline of data always consists of a single Publisher to begin the stream.

A *Subscriber* is the final stage of a Reactive Stream. The stream completes with a Subscriber; no further processing on that particular stream can occur.

A *Processor* combines Subscriber and Publisher to create a stage in the pipeline that continues the stream. It will manipulate and act on the data in the stream in any way, but it will not create or end the stream it's acting on.

In its simplest form, a stream consists of a Publisher and a Subscriber. Complex streams can consist of many Processors between a Publisher and a Subscriber, as shown in figure 8.3. There is no limit to the number of Processors that a stream can contain.

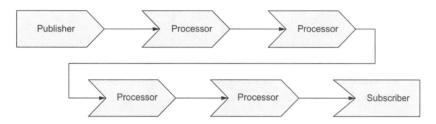

Figure 8.3   A complex Reactive Stream

Understanding these fundamental building blocks of a Reactive Stream is one part, but it's not the only part. *Back pressure* is a key aspect to Reactive Streams and their performance.

8.2.2   The importance of back pressure

What is back pressure exactly? Let's start by looking at a stream where service A is a publisher and service B is a subscriber. Figure 8.4 is an example of a situation where there is no restriction on the number of messages that service A can send to service B. Is that a problem? Maybe it isn't, which would be very lucky—usually it would be a big problem.

When service B is unable to process the messages it's receiving in a timely manner, the following problems can occur:

- The response time for service B can increase, because it's under heavy load.
- Service B can become unresponsive and fail. Depending on the deployment environment, it might mean there are no service B instances available for use. If there are no instances available, there can be a cascade of failures from service B to service A, and on to whatever called service A.
- Congestion on the network between services A and B will increase the latency of any communication on the same network path. This will lead to response time impacts on other services unrelated to service B.

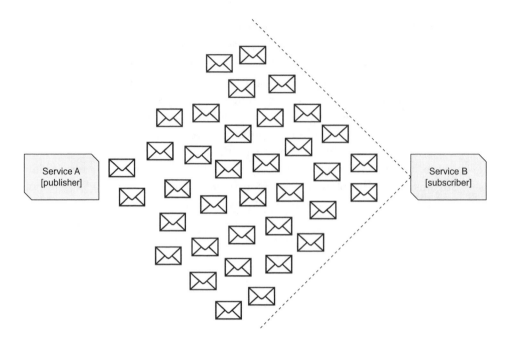

Figure 8.4   Overloading service B and the network

Overall, it's a bad situation. One service becoming unavailable is bad, but the impact on other unrelated services makes it even worse.

What should the flow of messages to a service look like? In figure 8.5, service B is still receiving a stream of messages from service A, but in such a way that service B never becomes overwhelmed with too many messages, enabling service B to remain in service and be more responsive to requests. It may appear service B is not being very responsive because it's handling fewer messages than in figure 8.4, but it's more responsive than being unavailable because it was unable to handle the load.

Figure 8.5   A steady stream of messages to service B

This is how back pressure can help to limit the possibility of the problems mentioned previously from occurring. Figure 8.6 outlines the process of implementing back pressure.

When service B subscribes to receive messages from service A, service A asks how many messages it would like. In this example, service B would like five messages.

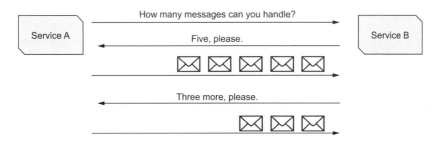

Figure 8.6 A steady stream of messages to service B

Service A dutifully sends across five messages for processing. Once service B has finished processing some of these messages, three in this case, service A will send three more messages. Notice that service A never sends more messages than service B has said it can process at once.

This section described Publishers, Subscribers, and Processors as the key components of Reactive Streams that developers must combine effectively to create pipelines for processing data. We also covered how the common problem associated with overloading Reactive Streams—sending too many messages—can be remedied using back pressure. In the next section, we introduce how Quarkus enables developers to integrate Reactive Streams into applications with Reactive Messaging.

8.3   *Reactive Messaging in Quarkus*

Quarkus enables developers to take advantage of Reactive Messaging, as well as the other aspects of reactive programming, while still utilizing the Java knowledge they've developed over the years with Java EE, and now Jakarta EE. This allows developers to convert small pieces of an application to use reactive concepts, without needing to develop an entirely reactive application.

Developers can steadily include more reactive aspects into their applications as their experience grows, without needing to switch between frameworks. This section explains the various ways a developer can use Quarkus to program with Reactive in their applications.

Let's start by copying the Account service from a previous chapter. Now add the following dependency to pom.xml:

```
<dependency>
  <groupId>io.quarkus</groupId>
  <artifactId>quarkus-smallrye-reactive-messaging-kafka</artifactId>
</dependency>
```

Quarkus offers Reactive Messaging extensions for Apache Kafka, AMQP, and MQTT. In this case, we chose the extension for Apache Kafka.

8.3.1   Bridging from imperative to reactive with emitters

Imperative programming uses a sequence of commands to alter state but does so in a step-by-step fashion where the developer defines the execution path. Imperative programming clearly defines what should happen, but also when it should happen, to achieve a desired result.

Change the Account service by modifying `Account` to have a `BigDecimal` field named `overdraftLimit`. The field will be used to track the current overdraft limit of an account, allowing it to be updated via events. With `Account` having another field, update `import.sql` to insert a value for the field into each record during startup. The code for the chapter sets it to `-200.00`, but the reader can set an alternative value.

The first challenge for developers is starting a Reactive Stream from imperative code. To start a Reactive Stream, a Publisher feeds the stream with messages. In the next example, an `Emitter` acts as a Publisher starting the Reactive Stream. Let's see how it works!

Listing 8.1   `AccountResource`

The name of the channel for emitting messages. The name of the channel in the application isn't required to match the name of the topic on Kafka.

Injects an Emitter for the Overdrawn message payload type

```
@Inject
@Channel("account-overdrawn")
Emitter<Overdrawn> emitter;

@PUT
@Path("{accountNumber}/withdrawal")
@Transactional
public CompletionStage<Account> withdrawal(@PathParam("accountNumber")
        Long accountNumber, String amount) {
  ...

    if (entity.accountStatus.equals(AccountStatus.OVERDRAWN)
        && entity.balance.compareTo(entity.overdraftLimit) <= 0) {
      throw new WebApplicationException("Account is overdrawn, no further
      withdrawals permitted", 409);
    }

    entity.withdrawFunds(new BigDecimal(amount));

    if (entity.balance.compareTo(BigDecimal.ZERO) < 0) {
      entity.markOverdrawn();
      entity.persist();
      Overdrawn payload =
        new Overdrawn(entity.accountNumber, entity.customerNumber,
        entity.balance, entity.overdraftLimit);
      return emitter.send(payload)
        .thenCompose(empty -> CompletableFuture.completedFuture(entity));
    }
    return entity;
}
```

The return type must be CompletionStage because the entity used in the Kafka message is still inside a transaction.

Throws an exception if the account has already passed the overdraftLimit amount

Creates an Overdrawn instance as the message payload

Sends a message containing the Overdrawn payload

Forces the entity to persist before sending it in the message

Chains the CompletionStage from emitter.send() to return one with the account entity

Listing 8.1 is an example of bridging between imperative and reactive programming. While inside a JAX-RS resource method—imperative programming—the application sends a message onto a channel—reactive programming—bridging from one programming model to the other. Section 8.3.3 details how listing 8.1 can be tested.

Being able to combine imperative and reactive programming into a single application is incredibly powerful. No longer is a developer restricted to utilizing only one part of their toolbox in developing an application. Now they can include as many parts of their toolbox as they need, or desire, in any given application, irrespective of whether it requires imperative or reactive programming. With Quarkus, developers are no longer required to choose between imperative or reactive programming for a project; they are able to use Quarkus in whichever direction the project might take.

Looking at the code in listing 8.1, we see the `Emitter` has a type of `Overdrawn`. An instance of `Overdrawn` will be the payload of the message that is sent to Apache Kafka, as shown next.

Listing 8.2 `Overdrawn`

```java
public class Overdrawn {
  public Long accountNumber;
  public Long customerNumber;
  public BigDecimal balance;
  public BigDecimal overdraftLimit;

  public Overdrawn(Long accountNumber, Long customerNumber, BigDecimal
    balance, BigDecimal overdraftLimit) {
    this.accountNumber = accountNumber;
    this.customerNumber = customerNumber;
    this.balance = balance;
    this.overdraftLimit = overdraftLimit;
  }
}
```

Injecting a `@Channel` can start a Reactive Stream within the same application or connect to an external system, such as Apache Kafka. In this case, it needs to connect to an external Apache Kafka topic. For that, the application needs to configure the channel indicated with the `@Channel` annotation, as illustrated in the next listing.

Listing 8.3 application.properties

Connects to the overdrawn topic to send messages

Uses the smallrye-kafka connector for the channel. This equates to sending the messages to Apache Kafka.

```
mp.messaging.outgoing.account-overdrawn.connector=smallrye-kafka
mp.messaging.outgoing.account-overdrawn.topic=overdrawn
mp.messaging.outgoing.account-overdrawn.value.serializer=
    io.quarkus.kafka.client.serialization.JsonbSerializer
```

Uses the Quarkus JSON-B serializer to convert the Overdrawn instance to JSON

The keys used in application.properties in this example do have special meaning, so let's discuss the various parts to them. The key format follows:

```
mp.messaging.<incoming|outgoing>.<channel_name>.<key_name>
```

The first variable aspect to the key is whether it represents an incoming or outgoing connection. In listing 8.1, a message will be sent from an application to Kafka, requiring listing 8.3 to use outgoing. The next variable is channel_name. Listing 8.1 specified the Emitter with @Channel("account-overdrawn"). Thus, all keys need to use the channel name account-overdrawn. Lastly is the variable key component identifying the specific piece of functionality being configured. In the next code listing, it includes connector, topic, and value.serializer. The full list of possible configuration keys for Apache Kafka with outgoing channels (http://mng.bz/OQeo) and incoming channels (http://mng.bz/YwWK) are in the SmallRye Reactive Messaging documentation (http://mng.bz/GOvR).

> **NOTE** If the channel name used within the application matched the topic on Apache Kafka, the key for topic can be skipped because it assumes the topic name is the channel name if not present.

Instead of emitting only the payload of a message, it's also possible to send the entire Message, including handlers for an acknowledgment, successful and failure, as shown here.

Listing 8.4 `AccountResource`

Uses Message.of() to construct an immutable message. The payload is the same content as the previous usage with emitter.send(payload).

A CompletableFuture is needed as the return type.

```
int ackedMessages = 0;
List<Throwable> failures = new ArrayList<>();
...
CompletableFuture<Account> future = new CompletableFuture<>();
emitter.send(Message.of(payload,
    () -> {
        future.complete(entity);
        return CompletableFuture.completedFuture(null);
    },
    reason -> {
        failures.add(reason);
        future.completeExceptionally(reason);
        return CompletableFuture.completedFuture(null);
    })
);
return future;
```

Completes the future with the account entity

A negative acknowledgment function where Throwable is a parameter and returns a CompletionStage<Void>. The example function captures the failure reason returned from the negative acknowledgment.

Defines an acknowledgment handler supplying a CompletionStage<Void> as the result. This handler increases a count of acknowledged messages.

Completes the future exceptionally

This section introduced how to bridge from imperative to reactive code with emitters, enabling developers to send messages from a JAX-RS resource method and transmit them to a destination—in this case, an Apache Kafka topic—using `@Channel` on the `Emitter` injection point, to indicate the topic.

8.3.2 What about blocking?

When developing reactive code, it's extremely important to not block the execution loop, also referred to as the event loop or IO thread. Blocking on the execution loop prevents other methods from executing at the same time, resulting in reduced throughput because the framework is not able to switch between inactive and active processes.

Figure 8.7 is a representation of the execution loop, showing it processing incoming requests with a single thread. Requests are all processed on the execution loop, but there are times when it's necessary to perform work that can be slower, such as writing to a database. In such a situation, it's critical to offload the slower work from the execution loop; otherwise, the single thread handling all requests will be prevented from doing anything except processing the slower work. When slower work is offloaded to other threads, the execution loop can handle a significantly higher request load.

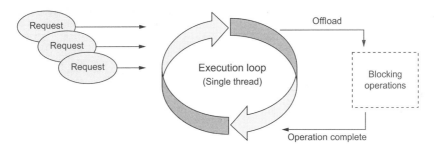

Figure 8.7   The execution loop

For these situations, developers need the ability to indicate which code is blocking, allowing the framework to offload the blocking code into a separate thread. Quarkus enables this with the `@Blocking` annotation for reactive messaging, as shown next.

Listing 8.5   `AccountResource`

Indicates that the method acts as a Subscriber by receiving messages but not sending any out. Just like @Channel, @Incoming contains the name of the channel, or topic, from which to read messages.

The method executes blocking code and runs the method on a thread that is not the execution loop thread.

```
@Incoming("overdraft-update")
@Blocking
@Transactional
```

```
public void processOverdraftUpdate(OverdraftLimitUpdate overdraftLimitUpdate) {
    Account account =
        Account.findByAccountNumber(overdraftLimitUpdate.accountNumber);
    account.overdraftLimit = overdraftLimitUpdate.newOverdraftLimit;
}
```

**Updates the Account with
the new overdraft limit**

**OverdraftLimitUpdate is the
payload from the message
that was received.**

NOTE   Section 8.4.2 explains the acknowledgment policies of `@Incoming`.

`OverdraftLimitUpdate` is a POJO with `accountNumber` and `newOverdraftLimit` as
fields. The source for `OverdraftLimitUpdate` is in /chapter8/account-service/.

`@Blocking` is a great annotation because it enables developers to utilize Reactive
Streams, while still executing more imperative, but blocking, code. Without the annotation, executing blocking code would need an `Executor` to spawn another thread to
perform the work and deal with propagating contexts between threads for CDI beans,
database transactions, or any other context that might be on the current thread that is
required to execute the method.

Listing 8.6   application.properties

**Reads the message from
the new-limit topic**

**Sets the Kafka broker location for production. In
development, the value defaults to localhost:9092,
making it unnecessary to set in most situations.**

```
%prod.kafka.bootstrap.servers=my-cluster-kafka-bootstrap.kafka:9092
mp.messaging.incoming.overdraft-update.connector=smallrye-kafka
mp.messaging.incoming.overdraft-update.topic=new-limit
mp.messaging.incoming.overdraft-update.value.deserializer=
    quarkus.accounts.OverdraftLimitUpdateDeserializer
```

**Specifies the deserializer used to convert the JSON
payload into an instance of OverdraftLimitUpdate**

These settings are similar to those from listing 8.3, but they configure an incoming
channel. Notice that `incoming` replaces `outgoing` in the key, and the channel name
`overdraft-update` replaces `account-overdrawn`.

Listing 8.6 specified a deserializer for `OverdraftLimitUpdate`. Let's take a look at
what it does, as shown next.

Listing 8.7   `OverdraftLimitUpdateDeserializer`

```
public class OverdraftLimitUpdateDeserializer extends
    JsonbDeserializer<OverdraftLimitUpdate> {
    public OverdraftLimitUpdateDeserializer() {
        super(OverdraftLimitUpdate.class);
    }
}
```

**In the default constructor, passes the
class type to the superclass constructor**

**The deserializer needs to
extend JsonbDeserializer for
JSON-B content. If using Jackson,
ObjectMapperDeserializer would
need to be extended instead.**

There's not much to the deserializer, but it handles the JSON-to-POJO conversion for developers. Developers don't need to use object mappers or interact with JSON objects—they can use the POJO directly in the method that receives a message.

This section introduced the `@Blocking` annotation for Reactive Messaging methods where developers know it could block and, therefore, needs to run in a separate thread. In addition, we covered using `@Incoming` to indicate a Subscriber of a Reactive Stream.

8.3.3 Testing "in memory"

Though it's important to test the integration with Apache Kafka, there is also benefit in being able to test quickly without it. To support testing of channels without Apache Kafka, the *in-memory* connector can be used instead. The in-memory connector replaces the `smallrye-kafka` connector for handling interaction with topics.

To use the in-memory connector, the following dependency is needed:

```
<dependency>
  <groupId>io.smallrye.reactive</groupId>
  <artifactId>smallrye-reactive-messaging-in-memory</artifactId>
  <scope>test</scope>
</dependency>
```

> **NOTE** The dependency is in `test` scope because it's not required for compilation, and it shouldn't be packaged into the final application.

The in-memory connector works by redefining the configuration of the channels in the application. To be able to do that, a `QuarkusTestResourceLifecycleManager`, shown in the next code listing, is needed.

Listing 8.8 InMemoryLifecycleManager

```
public class InMemoryLifecycleManager implements
    QuarkusTestResourceLifecycleManager {          Alters the incoming channel
  @Override                                        named overdraft-update to
  public Map<String, String> start() {             use the in-memory connector
    Map<String, String> env = new HashMap<>();
    env.putAll(InMemoryConnector.switchIncomingChannelsToInMemory(
    "overdraft-update"));
    env.putAll(InMemoryConnector.switchOutgoingChannelsToInMemory(
    "account-overdrawn"));          ◁──      The outgoing channel account-
    return env;                              overdrawn switches to use the
  }                                          in-memory connector.

  @Override
  public void stop() {                       Resets the configuration for any
    InMemoryConnector.clear();     ◁──       channels that were switched to
  }                                          the in-memory connector.
}
```

Now let's use this class in a test, illustrated next, to verify that an account going overdrawn triggers an event.

Listing 8.9   AccountResourceEventsTest

```
@QuarkusTest
@QuarkusTestResource(InMemoryLifecycleManager.class)    ⊲  Uses the InMemoryLifecycle-
public class AccountResourceEventsTest {                   Manager with the test to switch
                                                           the channels to in-memory

    @Inject @Any                        Injects an InMemoryConnector into the test for
    InMemoryConnector connector;    ⊲   interacting with a channel. @Any on the injection
                                        point is needed because the instance to be injected
                                        has a qualifier present, indicating any qualifiers
    @Test                               can be ignored.
    void testOverdraftEvent() {
        InMemorySink<Overdrawn> overdrawnSink = connector.sink("account-overdrawn");  ⊲

        Account account =                               Retrieves the sink for
            given()                                      the account-overdrawn
                .when().get("/accounts/{accountNumber}", 78790)   channel from the
                .then().statusCode(200)                  InMemoryConnector. The
                .extract().as(Account.class);            sink receives any events
                                                         sent to the channel.

        BigDecimal withdrawal = new BigDecimal("23.82");
        BigDecimal balance = account.balance.subtract(withdrawal);    ⊲

        account =                                       Sets a withdrawal amount that
            given()                                     will not cause the account to
                .contentType(ContentType.JSON)          become overdrawn
                .body(withdrawal.toString())
                .when().put("/accounts/{accountNumber}/withdrawal", 78790)
                .then().statusCode(200)
                .extract().as(Account.class);

        // Asserts verifying account and balance have been removed.

        assertThat(overdrawnSink.received().size(), equalTo(0));    ⊲

        withdrawal = new BigDecimal("6000.00");         Verifies that the sink for the
        balance = account.balance.subtract(withdrawal); channel has not received any
                                                        events. It shouldn't because
        account =                                       the account is not overdrawn.
            given()
                .contentType(ContentType.JSON)
                .body(withdrawal.toString())
                .when().put("/accounts/{accountNumber}/withdrawal", 78790)
                .then().statusCode(200)
                .extract().as(Account.class);

        // Asserts verifying account and customer details have been removed.
        assertThat(account.accountStatus, equalTo(AccountStatus.OVERDRAWN));
        assertThat(account.balance, equalTo(balance));
                                                        The channel
        assertThat(overdrawnSink.received().size(), equalTo(1));  ⊲  should have
                                                        received an
                                                        event.
```

Makes another account withdrawal that will trigger it being overdrawn

Asserts the account status is OVERDRAWN

```
    Message<Overdrawn> overdrawnMsg = overdrawnSink.received().get(0);   ◁┐
    assertThat(overdrawnMsg, notNullValue());                         ◁
    Overdrawn event = overdrawnMsg.getPayload();              ◁
    assertThat(event.accountNumber, equalTo(78790L));
    assertThat(event.customerNumber, equalTo(444222L));
    assertThat(event.balance, equalTo(balance));
    assertThat(event.overdraftLimit, equalTo(new BigDecimal("-200.00")));
  }
  ...
}
```

Verifies the contents of the Overdrawn payload have the appropriate values for the account

Retrieves the event, Message instance, from the channel sink

Listing 8.9 tests the use of `Emitter` in `AccountResource.withdrawal()` by verifying that an event is sent to the `Emitter`, but only when the account becomes overdrawn, and not before.

Next, let's see the test for `@Incoming`.

Listing 8.10 `AccountResourceEventsTest`

```
public class AccountResourceEventsTest {
  ...
  @Test
  void testOverdraftUpdate() {
    InMemorySource<OverdraftLimitUpdate> source =
     connector.source("overdraft-update");                 ◁

    Account account =
        given()
          .when().get("/accounts/{accountNumber}", 123456789)
          .then().statusCode(200)
          .extract().as(Account.class);

    // Asserts verifying account and balance have been removed.
    assertThat(account.overdraftLimit, equalTo(new BigDecimal("-200.00")));

    OverdraftLimitUpdate updateEvent = new OverdraftLimitUpdate();   ◁
    updateEvent.accountNumber = 123456789L;
    updateEvent.newOverdraftLimit = new BigDecimal("-600.00");

    source.send(updateEvent);

    account =
        given()
          .when().get("/accounts/{accountNumber}", 123456789)
          .then().statusCode(200)
          .extract().as(Account.class);

    // Asserts verifying account and balance have been removed.
    assertThat(account.overdraftLimit, equalTo(new BigDecimal("-600.00")));  ◁
  }
}
```

Retrieves the source for the overdraft-update channel from the InMemoryConnector. The source can send events to the channel.

Ensures the current overdraft limit on the account is the default -200.00

Sends the event to the channel using the source

Creates an OverdraftLimitUpdate instance with the account number and new overdraft limit

After retrieving the account, verifies the overdraft limit has been updated to -600.00

To see the tests run, open a terminal and change to /chapter8/account-service/ directory and run the following:

```
mvn verify
```

If everything worked as expected, the tests pass without error.

With the 2.x release of Quarkus, an alternative to in-memory testing is available for Kafka. When a Docker instance is available, the new Dev Services (https://quarkus .io/guides/kafka-dev-services) facility will start a Kafka broker using Redpanda (https:// vectorized.io/redpanda).

This section revealed how to test Reactive Messaging applications without needing to run an external messaging broker, such as Apache Kafka. Whether application code uses an `Emitter`, `@Incoming`, or any method annotation for reactive messaging, the code can be unit tested. Though there is still a need for integration testing, being able to unit test code provides a faster feedback loop for issues.

8.4   How does it work?

The previous section covered some examples using Reactive Messaging, but now let's take a look at what underpins the examples. Readers will learn about the MicroProfile Reactive Messaging specification, which is where the annotations from the examples are defined, and what a Reactive Stream looks like.

8.4.1   *MicroProfile Reactive Messaging specification*

The specification defines the means to build distributed systems enforcing asynchronous communication by promoting location transparency and temporal decoupling. Temporal decoupling refers to separating two different actions, or steps of execution, such that they can occur at different times. Location transparency requires not hard-coding physical addresses of one service into another but enabling the physical location of services to shift over time and still be addressable.

Synchronous communication, often through HTTP, can have a level of location transparency through the use of DNS records or service registries. For example, Kubernetes uses DNS for location transparency to abstract which node in the cluster is hosting a service instance. However, there is no way to avoid temporal coupling between services because the very nature of synchronous communication requires it.

How does Reactive Messaging differ from the message-driven beans of JMS? JMS was designed at a time when message brokers were present at the edges of application architectures, not as an integral piece of an application's architecture. If a developer wants to use messages with JMS within their application, it requires a message to be published to an external broker, before the same application then receives the same message from an external broker. When dealing with intra-application messaging, message brokers built for operating at the edges of a system would be overweight. The Reactive Messaging specification brings this functionality to developers by not requiring external brokers to create Reactive Streams within an application.

Over the following sections, the reader will learn about the specification, including how messages, channels, connectors, and streams work together as part of a distributed system.

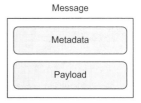

Figure 8.8   Content of a Message

8.4.2   *Message content and metadata*

The core of the specification is a Message, representing the data that's transmitted, as shown in figure 8.8. As seen from the examples earlier in the chapter, the Message wraps the specific payload being sent.

The Message interface provides methods that readers have already seen in earlier examples, including the following:

- getPayload—Retrieves the payload from the message wrapper. Examples of payload are OverdraftLimitUpdate and Overdrawn.
- getMetadata—Accesses the metadata from within the message wrapper. Depending on the underlying message type, the available metadata will differ. When using Apache Kafka, getMetadata(IncomingKafkaRecordMetadata.class) can be called on Message. IncomingKafkaRecordMetadata offers methods to access details of the underlying Kafka record, such as getTopic, getKey, and getTimestamp.
- ack—For acknowledging the completion of message processing.
- nack—To negatively acknowledge message processing. This indicates there was a failure in processing the message, and the publisher of the message needs to determine the appropriate handling of the failed message.

IMPORTANT   A Subscriber or Processor must properly acknowledge the processing of a message. Doing so assists in preventing the reprocessing of successful messages. With Quarkus, in many situations acknowledgment happens automatically for the developer. When a method has a Message parameter, developers must manually call ack() on the message. In other situations, acknowledgment occurs as long as no exception is thrown.

NOTE   Negative acknowledgment, the nack() method, is an experimental feature of SmallRye Reactive Messaging in Quarkus. If feedback from the community is positive, the method will be proposed to the specification.

When more control over automatic acknowledgment of a message is needed, the developer can annotate a method with @Acknowledgement. @Acknowledgement provides the following four options for configuring the type of acknowledgment:

- POST_PROCESSING—Acknowledgment of an incoming message does not occur until any produced message has been acknowledged. If service A sends a message to service B, which in turn sends a message to service C, service B will not acknowledge the message it received from service A until service C has acknowledged the message service B sent.

- PRE_PROCESSING—The incoming message is acknowledged before method execution.
- MANUAL—The developer has full control over executing `ack()` on the `Message`.
- NONE—No acknowledgment of any kind is performed.

Now let's see in the next code listing some methods that interact with message metadata by adding it to a message and then retrieving it in a subsequent method.

Listing 8.11   `OverdraftResource`

Receives a Message with an Overdrawn payload, and returns an identical message and payload combination, though not the same message content in this case

An incoming channel connected to the topic that receives messages from AccountResource

An internal application channel for passing a message to ProcessOverdraftFee in listing 8.12

```
@Incoming("account-overdrawn")
@Outgoing("customer-overdrafts")
public Message<Overdrawn> overdraftNotification(Message<Overdrawn> message) {
    Overdrawn overdrawnPayload = message.getPayload();

    CustomerOverdraft customerOverdraft =
        customerOverdrafts.get(overdrawnPayload.customerNumber);
    // Create a new CustomerOverdraft if it's null. Full content in chapter
      source

    AccountOverdraft accountOverdraft =
      customerOverdraft.accountOverdrafts.get(overdrawnPayload.accountNumber);
    // Create a new AccountOverdraft if it's null. Full content in chapter
      source
    customerOverdraft.totalOverdrawnEvents++;
    accountOverdraft.currentOverdraft = overdrawnPayload.overdraftLimit;
    accountOverdraft.numberOverdrawnEvents++;

    return message.addMetadata(customerOverdraft);
}
```

Updates the customer and account overdraft events

Gets the current set of overdraft events for the customer

Retrieves the Overdrawn payload from inside the message

Returns a new Message instance containing the same payload, but with CustomerOverdraft as metadata in the message

Listing 8.11 is a Publisher, defined earlier in the chapter, because it includes both `@Incoming` and `@Outgoing` on the method. In the next code listing, we extract the customer overdraft details to determine the appropriate fee, then we create an `Account-Fee` that is packaged into a message and sent to the outgoing channel.

Listing 8.12   `ProcessOverdraftFee`

A CDI bean with an application scope means only one will be created.

Receives the messages from the customer-overdrafts channel that were added in listing 8.11

```
@ApplicationScoped
public class ProcessOverdraftFee {
  @Incoming("customer-overdrafts")
  @Outgoing("overdraft-fee")
```

Creates a message to be sent to the overdraft-fee channel

```
   public AccountFee processOverdraftFee(Message<Overdrawn> message) {
      Overdrawn payload = message.getPayload();
      CustomerOverdraft customerOverdraft =
          message.getMetadata(CustomerOverdraft.class).get();

      AccountFee feeEvent = new AccountFee();
      feeEvent.accountNumber = payload.accountNumber;
      feeEvent.overdraftFee = determineFee(payload.overdraftLimit,
       customerOverdraft.totalOverdrawnEvents,
          customerOverdraft.accountOverdrafts.get(payload.accountNumber)
       .numberOverdrawnEvents);
      return feeEvent;
   }
}
```

AccountFee is the payload that will be included in the new message the method produces.

Accepts a Message with Overdrawn payload, and returns an AccountFee payload that will be wrapped into a message

Retrieves the CustomerOverdraft metadata from the Message, which was added in listing 8.11

`OverdraftResourceEventsTest` tests these interactions, which is in the chapter source in the /chapter8/overdraft-service/src/test/java/quarkus/overdraft_ directory. Because the content of `OverdraftResourceEventsTest` is quite similar to listing 8.9, it was not included for brevity.

Running `mvn verify` in the /chapter8/overdraft-service/ directory runs the test. Everything should pass without a problem.

Because the test used the in-memory connector, there was no need to configure any of the channels with properties. However, they are needed when connecting with Kafka, as shown next.

Listing 8.13 application.properties

```
mp.messaging.incoming.account-overdrawn.connector=smallrye-kafka
mp.messaging.incoming.account-overdrawn.topic=overdrawn
mp.messaging.incoming.account-overdrawn.value.deserializer=
    quarkus.overdraft.OverdrawnDeserializer

mp.messaging.outgoing.overdraft-fee.connector=smallrye-kafka
mp.messaging.outgoing.overdraft-fee.topic=account-fee
mp.messaging.outgoing.overdraft-fee.value.serializer=
    io.quarkus.kafka.client.serialization.JsonbSerializer

mp.messaging.outgoing.overdraft-update.connector=smallrye-kafka
mp.messaging.outgoing.overdraft-update.topic=new-limit
mp.messaging.outgoing.overdraft-update.value.serializer=
    io.quarkus.kafka.client.serialization.JsonbSerializer
```

OverdrawnDeserializer converts JSON into an Overdrawn instance and is nearly identical to listing 8.7.

IMPORTANT Listing 8.13 does not include a channel definition for `customer-overdrafts`. `customer-overdrafts` is purely an internal application channel; `@Outgoing` and `@Incoming` are present in the same application deployment, so there is no need for it to be defined in configuration. Quarkus will automatically create a Reactive Stream connecting them.

This section introduced the `Message` interface with methods for accessing the payload, acknowledging a message, and retrieving metadata from the message. `Message` consists of the payload with additional metadata wrapped together.

8.4.3   *Messages in the stream*

How does a `Message` fit within a Reactive Stream?

Figure 8.9 shows an internal view of an application where several CDI beans publish, process, and subscribe to messages, creating a Reactive Stream between them. Between each CDI bean is a *channel*, enabling methods on CDI beans to be connected together in a chain, where they can pass messages.

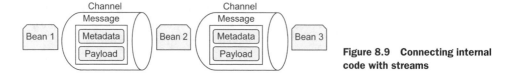

Figure 8.9   **Connecting internal code with streams**

A channel can be within an application between components, as in figure 8.9, or connect to remote brokers or message transport layers.

The architecture in figure 8.10 is an application receiving messages with one connector and publishing messages to another connector.

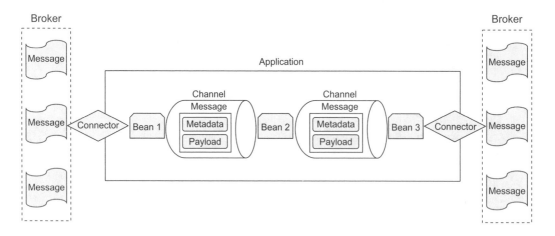

Figure 8.10   **Integrating streams between microservices**

In this architecture, channels connect external brokers to the application and between components of the application internally. The connector transport could be of the same or different types, such as a Kafka cluster or an AMQP broker. If the connector transport utilizes a Kafka cluster, an external channel is a representation of a Kafka topic. An example of this architecture can be seen in listing 8.11 and listing 8.12.

8.5   *Deploying to Kubernetes*

To be able to deploy the application to Kubernetes, it's necessary to have an Apache Kafka cluster to send to and receive messages from topics.

8.5.1   *Apache Kafka in Minikube*

The Strimzi (https://strimzi.io/) project is a great way to run an Apache Kafka cluster on Kubernetes. We will use it with Minikube for testing the application for the chapter. Strimzi includes the following great features by default:

- Secured by default, with support for TLS
- Options for configuring NodePort, LoadBalancer, and Ingress
- Dedicated Kafka nodes
- Operation-based deployment

If Minikube is already running, stop it and run `minikube delete` before restarting it. It is recommended to use more than the default 2 GB RAM for Minikube when running Apache Kafka.

To keep all the Kafka components separate from the applications, let's put them into their own namespace as follows:

```
kubectl create namespace kafka
```

Now install the Strimzi Kubernetes operator, as shown here:

```
kubectl apply -f 'strimzi-cluster-operator-0.25.0.yaml' -n kafka
```

> **NOTE** Operators are software extensions to Kubernetes that utilize custom resources to manage applications or their components. In this instance, the operator is managing an Apache Kafka cluster.

To create the cluster, some YAML, shown in the next code listing, is required to inform the Strimzi operator of the type of cluster needed.

Listing 8.14   kafka_cluster.yml

```
apiVersion: kafka.strimzi.io/v1beta2
kind: Kafka                          ◁──  Sets the resource kind to Kafka, which
metadata:                                 is recognized by the Strimzi operator
  name: my-cluster    ◁─────────────
spec:                                     Indicates the name
  kafka:                                  for the cluster
```

```
    replicas: 2          ◁        Number of Kafka
    listeners:                    replicas to create
      - name: plain      ◁
        port: 9092                Defines the plain
        type: internal           and tls listeners
        tls: false               for the broker
      - name: tls
        port: 9093
        type: internal
        tls: true
  ...                            Number of Zookeeper replicas. Zookeeper
zookeeper:                       is a key-value store used in distribution
  replicas: 2          ◁         systems for storing configuration.
  ...
```

NOTE   In a production environment, it is recommended to have three repli-cas of Kafka and Zookeeper, at a minimum, for failover purposes. However, in the constrained environment of a local machine, two replicas shouldn't overwhelm the local system while still showcasing multiple brokers.

Now create the cluster defined in listing 8.14 as follows:

```
kubectl apply -f kafka_cluster.yml -n kafka
```

Creating the cluster can take a few minutes because it needs to download container images for Kafka and Zookeeper and configure all the instances. There are a couple of alternatives to wait for it to be ready. Run a `wait` command that will complete when the cluster is ready like so:

```
kubectl wait kafka/my-cluster --for=condition=Ready --timeout=300s -n kafka
```

Or keep checking the status of the Kubernetes Pods as follows:

```
kubectl get pods -n kafka
```

The expected result of the above command is shown here:

```
NAME                                            READY   STATUS    RESTARTS   AGE
my-cluster-entity-operator-574bcbc568-xb4xr     3/3     Running   0          86s
my-cluster-kafka-0                              1/1     Running   0          115s
my-cluster-kafka-1                              1/1     Running   0          115s
my-cluster-zookeeper-0                          1/1     Running   0          3m2s
my-cluster-zookeeper-1                          1/1     Running   0          3m2s
strimzi-cluster-operator-54ff55979f-895lj       1/1     Running   0          4m14s
```

Let's run a quick test to verify the Kafka cluster is operating correctly. First, start a pro-ducer that accepts messages in the terminal as follows:

```
kubectl -n kafka run kafka-producer -ti
  --image=quay.io/strimzi/kafka:0.25.0-kafka-2.8.0 --rm=true
  --restart=Never -- bin/kafka-console-producer.sh --broker-list
  my-cluster-kafka-bootstrap.kafka:9092 --topic my-topic
```

When the producer is ready to accept input, it will display ">" on the left-hand side of the terminal window. To send a message, type anything into the terminal and press Enter. Pressing Enter creates a message, adding it to the `my-topic` topic.

Now run the consumer in a different terminal to read the messages, as shown next:

```
kubectl -n kafka run kafka-consumer -ti
  --image=quay.io/strimzi/kafka:0.25.0-kafka-2.8.0 --rm=true
  --restart=Never -- bin/kafka-console-consumer.sh --bootstrap-server
  my-cluster-kafka-bootstrap.kafka:9092 --topic my-topic --from-beginning
```

A delay of a few seconds occurs while it downloads and starts the container image. Once started, the messages entered into the producer appear in the order they were entered. When the messages have been received, stop the consumer and producer by typing Ctrl-C in each terminal window.

For the Account service and Overdraft service to operate, topics in Kafka are needed, so add them as follows:

```
kubectl apply -f kafka_topics.yml -n kafka
```

The kafka_topics.yml asks for three topics to be created, named `overdrawn`, `new-limit`, and `account-fee`. Each topic defines three partitions and two replicas. The kafka_topics.yml can be found in the /chapter8 directory.

In the next section, we retrieve messages directly from a Kafka topic.

8.5.2 *Putting it all together*

With the Apache Kafka cluster in place, it's time to deploy the Account service and Overdraft service. Before deploying the services, we need the following PostgreSQL database:

```
kubectl apply -f postgresql_kubernetes.yml
```

> **NOTE** Run `eval $(minikube -p minikube docker-env)` before the next command to ensure the container image build uses Docker inside Minikube.

Next, deploy the Account service. Change to the /chapter8/account-service/ directory in a terminal and run the following code:

```
mvn verify -Dquarkus.kubernetes.deploy=true
```

Next, deploy the Overdraft service in the same manner.

When complete, run `minikube service list` to show the deployed services, as shown in the next code listing.

Listing 8.15 Services present in Minikube

```
|------------|------------------------------------|-------------------|---------------------------|
| NAMESPACE  |                NAME                | TARGET PORT       |           URL             |
|------------|------------------------------------|-------------------|---------------------------|
| default    | account-service                    | http/80           | http://192.168.64.15:30704 |
| default    | kubernetes                         | No node port      |                           |
| default    | overdraft-service                  | http/80           | http://192.168.64.15:31621 |
| default    | postgres                           | http/5432         | http://192.168.64.15:31615 |
| kafka      | my-cluster-kafka-bootstrap         | No node port      |                           |
| kafka      | my-cluster-kafka-brokers           | No node port      |                           |
| kafka      | my-cluster-zookeeper-client        | No node port      |                           |
| kafka      | my-cluster-zookeeper-nodes         | No node port      |                           |
| kube-system| kube-dns                           | No node port      |                           |
|------------|------------------------------------|-------------------|---------------------------|
```

With everything in place it's time to test it all out!

Let's withdraw $600 from an account that will make it overdrawn. Open a terminal and run the following:

```
ACCOUNT_URL=`minikube service --url account-service`
curl -H "Content-Type: application/json" -X PUT -d "600.00"
      ${ACCOUNT_URL}/accounts/123456789/withdrawal
```

The response we should receive is shown in the next code sample.

Listing 8.16 Account details response

```
{
    "id":1,
    "accountNumber":123456789,
    "accountStatus":"OVERDRAWN",     <--  Status of the account is OVERDRAWN.
    "balance":-49.22,                <--  The account is reduced from $550.78 to -$49.22.
    "customerName":"Debbie Hall",
    "customerNumber":12345,
    "overdraftLimit":-200.00
}
```

With an account becoming overdrawn, a message should have been added to the `account-fee` topic. To find out if there is one, use the `kafka-console-consumer.sh` script from the Kafka installation. In a terminal run the following:

Uses the topic consumer script within the instance | Runs an interactive instance named kafka-consumer | Uses the Strimzi Kafka container image

```
kubectl -n kafka run kafka-consumer -it \
    --image=strimzi/kafka:0.25.0-kafka-2.8.0 \
    --rm=true --restart=Never \
    -- bin/kafka-console-consumer.sh \
    --bootstrap-server my-cluster-kafka-bootstrap.kafka:9092 \
```

Doesn't restart the container and remove it when done

The Kafka bootstrap server

```
--topic account-fee \
--from-beginning
```

Reads messages from offset 0 of the topic

Connects to the account-fee topic

NOTE Ensure the `kafka-consumer` from earlier in the chapter was stopped first to prevent errors.

Assuming the message was correctly sent to the Kafka topic, the result of the previous command should be the following:

```
{
  "accountNumber":123456789,
  "overdraftFee":15.00
}
```

For the same account, now verify what the current overdraft limit is set to as follows:

```
curl -X GET ${ACCOUNT_URL}/accounts/123456789
```

The response should be the same as listing 8.16. It will show a current `overdraft-Limit` of `-200.00`. Now call the Overdraft service to adjust the limit as follows:

```
OVERDRAFT_URL=`minikube service --url overdraft-service`
curl -H "Content-Type: application/json" -X PUT -d "-600.00"
    ${OVERDRAFT_URL}/overdraft/123456789
```

Now verify a message was sent through Kafka and the limit is updated in the Account service, as shown next:

```
curl -X GET ${ACCOUNT_URL}/accounts/123456789
```

The response should be the following:

```
{
  "id":1,
  "accountNumber":123456789,
  "accountStatus":"OVERDRAWN",
  "balance":-49.22,
  "customerName":"Debbie Hall",
  "customerNumber":12345,
  "overdraftLimit":-600.00
}
```

The overdraftLimit for the account has been updated to -$600.00.

This section explained how to use the Strimzi operator for creating an Apache Kafka cluster. Whether in Minikube or a production Kubernetes cluster, the Strimzi operator can be used for it all. With a Kafka cluster in place, we can create topics with the Strimzi operator. With the services deployed, the reader ran `curl` commands to interact with the different services for interacting with the topics.

> **Exercise for the reader**
>
> Copy the Transaction service from a previous chapter, and modify it to process messages from the `account-fee` topic in Kafka. The messages on the topic will have `AccountFee` instances as a payload. Retrieve the content of `AccountFee`, and create a transaction against the `accountNumber` with the specified amount.

Summary

- Reactive Streams consist of a Publisher to create a message, a Subscriber to receive a message terminating the stream, and any number of Processors in between.
- By adding `@Incoming` to a method, a Subscriber listens to messages from a Reactive Stream.
- Whether connecting to Apache Kafka, AMQP brokers, MQTT brokers, or other types of messaging systems, developers are able to switch configuration between them without needing to modify application code.
- Include `@Blocking` on a method to indicate it should occur on a separate thread, because the work required is potentially blocking. An example is storing records in a database.
- Use the Strimzi operator for creating an Apache Kafka cluster in Kubernetes, or Minikube, and creating topics.

Developing Spring
microservices with Quarkus

This chapter covers

- Comparing Spring and Quarkus/MicroProfile APIs
- Replacing Quarkus/MicroProfile APIs with Spring APIs
- How Quarkus implements Spring API compatibility

Spring is a popular Java microservices runtime with a large developer base that has invested a lot of time learning Spring APIs. By offering compatibility with commonly used Spring APIs, Quarkus enables Spring developers to leverage that investment and get started quickly. Spring developers can then benefit from Quarkus development features like live coding and production efficiencies like low memory usage and fast boot time. This chapter is intended for experienced Spring developers and will not cover Spring APIs in depth. The examples for this chapter update the examples from chapters 3 and 7 to use Spring APIs where possible. By updating existing examples, the following two concepts will become apparent:

- Spring APIs can be used side by side with Quarkus and MicroProfile APIs.
- Spring APIs and Quarkus/MicroProfile APIs have similar programming models.

The next section gives a more in-depth overview of the compatibility between Quarkus and Spring APIs.

9.1 *Quarkus/Spring API compatibility overview*

When adopting Quarkus, Spring developers can bring their existing API knowledge with them. The list of Quarkus/Spring compatibility extensions follows:

- Quarkus Extension for Spring Boot properties
- Quarkus Extension for Spring Cache API (not covered in this chapter)
- Quarkus Extension for Spring Cloud Config Client
- Quarkus Extension for Spring DI API
- Quarkus Extension for Spring Data JPA API
- Quarkus Extension for Spring Scheduled (not covered in this chapter)
- Quarkus Extension for Spring Security API
- Quarkus Extension for Spring Web API

The Spring and Quarkus ecosystems are much larger in scope than the extensions outlined in this list. Migrating existing Spring applications to Quarkus using the Spring compatibility APIs is not a primary goal of the Spring compatibility APIs. The goal is to offer enough of the Spring ecosystem APIs to make Spring developers immediately comfortable and productive with Quarkus. Regardless, organizations have been using the compatibility APIs to facilitate the migration of existing Spring applications where sufficient API coverage is available and supported APIs, like MicroProfile Fault Tolerance, are available.

Once familiar with Quarkus, some developers decide to switch from the Spring APIs to the Quarkus and MicroProfile APIs because the APIs are similar and they prefer developing to industry standards when possible. For example, table 9.1 shows a simple method using both the JAX-RS and Spring Web APIs. The APIs are similar, and both can run on Quarkus.

Table 9.1 Comparing a method written using JAX-RS vs. Spring Web annotations

JAX-RS	Spring Web

``
@GET
@Path("/{accountNumber}/balance")
public BigDecimal getBalance(
      @PathParam("accountNumber")
Long accountNumber) {
  ...
}
``
	``
	@GetMapping("/{accountNumber}/balance")
	public BigDecimal getBalance(
	        @PathVariable("accountNumber")
	Long accountNumber) {
	  ...
	}
	``

The following sections focus on applying the Spring compatibility APIs to the Bank service, Account service, and Transaction service. To a surprising degree, it is a simple mapping, similar to table 9.1.

9.2 Spring dependency injection and configuration compatibility

Spring popularized Java dependency injection more than a decade ago, and CDI popularized annotation-based dependency injection a few years later. Today, both frameworks offer annotation-based dependency injection with similar functionality. The configuration annotations are also similar between Spring and Quarkus. Table 9.2 shows how Quarkus converts Spring annotations to CDI and MicroProfile Config annotations during compilation.

Table 9.2 Spring-to-CDI/MicroProfile annotation compile-time conversions

Spring	CDI/MicroProfile	Comments
@Autowire	@Inject	Injects a component.
@Bean	@Produces	Defines a factory method.
@Configuration	@ApplicationScoped	
@ConfigurationProperties	@ConfigProperties	Injects multiple properties.
@Qualifier	@Named	Differentiates between different beans of the same type in the same scope.
@Value	@ConfigProperty	Injects a property value; @Value provides expression language support.
@Component @Service @Repository	@Singleton	By default, Spring stereotypes are singletons.

The next section will set up a Spring Cloud Config Server as a configuration source for the Bank service, followed by a section that uses Spring DI annotations to obtain properties from the Spring Cloud Config Server.

9.2.1 Setting up the Spring Cloud Config Server

The Spring Cloud Config Server (Config Server) is a configuration source that provides common access to configurations stored in Git repositories, Redis, Vault, and more. By supporting the Config Server, Quarkus applications can more easily run in existing Spring environments. The instructions for installing the Config Server are available from the Spring community (https://spring.io/guides/gs/centralized-configuration).

> **NOTE** Optionally, use the Config Server included in the book's Git repository in the chapter 9 spring-config-server subdirectory.

Listing 9.1 shows the properties from the chapter 3 Bank service that have been added to the Config Server Git repository at https://github.com/jclingan/banking-config-repository in the bank-service.properties file. The properties have minimal differences, like the ("Config Server") text appended to some properties to make the configuration source apparent.

Listing 9.1   Config Server bank-service.properties

```
# Configuration file
# key = value

# Bank names
bank.name=Bank of Quarkus (Config Server)
%dev.bank.name=Bank of Development (Config Server)
%prod.bank.name=Bank of Production  (Config Server)

# Using @ConfigProperties
bank-support.email=support@bankofquarkus.com (Config Server)
bank-support.phone=555-555-5555 (Config Server)

# Devmode properties for expansion below
username=quarkus_banking
password=quarkus_banking

# Property expansion
db.username=${username}
db.password=${password}
```

The next listing shows the required properties to configure the Config Server in src/main/resources/application.properties.

Listing 9.2   Config Server application.properties

```
                                    Specifies a port that does not
                                    conflict with other services
server.port=18888        ⊲─┘
spring.cloud.config.server.git.uri=https://github.com/jclingan/banking-
     config-repository/        ⊲──┐
                                   The location of the Git repository
                                   that defines properties used by
                                   the Bank service
```

Package the Config Server using `mvn package`, and then start it with `java -jar target/ spring-config-server-0.0.1-SNAPSHOT.jar`. With the Config Server running, the next step is to update the Bank service to use the server as a configuration source.

9.2.2   *Using the Spring Config Server as a configuration source*

The Bank service requires updates to use the Config Server. First, run `mvn quarkus: add-extension -Dextensions=quarkus-spring-cloud-config-client` to add the Config Server as a configuration source.

The Config Server will provide most of the properties defined in the chapter 3 Bank service. However, the Bank service properties outlined in the next code listing have to be defined locally because they are Quarkus build-time properties.

Listing 9.3 Bank service application.properties

Enables the Config Server as a configuration source

The Config Server selects the configuration based on the application name. This maps to bank-service.properties in the Git repository.

```
# Spring Cloud Config Server Client configuration

quarkus.application.name=bank-service
quarkus.spring-cloud-config.enabled=true
quarkus.spring-cloud-config.url=http://localhost:18888
%prod.quarkus.spring-cloud-config.url=http://spring-config-server:18888
```

Provides the URL to the Config Server when running locally during development

Provides the URL to the Config Server when running in Minikube

From the bank-service directory, test the results by running `mvn quarkus:dev`, and then check an endpoint using `curl localhost:8080/bank/secrets`.

The output should match the text in the next listing.

Listing 9.4 Bank service application.properties

```
{"password":"quarkus_banking","db.password":"quarkus_banking","db.username":"
    quarkus_banking","username":"quarkus_banking"}
```

9.2.3 Converting the Bank service to use Spring Configuration APIs

To use the Spring DI and Spring Boot Configuration APIs, add the quarkus-spring-di and quarkus-spring-boot-properties extensions using `mvn quarkus:add-extension -Dextensions=quarkus-spring-di,quarkus-spring-boot-properties`.

Referring to table 9.2, update the BankSupportConfig.java source code to use Spring's `@ConfigurationProperties` annotation as shown next.

Listing 9.5 Converting to Spring's `@ConfigurationProperties`

```
@ConfigurationProperties
public class BankSupportConfig {
    ...
}
```

Changes the MicroProfile @ConfigProperties annotation to Spring Boot's @ConfigurationProperties

Update BankResource.java to replace MicroProfile's `@ConfigProperty` annotation with Spring's `@Value` annotation as shown in the following code.

Listing 9.6 Converting to Spring's `@Value` annotation in BankResource.java

```
@Value("${bank.name:Bank of Default}")
    String name;

    @Value("${db.username:Missing}")
    String db_username;
```

Replaces @ConfigProperty with @Value. The @ConfigProperty defaultValue parameter value is now defined in the @Value expression.

```
@Value("${db.password:Missing}")       <───┐
String db_password;                         │
                                            │
@Value("app.mobilebanking")            <─── │  Replaces @ConfigProperty with
Optional<Boolean> mobileBanking;            │  @Value. The @ConfigProperty
                                            │  defaultValue parameter value is now
@Value("username")                     <─── │  defined in the @Value expression.
String username;                            │
                                            │
@Value("password")                     <───┘
String password;
```

Check an endpoint using `curl localhost:8080/bank/secrets`. The output should match the earlier output in listing 9.4. Stop the Bank service to avoid port conflicts with upcoming services.

As shown, converting the Bank service to using Spring property and DI annotations is seamless, including using a Config Server as a configuration source.

> ### Exercise for the reader
> Update the remaining services to Spring DI APIs. The book's Git repository contains working updated code for the Bank service, Account service, and Transaction service.

The next section will convert the Account service to use Spring Web APIs.

9.3   *Quarkus/Spring Web API compatibility*

This section will change JAX-RS APIs in the Account service to their Spring Web equivalents. As with using Spring configuration and DI annotations, the JAX-RS and Spring Web APIs are similar enough to make the conversion straightforward. A list of Spring Web annotations supported by Quarkus follows:

- `@CookieValue`
- `@DeleteMapping`
- `@ExceptionHandler` (with Quarkus, usable only in the `@RestControllerAdvice` class)
- `@MatrixVariable`
- `@RequestBody`
- `@RequestMapping`
- `@RequestParam`
- `@ResponseStatus`
- `@RestController`
- `@RestControllerAdvice` (with Quarkus, supports only the `@ExceptionHandler` capability)
- `@PatchMapping`
- `@PathVariable`

- @PostMapping
- @PutMapping

Before updating the code to Spring Web APIs, execute the following steps:

1 *Add Spring Web compatibility*—From the account-service directory, add the quarkus-spring-web extension to the Account service to enable the Spring Web annotations. Run `mvn quarkus:add-extension -Dextensions=quarkus-spring-web`.

2 *Start the PostgreSQL database*—The Account service requires the PostgreSQL database. If it is not already running, deploy the PostgreSQL database to Minikube by running `kubectl apply -f postgresql_kubernetes.yml` from the chapter 9 top-level directory.

3 *Proxy database requests*—To forward local database requests to the Minikube PostgreSQL instance, run `kubectl port-forward service/postgres 5432:5432`.

The next code listing converts AccountResource.java to the Spring Web APIs.

Listing 9.7 Converting the Account service to Spring Web APIs

@RestController replaces the @ApplicationScoped annotation.

@RestMapping and its parameters replace JAX-RS @Path, @Produces, and @Consumes annotations.

```
@RestController
@RequestMapping(path = "/accounts",
                produces=MediaType.APPLICATION_JSON_VALUE,
                consumes=MediaType.APPLICATION_JSON_VALUE)
public class AccountResource {

    @GetMapping
    public String hello() {
        return "hello";
    }

    @PostMapping("{accountNumber}/transaction")
    @Transactional
    public Map<String, List<String>>
        transact(@RequestHeader("Accept") String acceptHeader,
        @PathVariable("accountNumber") Long accountNumber,
        @RequestBody BigDecimal amount) {
    ...
    if (account == null) {
      throw new ResponseStatusException(HttpStatus.NOT_FOUND,
            "Account with " + accountNumber + " does not exist.");
    }

    if (entity.getAccountStatus().equals(AccountStatus.OVERDRAWN)) {
      throw new ResponseStatusException(HttpStatus.CONFLICT,
            "Account is overdrawn, no further withdrawals permitted");
    }

    ...
```

@GetMapping replaces JAX-RS @GET.

@PostMapping replaces JAX-RS @PATH and @POST annotations.

@RequestHeader replaces @Context HttpHeaders. For the moment, directly injecting a @RequestHeader MultiValueMap is not supported. This will be addressed in a Quarkus update.

@PathVariable replaces @PathParam.

@RequestBody has no JAX-RS equivalent. By default, JAX-RS attempts to bind JSON to a specified data type.

ResponseStatusException replaces JAX-RS WebApplicationException.

```
        List<String> list = new ArrayList<>();

        list.add((acceptHeader));
        Map<String,List<String>> map = new HashMap<String,List<String>>();
        map.put("Accept", list);

        ...
    }

    @GetMapping("/{accountNumber}/balance")                    ◁ ──┐
    public BigDecimal getBalance(@PathVariable("accountNumber") Long   ◁──┐
        accountNumber) {
        ...
        if (account == null) {
          throw new ResponseStatusException(HttpStatus.NOT_FOUND,   ◁──┐
                "Account with " + accountNumber + " does not exist.");
        }
    }
}
```

@GetMapping replaces JAX-RS @GET.

@PathVariable replaces JAX-RS @PathParam.

ResponseStatusException replaces JAX-RS WebApplicationException and uses Spring's HttpStatus class to return the HTTP status code.

This section of code "manually" creates Spring's MultiValueMap with one entry that can be returned to the caller. This code will be removed once MultiValueMap injection is supported in a future Quarkus update (https://github.com/quarkusio/quarkus/issues/14051).

AccountResource.java also defines an exception handler, which catches application exceptions and returns an HTTP 500 status code. This code is slightly more complex than previous examples because the annotations do not map one to one, and some new data types are involved, such as `ResponseEntity`. The next code snippet replaces the JAX-RS `ExceptionMapper` with a Spring Web `@RestControllerAdvice` class.

Listing 9.8   Converting `ExceptionMapper` to `@RestControllerAdvice`

The JAX-RS ExceptionMapper interface is converted to a Spring Web @RestControllerAdvice annotation and also replaces the JAX-RS @Provider annotation.

The JAX-RS toResponse() interface method is converted to a method annotated with the Spring Web @ExceptionHandler annotation.

```
    @RestControllerAdvice
        public static class ErrorMapper {
          @ExceptionHandler(Exception.class)                      ◁──
          public ResponseEntity<Object> toResponse(Exception exception) {

            HttpStatus code = HttpStatus.INTERNAL_SERVER_ERROR;
            if (exception instanceof ResponseStatusException) {
              code = ((ResponseStatusException) exception).getStatus();
            }

            JsonObjectBuilder entityBuilder = Json.createObjectBuilder()
                .add("exceptionType", exception.getClass().getName())
                .add("code", code.value());

            if (exception.getMessage() != null) {
              entityBuilder.add("error", exception.getMessage());
            }
```

Spring HttpStatus replaces integer status code.

```
        return new ResponseEntity(entityBuilder.build(), code);    ◄
    }                                                         Spring ResponseEntity
}                                                             replaces JAX-RS Response.
```

Listing 9.9   Searching for valid account

```
curl -i localhost:8080/accounts/444666/balance
```

Listing 9.10   Account balance

```
HTTP/1.1 200 OK
Content-Length: 7
Content-Type: application/json

3499.12
```

Test the POST endpoint and verify posting works as shown as follows.

Listing 9.11   POSTing to the account

```
curl -i \
        -H "Content-Type: application/json" \
        -X POST \
        -d "2.03" \
        localhost:8080/accounts/444666/transaction
```

Listing 9.12   Updating the account balance

```
HTTP/1.1 200 OK
Content-Length: 18
Content-Type: application/json

{"Accept":["*/*"]}
```

Listing 9.13   Getting the updated balance

```
curl -i localhost:8080/accounts/444666/balance
```

Listing 9.14   Updating the account balance

```
HTTP/1.1 200 OK
Content-Length: 7
Content-Type: application/json

3501.15
```

Exercise for the reader
Update the remaining services to Spring Web APIs. The book's Git repository contains working converted code for the Bank service and the Transaction service.

With the Spring DI and Spring Web conversions completed, the next section covers updating Hibernate ORM with Panache to Spring Data JPA.

9.4   *Quarkus/Spring Data JPA compatibility*

The final major Quarkus/Spring compatibility API to cover is the Spring Data JPA API to persist data. The Hibernate ORM with Panache repository pattern is based on the repository pattern popularized by Spring Data JPA, giving the two comparable functionality and a similar API. The following Spring Data JPA repositories, and the interfaces that extend them, are supported:

- Repository
- CrudRepository
- PagingAndSortingRepository
- JpaRepository

To use the Spring Data JPA APIs, add the quarkus-spring-data-jpa extension using `mvn quarkus:add-extension -Dextensions=quarkus-spring-data-jpa`.

Use the following three steps to update the current Account service to use the Spring Data JPA APIs:

1   Create the `AccountRepository` interface.
2   Revert the Hibernate ORM with Panache entity to a JPA entity.
3   Update Account service to use the Spring Repository APIs.

First, create the `AccountRepository` as shown next.

Listing 9.15   Creating the `AccountRepository` interface

```
public interface AccountRepository extends JpaRepository<Account, Long> {
    public Account findByAccountNumber(Long accountNumber);
}
```

findByAccountNumber is updated to follow the JpaRepository interface method-naming pattern using query creation keywords. The query creation keywords are available in the Spring Data JPA documentation (http://mng.bz/Zx85).

The JpaRepository replaces the PanacheRepository covered in chapter 4. Hibernate ORM with Panache is implemented as a class, whereas JpaRepository is an interface.

Next, update the `Account` class to follow JPA entity rules as shown in the following listing. This is the same entity defined in the JPA example in chapter 4.

Listing 9.16   Reverting Account.java to a JPA entity

```
@Entity
public class Account {
    @Id
    @GeneratedValue
    private Long id;
```

Creates a JPA entity ID field that was provided by the Hibernate ORM with Panache entity

```
private Long accountNumber;
private Long customerNumber;
private String customerName;
private BigDecimal balance;
private AccountStatus accountStatus = AccountStatus.OPEN;


@Override
public int hashCode() {
  return Objects.hash(id, accountNumber, customerNumber);
}

public Long getId() {
  return id;
}

public void setId(Long id) {
  this.id = id;
}

public Long getAccountNumber() {
  return accountNumber;
}

public void setAccountNumber(Long accountNumber) {
  this.accountNumber = accountNumber;
}

public Long getCustomerNumber() {
  return customerNumber;
}

public void setCustomerNumber(Long customerNumber) {
  this.customerNumber = customerNumber;
}

public String getCustomerName() {
  return customerName;
}

public void setCustomerName(String customerName) {
  this.customerName = customerName;
}

public BigDecimal getBalance() {
  return balance;
}

public void setBalance(BigDecimal balance) {
  this.balance = balance;
}

public AccountStatus getAccountStatus() {
  return accountStatus;
}
```

Although not required, changes field access modifiers from public to private as the code reverts back to traditional JPA entities

Creates field accessors

```
public void setAccountStatus(AccountStatus accountStatus) {        Creates field
  this.accountStatus = accountStatus;                              accessors
}


@Override
public boolean equals(Object o) {
  if (this == o) return true;
  if (o == null || getClass() != o.getClass()) return false;
  Account account = (Account) o;
  return id.equals(account.id) &&
      accountNumber.equals(account.accountNumber) &&
      customerNumber.equals(account.customerNumber);
}
}
```

Note that, developers have successfully used Lombok with Quarkus. However, edge case issues exist, and Lombok is not included in the Quarkus test suite. For these reasons, Lombok is not shown here.

Last, update the Account service to use the repository as shown in the following code sample, which is similar to the `panache-repository` example in chapter 4.

Listing 9.17   Updating the Account service to use the Spring Data JPA repository

The Account service currently uses the active record data access pattern, introduced in chapter 4, to invoke methods on the entity directly. The Account service needs to be updated to use the Spring Data JPA repository pattern for data access. Spring Data JPA requires a repository instance to access the entity.

```
@RestController
@RequestMapping(path = "/accounts",
               produces=MediaType.APPLICATION_JSON_VALUE,
               consumes=MediaType.APPLICATION_JSON_VALUE)
public class AccountResource {

  AccountRepository repository;
                                                               Injects an
                                                               instance of the
  public AccountResource(AccountRepository repository) {       AccountRepository
    this.repository = repository;                              using constructor
  }                                                            injection

  @GetMapping
  public String hello() {
    return "hello";
  }

  @GetMapping("/{accountNumber}/balance")
  public BigDecimal getBalance(
                   @PathVariable("accountNumber") Long accountNumber) {
```

```
    Account account = repository.findByAccountNumber(accountNumber);    ◁─────┐
    ...
}

@PostMapping("{accountNumber}/transaction")              Finds the accountNumber
@Transactional                                            by calling the repository
public Map<String, List<String>> transact(               findByAccountNumber()
        @RequestHeader("Accept") String acceptHeader,            method
        @PathVariable("accountNumber") Long accountNumber,
        @RequestBody BigDecimal amount) {
    Account entity = repository.findByAccountNumber(accountNumber);    ◁─────┘

    ...

    entity.setBalance(entity.getBalance().add(amount));    ◁───┐
    repository.save(entity);    ◁───┐
                                    │          Updates the entity
    ...              Persists the   │          using an entity field
                   updated entity   │          accessor method
}
}
```

To test the JPA repository, run the following commands. These are the same commands that are provided in the previous section.

Listing 9.18 Searching for valid account

```
curl -i localhost:8080/accounts/444666/balance
```

Listing 9.19 Account balance

```
HTTP/1.1 200 OK
Content-Length: 7
Content-Type: application/json

3499.12
```

Listing 9.20 POSTing to the account

```
curl -i \
        -H "Content-Type: application/json" \
        -X POST \
        -d "2.03" \
        localhost:8080/accounts/444666/transaction
```

Listing 9.21 Updating the accountBalance

```
HTTP/1.1 200 OK
Content-Length: 18
Content-Type: application/json

{"Accept":["*/*"]}
```

Listing 9.22   Getting the updated balance

```
curl -i localhost:8080/accounts/444666/balance
```

Listing 9.23   The updated balance

```
HTTP/1.1 200 OK
Content-Length: 7
Content-Type: application/json

3501.15
```

This completes the conversion of the Quarkus and MicroProfile APIs to the Spring API equivalents, all running on Quarkus! The next section gives more detail on how Quarkus implements the Spring API compatibility.

> **NOTE**   The completed examples for this chapter in the Git repository use Spring APIs for most functionality in the Bank service, Account service, and Transaction service. The primary API exceptions are the MicroProfile Fault Tolerance APIs and MicroProfile Rest Client, which do not have equivalent Spring compatibility APIs. However, the MicroProfile Rest Client and Micro-Profile Fault Tolerance APIs can be used side by side with the Spring compatibility APIs.

9.5   *Deploying to Kubernetes*

With everything running successfully locally, deploy the services to Kubernetes using the following steps:

1   *Use Minikube Docker daemon*—Run `eval $(/usr/local/bin/minikube docker-env)` to use the Docker daemon running in Minikube. This needs to be run for any terminal that is used to deploy the Bank, Account, or Transaction services.

2   *Create the Config Server container image*—From the spring-config-server directory, run `mvn package` to create the uber-JAR, and then `docker build -t quarkus-mp/spring-config-server:0.0.1-SNAPSHOT` . to generate the container image. This will build the image using the Minikube Docker registry.

3   *Deploy the Config Server*—From the spring-config-server directory, run `kubectl apply -f minikube.yml`.

4   *Deploy the Bank service*—From the bank-service directory, deploy the Bank service to Kubernetes with `mvn clean verify -Dquarkus.kubernetes.deploy=true`.

   Test the service using the following commands:

Gets the service URL from Minikube (repeat for each service below)

```
export  BANK_SERVICE_URL=`minikube service bank-service --url`
curl $BANK_SERVICE_URL/bank/secrets
```

Accesses the service (repeat for each service below)

5 *Deploy the Account service*—From the account-service directory, deploy the Account service to Kubernetes with `mvn clean verify -Dquarkus.kubernetes.deploy =true`.

Test the service using the following commands:

```
export  ACCOUNT_SERVICE_URL=`minikube service account-service --url`
curl -i $ACCOUNT_SERVICE_URL/accounts/444666/balance
```

6 *Deploy the Transaction service*—From the transaction-service directory, deploy the Transaction service to Kubernetes with `mvn clean verify -Dquarkus.kubernetes .deploy=true`.

Test the service using the following commands:

```
export TRANSACTION_SERVICE_URL=`minikube service transaction-service --url`
curl -i $TRANSACTION_SERVICE_URL/transactions/444666/balance
```

9.6   *How Quarkus implements Spring API compatibility*

Due to their similarity, using the Spring APIs in place of the existing Quarkus APIs (and vice versa) is straightforward. This section adds details that are helpful to know when using the Spring Compatibility APIs.

Quarkus implements Spring APIs in a Quarkus-native manner so developers have a consistent developer experience when combining Spring APIs with Quarkus and Micro-Profile APIs. To accomplish this, Quarkus implements Spring compatibility using the following three techniques:

- *Annotation substitution*—Quarkus replaces Spring annotations with annotations supported by existing extensions during compilation. For example, Spring Dependency Injection annotations are replaced with CDI annotations during compilation.
- *Interface implementation*—Quarkus provides implementations for Spring interfaces. Its support of Spring Data JPA takes this approach, leveraging Hibernate and Hibernate with Panache framework functionality to implement Spring Data interfaces.
- *Spring-aware extensions*—Update Quarkus-supported extensions to understand Spring annotations and Spring concepts. For example, RESTEasy and Quarkus Cache extensions were updated to understand Spring Web and Spring Cache APIs.

9.7   *Common Quarkus/Spring compatibility questions*

Answers to a few common Spring Compatibility API questions follow:

- *Can Spring Starters be used with Quarkus?* Spring framework .jar files, like those that are defined in Spring Starters, are not compatible with Quarkus. The two frameworks take very different application-bootstrapping approaches, for example. The next section compares the two application bootstrapping approaches in more detail.

- *Which versions of Spring is Quarkus compatible with?* The Quarkus Spring API compatibility does not target a specific minor version of Spring, but it generally targets Spring 5 and Spring Boot 2 APIs. Quarkus can be updated as Spring APIs evolve to remain compatible.

- *What is the Spring compatibility performance overhead?* Because the Spring APIs are implemented in a Quarkus-native manner, no performance penalty exists for using the Spring compatibility extensions with Quarkus. In fact, as covered in chapter 1, the result is faster startup time with lower memory utilization.

- *Can Spring properties like* `server.port` *be used?* No. Only Quarkus properties, which begin with `quarkus.*`, can be used. However, the "Quarkus: All Configuration Options" guide (https://quarkus.io/guides/all-config) contains a search field for helpful lookup of Quarkus properties that can help to find a Quarkus equivalent.

9.8   Comparing the Spring Boot and Quarkus startup processes

Quarkus and Spring Boot optimize application bootstrapping differently. Spring Boot optimizes for late binding, where it makes dynamic decisions based on its environment while it is starting. Figure 9.1 illustrates the Spring Boot startup process.

1 Spring Boot does very little during build time.
2 The application is compiled. Java class files and static content are packaged into a .jar file.
3 Spring Boot conducts most of its work during startup (run time). The .jar file is booted using `java -jar`. The process is similar for Spring Boot .war deployments.
4 The application configuration is loaded and parsed.
5 The classpath is scanned for annotated classes.
6 The metamodel (Spring application context) is created.
7 Business logic is executed.

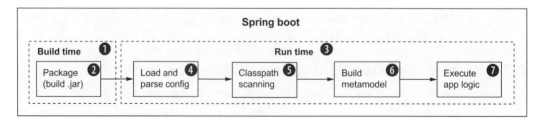

Figure 9.1 The Spring Boot startup processing

The run-time steps occur every time a Spring Boot application is started.

Quarkus, as shown in Figure 9.2, optimizes for immutable containers and Kubernetes infrastructure using *ahead-of-time* (AOT) compilation:

1 Quarkus does most of the work up front during the application build.
2 The configuration is loaded and parsed.
3 The classpath is scanned for annotations.
4 Quarkus builds the metamodel based on the parsed configuration and scanned annotations. The metamodel is stored as precompiled bytecode in generated .class files.
5 Package the precompiled metamodel, class files, and static content in the .jar file. Quarkus extension designers use build-time configuration properties, discussed in chapter 3, to enable or disable extension features to achieve a form of "dead code elimination," which eliminates startup code that might otherwise be executed.
6 Quarkus does very little work during startup (run time).
7 The precompiled metamodel is loaded and followed by application business logic execution.

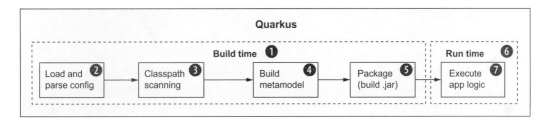

Figure 9.2 The Quarkus startup processing

Quarkus optimizes its Spring API compatibility for AOT (build-time) compilation, often delivering significant startup time improvement. Quarkus AOT compilation can also significantly reduce run-time memory consumption by avoiding the heap memory associated with run-time configuration parsing and annotation scanning.

Summary

- Quarkus offers Spring compatibility for popular Spring APIs.
- Spring developers can quickly become productive with Quarkus.
- Spring APIs can be used side by side with Quarkus and MicroProfile APIs in the same application and even in the same Java class.

- With Spring Cloud Config Server support, Quarkus applications can be more easily run side by side with Spring Boot applications on the same infrastructure.
- Spring Starters do not run properly with Quarkus due to Quarkus relying more heavily on build-time annotation scanning and Spring relying more heavily on run-time annotation scanning. Use the available Quarkus Spring Compatibility extensions (https://quarkus.io/guides/#compatibility) instead.

Part 3

Observability,
API definition, and
security of microservices

Part 3 dives into key topics beyond the mere development of microservices. This part covers key pillars for observability, metrics and tracing, microservice API definitions with OpenAPI, and, finally, securing microservices.

Capturing metrics

This chapter covers

- The role of metrics in a microservices architecture
- Types of metrics
- Creating custom metrics
- Metrics scopes
- Viewing metrics in Grafana
- MicroProfile Metrics and Micrometer metrics

MicroProfile Metrics exposes runtime metrics like CPU and memory utilization and can also expose custom application performance and business metrics. We can forward exposed metrics to graphing systems like Grafana and view them in dashboards representing a live view of running microservices. A live view of metrics can improve business performance and improve application availability.

In this chapter, we instrument the chapter 7 Account service and Transaction service with metrics using MicroProfile Metrics APIs, with a section covering the Quarkus Micrometer metrics extension.

The following section explains the benefits of metrics.

10.1   *The role of metrics in a microservices architecture*

Instrumenting runtimes and applications with metrics offer benefits such as the following:

- *Facilitate troubleshooting*—Instrumenting runtimes and applications with metrics gives administrators and developers insights into microservice failures and hopefully avoids failures before they occur. For example, a microservice continually approaching maximum allocated resources like memory or CPU gives administrators insights into Kubernetes cluster resource allocation.
- *Monitor telemetry and generate alerts*—Telemetry delivers a continuous stream of live data to provide a basis for decision making. As an analogy, modern automobiles constantly monitor their state in the context of their environment. More concretely, lane departure assist nudges the steering wheel to inform the driver to stay in the proper lane. Similarly, Prometheus alerts can monitor a live system instrumented with metrics and react to predefined conditions and thresholds. Alerts can take actions as simple as sending warning messages to an actively monitored Slack channel or scaling a service by adding instances to a Kubernetes cluster.
- *Monitor service level agreement (SLA) compliance*—Service deployments are often accompanied by SLAs agreed to by business units, developers, and administrators. Metrics like requests per second and average service request time often form the foundation for SLAs.

With these benefits in mind, let's quickly look at metrics in action.

10.2   *Getting started with MicroProfile Metrics*

This section will enable Account service and Transaction service metrics provided by Quarkus extensions and give some context for the remainder of the chapter.

The services require the PostgreSQL database to be running. To start the database in Minikube, run the following commands from the chapter10 directory in a new terminal window.

Listing 10.1   Starting PostgreSQL

```
kubectl apply -f postgresql_kubernetes.yml

# Wait for the pod to start running (CTRL-C to exit)
kubectl get pods -w

# Forward requests from localhost to PostgreSQL running in minikube
kubectl port-forward service/postgres 5432:5432
```

With the database up and running, add the quarkus-smallrye-metrics extension to each service and start the service in a new terminal window, as shown in the next listing. This extension implements MicroProfile Metrics.

Listing 10.2   Adding the quarkus-smallrye-metrics extension and starting the services

```
cd account-service
mvn quarkus:add-extension -Dextensions="io.quarkus:quarkus-smallrye-metrics"
mvn quarkus:dev

# In another terminal window
cd ../transaction-service
mvn quarkus:add-extension -Dextensions="io.quarkus:quarkus-smallrye-metrics"
mvn quarkus:dev -Ddebug=5006
```

As shown in listing 10.2, in a new terminal window, repeat these commands, replacing `account-service` with `transaction-service` and specifying a different debugging port that doesn't conflict with the default port used by the Account service.

MicroProfile Metrics requires that runtimes expose metrics at the `/metrics` endpoint. Quarkus does this indirectly by redirecting the HTTP call to `/q/metrics`, as shown in the next code sample.

Listing 10.3   Requesting metrics from the Account service `/metrics` endpoint

```
curl -i localhost:8080/metrics
```

Listing 10.4   Metrics redirect output

```
HTTP/1.1 301 Moved Permanently
location: /q/metrics
content-length: 0
```

In Quarkus, all non-application HTTP/s endpoints are on the `/q/` subpath with a similar redirect. Next, make an HTTP request to the `/q/metrics/` endpoint directly, as shown in the next listings, with detailed explanations to follow.

Listing 10.5   Requesting metrics from the Account service `/q/metrics` endpoint

```
curl -i localhost:8080/q/metrics
```

Listing 10.6   Metrics request output (explained in more detail later)

```
                                                          Metric HELP metadata
# HELP base_classloader_loadedClasses_count Displays the number of classes ◁─┘
that are currently loaded in the Java virtual machine.
# TYPE base_classloader_loadedClasses_count gauge     ◁───── Metric TYPE metadata
base_classloader_loadedClasses_count 13010.0          ◁─┐ Metric name
...          ◁──────                                     │ and value
                    The output has been shortened to display only the
                    first metric. In a real-world running system, there
                    could be hundreds of metrics!
```

NOTE   The output order may change across Quarkus versions. If this output is not easily found, then run `curl -i localhost:8080/q/metrics | grep base_classloader_loadedClasses_count`.

This command and its output look simple, and, on the surface, they are. However, we will explain in detail a lot of context and capability behind these in the remaining sections. Before digging deeper, let's install Prometheus and Grafana to graph the metric output to make viewing metrics easier to follow.

10.2.1 *Graphing metrics with Prometheus and Grafana*

Grafana graphs the Account service and Transaction service metrics using Prometheus as the time-series metrics data source, with the metrics flow shown in figure 10.1.

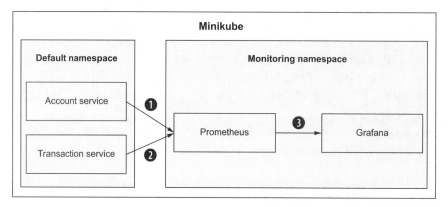

1. Prometheus scrapes the Account service metrics and stores them in its time-series database.
2. Prometheus scrapes the Transaction service metrics.
3. Grafana pulls the Account service and Transaction service metrics from Prometheus and graphs them.

Figure 10.1   Chapter 10 metrics visualization architecture

> **NOTE** This metrics architecture is based on scraping, or pulling, data. The Prometheus installation scrapes service metric endpoints every 3 seconds. Grafana scrapes Prometheus every 15 seconds. The Grafana graphs refresh every 5 seconds. Metrics data is never pushed from one service to another.

The source code for the book includes manifests for Prometheus and Grafana installation in the /chapter10/manifests-prometheus-grafana directory. These files are from the 0.7 release of https://github.com/prometheus-operator/kube-prometheus.

To ensure we have sufficient memory for all the components of Prometheus and Grafana, we start Minikube with at least 4 GB of memory as follows:

```
minikube start --memory=4g
```

With that done, change into the top-level /chapter10 directory of the book source and install Prometheus, Grafana, and ServiceMonitor *custom resource definitions* (CRDs; they specify how services should be monitored) with the provided manifests, as shown next.

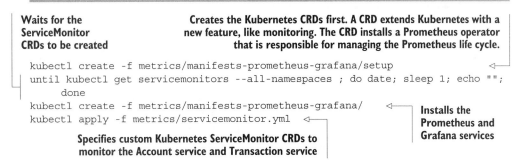

Listing 10.7 Installing Prometheus, Grafana, and the ServiceMonitor CRDs

Waits for the ServiceMonitor CRDs to be created

Creates the Kubernetes CRDs first. A CRD extends Kubernetes with a new feature, like monitoring. The CRD installs a Prometheus operator that is responsible for managing the Prometheus life cycle.

```
kubectl create -f metrics/manifests-prometheus-grafana/setup
until kubectl get servicemonitors --all-namespaces ; do date; sleep 1; echo "";
    done
kubectl create -f metrics/manifests-prometheus-grafana/
kubectl apply -f metrics/servicemonitor.yml
```

Installs the Prometheus and Grafana services

Specifies custom Kubernetes ServiceMonitor CRDs to monitor the Account service and Transaction service

The Prometheus Operator uses ServiceMonitor CRDs to determine which services to monitor. The next listing explains the ServiceMonitor CRD in more detail.

Listing 10.8 Transaction service ServiceMonitor CRD

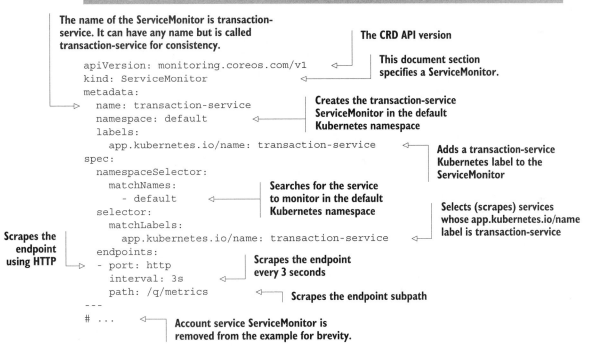

The name of the ServiceMonitor is transaction-service. It can have any name but is called transaction-service for consistency.

The CRD API version

This document section specifies a ServiceMonitor.

```
apiVersion: monitoring.coreos.com/v1
kind: ServiceMonitor
metadata:
  name: transaction-service
  namespace: default
  labels:
    app.kubernetes.io/name: transaction-service
spec:
  namespaceSelector:
    matchNames:
      - default
  selector:
    matchLabels:
      app.kubernetes.io/name: transaction-service
  endpoints:
  - port: http
    interval: 3s
    path: /q/metrics
---
# ...
```

Creates the transaction-service ServiceMonitor in the default Kubernetes namespace

Adds a transaction-service Kubernetes label to the ServiceMonitor

Searches for the service to monitor in the default Kubernetes namespace

Selects (scrapes) services whose app.kubernetes.io/name label is transaction-service

Scrapes the endpoint using HTTP

Scrapes the endpoint every 3 seconds

Scrapes the endpoint subpath

Account service ServiceMonitor is removed from the example for brevity.

Figure 10.2 explains the monitoring process, at a high level, from end to end:

1 During the installation outlined in listing 10.7, the Prometheus operator instructs Prometheus to monitor for ServiceMonitor definitions and to create a Prometheus configuration for it when one is found.

2 During installation, Grafana is preconfigured to scrape metric data from Prometheus.

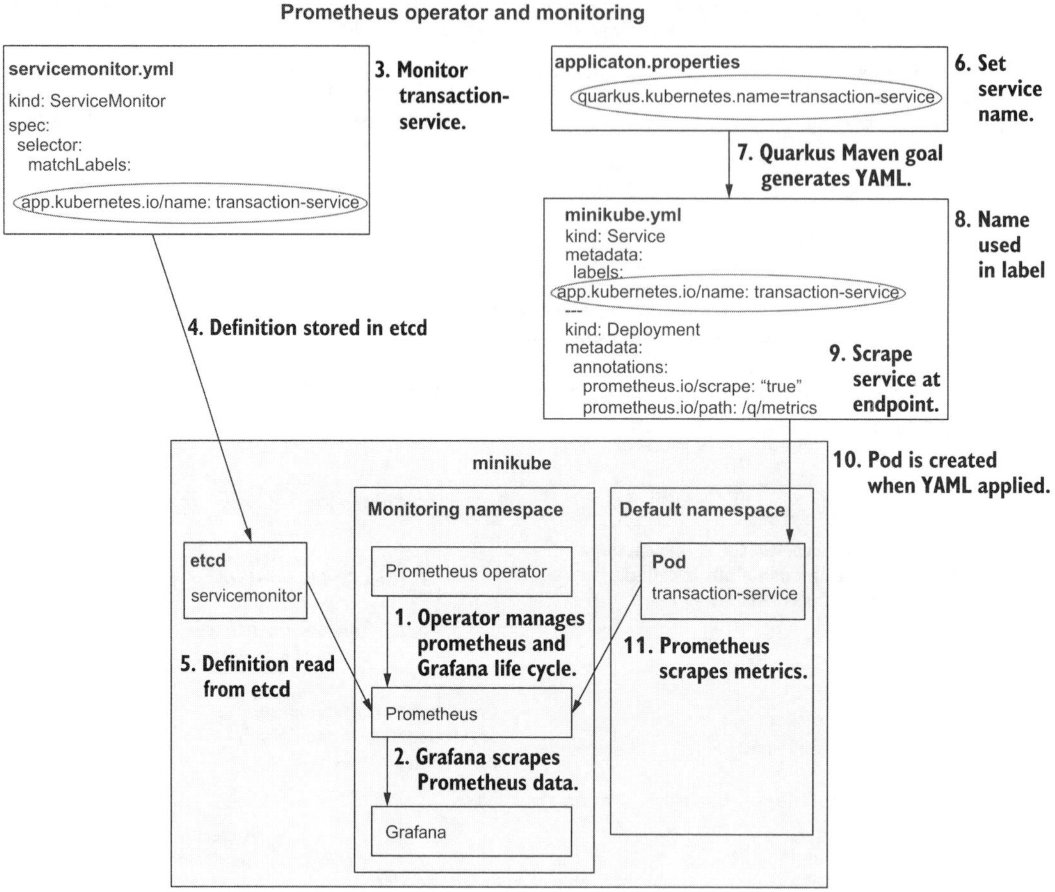

Prometheus operator and monitoring

Figure 10.2   **Monitoring flow**

3   The servicemonitor.yaml, shown in listing 10.8, defines the Transaction service
     ServiceMonitor. This definition instructs the consumer—Prometheus in this
     case—to search for Pods labeled with `app.kubernetes.io/name transaction-`
     `service`.

4   The servicemonitor.yaml is applied in listing 10.7. When applied, the Service-
     Monitor CRD (definition) is added to the Kubernetes etcd registry.

5   As defined in the ServiceMonitor, Prometheus waits for Pods labeled with
     `app.kubernetes.io/name transaction-service`.

6   The Transaction service application.properties define the Kubernetes name as
     `transaction-service`.

7   The Maven package phase (e.g., `mvn package`) generates minikube.yml. The
     `app.kubernetes.io/name` label value is defined by the `quarkus.kubernetes`
     `.name` property.

8   When applied, the Transaction service–related Kubernetes objects like `Service`, `Deployment`, and `Pod` are labeled with `app.kubernetes.io/name: transaction-service`.

9   The `prometheus.io/scrape="true"` and `prometheus.io/path: /q/metrics` deployment annotations inform Prometheus to scrape the service ("true") at the specified path (`/q/metrics`).

10   When the Transaction service is deployed (e.g., `mvn clean package -DskipTests -Dquarkus.kubernetes.deploy=true`), the Kubernetes objects are created, and the `transaction-service` Pod is created.

11   Prometheus identifies a new Pod based on the ServiceMonitor definition and begins to scrape the container metrics.

NOTE   The key to "binding" the Pod to the ServiceMonitor is the Pod label. The binding relationship is highlighted with a circle. The ServiceMonitor in step 3 is looking for an `app.kubernetes.io/name=transaction-service` match. In step 6, the `quarkus.kubernetes.name` specifies the `transaction-service` service name in application.properties. When building the Transaction service, Quarkus will generate the YAML in step 8, which generates the `app.kubernetes.io/name=transaction-service` key-value pair that will be matched by the ServiceMonitor, circled. Also, to simplify the diagram, only the Transaction service is shown. This flow applies to all services with a ServiceMonitor, like the Account service. Last, the monitoring processes are running in the `monitoring` namespace. Run `kubectl get pods -n monitoring` to see the running Pods related to monitoring.

To access Grafana in Minikube, port 3000 will need to be forwarded from the desktop to the cluster, as follows:

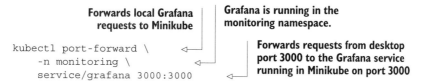

Open http://localhost:3000 in a browser, and log in with username "admin" and password "admin." Figure 10.3 shows the Grafana home page. When the URL first opens, it requires login credentials. Use "admin" for the username and password; it will ask to set a new password before opening the home page.

Next, load the preconfigured Grafana dashboard as shown in figure 10.4. Deploy the Account service and Transaction service to Minikube as shown in the listing 10.9.

Figure 10.3   Grafana home page

1. Click the + button to add a dashboard.

2. Import an existing dashboard.

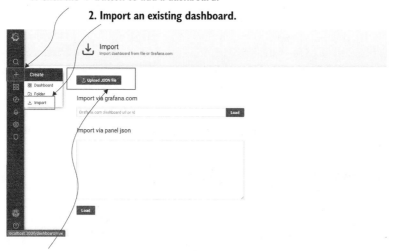

3. Upload Banking_Microservices_Dashboard.json located in the chapter10/metrics directory.

4. Click the Import button (not shown).

Figure 10.4   Import the Banking Microservices dashboard

Listing 10.9   Deploying services to Minikube

Uses the Docker engine running in Minikube

```
# In the account-service and transaction-service directories, run:
cd account-service
eval $(/usr/local/bin/minikube docker-env)
```

```
mvn clean package -DskipTests -Dquarkus.kubernetes.deploy=true    ◄─┐
                                                                     │  Deploys the
cd ../transaction-service                                            │  service to
mvn clean package -DskipTests -Dquarkus.kubernetes.deploy=true    ◄─┘  Kubernetes
```

View the dashboard and notice the Used Heap panel, shown in figure 10.5, is updated in 15 to 30 seconds with the JVM heap used by each service.

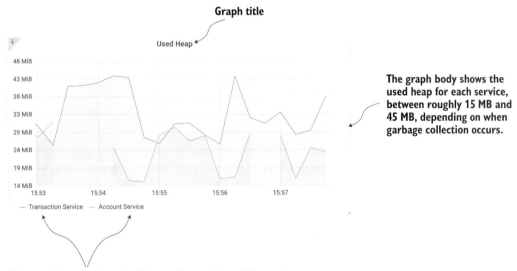

Figure 10.5 Grafana JVM Used Heap graph

> **NOTE** Only the JVM Used Heap panel will update. The remaining panels will update as we instrument the services with metrics throughout the remainder of this chapter.

With the successful deployment and graphing of the Banking microservices, it's time to dig into MicroProfile Metrics.

10.2.2 *MicroProfile Metrics*

The Java platform has shipped with the Java Management Extensions (JMX) since JDK 5. JMX does not meet the metric needs of modern Enterprise Java applications. For example, the JMX API is somewhat complex and was created before annotations were added to the Java platform. Also, JMX does not expose metric metadata, nor does it expose metrics in a modern cloud-friendly format. The MicroProfile community created MicroProfile Metrics to address all of these concerns.

MicroProfile Metrics output formats

MicroProfile Metrics requires implementations to support two output formats. The first is OpenMetrics (https://openmetrics.io) format, a standard text format defined under the Cloud Native Computing Foundation (CNCF). OpenMetrics is the default MicroProfile Metrics output format when the HTTP accept header is `text/plain`. As shown in listing 10.6, it contains useful metadata such as `HELP` and `TYPE`, which can be consumed by external metrics tooling. The next listing expands on listing 10.6.

Listing 10.10   OpenMetrics output explained

> OpenMetrics metadata begins with a hashtag ("#"). The first field, the metadata keyword HELP, offers help text that is used by external tooling. The second field in the HELP metadata is the metric name, base_classloader_loadedClasses_count. The remainder of the line describes the intent of base_classloader_loadedClasses_count.

```
# HELP base_classloader_loadedClasses_count Displays the number of classes      ◁
that are currently loaded in the Java virtual machine.
# TYPE base_classloader_loadedClasses_count gauge
base_classloader_loadedClasses_count 13010.0                                     ◁
```

The metric TYPE metadata. The second field, base_classloader_ loadedClasses_count, is the metric name. The third field is the metric type—gauge, in this case. We describe metric types in detail in an upcoming section.

The metric name and value. Quarkus had loaded 13010 classes into memory when this value was read.

Metrics output is machine readable, but the format is easy to understand, even for developers. Metrics are helpful when debugging an application by querying the `/q/metrics` endpoint. For example, to view the metric displayed in listing 10.10, run the `curl` command shown next.

Listing 10.11   Obtaining a metric directly using the metric name

```
curl -i localhost:8080/q/metrics/base/classloader.loadedClasses.count      ◁
```

> Note that the curl command is using the inherent metric name, whereas OpenMetrics replaces the '.' character with underscores, and MicroProfile Metrics prefixes base. Therefore, the OpenMetrics metric name equivalent is base_classloader_loadedClasses_count. We explain the MicroProfile Metrics naming convention in the next section.

MicroProfile also requires support for metrics output in JSON format. JSON-formatted metric output can be obtained by using the `application/json` HTTP request header, as shown in the following code snippet.

Listing 10.12   Requesting metrics in JSON-formatted output

```
curl -i \
    -H "Accept:application/json" \
    localhost:8080/q/metrics
```

Sample output is shown next, with some output excluded for brevity, as identified by the ellipses.

Listing 10.13 JSON-formatted metrics output

```
{
    "base": {
        "cpu.systemLoadAverage": 2.1865234375,
        "thread.count": 60,
        "classloader.loadedClasses.count": 9667,
        ...
    },
    "vendor": {
    ...
    }
    "application": {
    ...
    }
}
```

The output is in JSON format.

The output uses base, vendor, and application JSON objects. These objects will be explained in the next section.

Metrics are JSON name-value pairs. In this example, the Account service has created 60 threads.

The output uses base, vendor, and application JSON objects. These objects are explained in the next section.

Note that the JSON format does not include the TYPE and HELP metadata available in OpenMetrics format and instead focuses on the efficient machine-consumable JSON format. This chapter focuses on OpenMetrics output because it is a standard format easily consumed by Prometheus later in the chapter.

This section used the annotated MicroProfile Metrics naming convention. The following section explains the naming convention in more detail.

ANNOTATED METRICS NAMING CONVENTION

MicroProfile Metrics follows a naming convention. The naming convention shown in the next listing is explained in detail in table 10.1.

Listing 10.14 MicroProfile Metrics annotated metrics naming convention

```
<scope>.<class>.<method>.<name>l
```

Table 10.1 MicroProfile Metrics naming convention details

Convention	Description
Scope	Must be base, vendor, or application. Scopes are explained in the next section.
Class	The package and class name the annotation applies to.
Method	The method the annotation applies to.
Name	The name of the metric, like `classloader.loadedClasses.count`.

Upcoming sections discuss topics like tags, scope, and absolute that can influence the metric name. This section references scope a couple of times, so the next section digs into that a bit deeper.

MICROPROFILE METRICS SCOPES

MicroProfile categorizes metrics into the three scopes outlined in table 10.2.

Table 10.2   Metric scopes

Scope	Description
Base	Metrics required by all MicroProfile Metrics implementations. For example, the `base_thread_count` metric exposes the number of live threads in the running application process. Base metrics are portable across implementations.
Vendor	Metrics specific to a runtime. Vendor metrics are *not* portable across implementations. For example, the `vendor_cpu_processCpuTime_seconds` metric, which is specific to Quarkus, exposes the CPU time used by the application process. Each Quarkus extension exposes metrics specific to that extension. As the number of extensions used by an application grows, so does the number of available metrics.
Application	Metrics defined by the application or on behalf of the application.

Scopes can be queried directly by appending the scope to the metrics URL. For example, the next code listing requests only base metrics.

Listing 10.15   Requesting base metrics

```
curl -i localhost:8080/q/metrics/base
```

A few lines of query output is shown next. The list of required base metric names will be the same across all MicroProfile Metrics implementations, although the metric values will differ.

Listing 10.16   Requesting base metrics output

```
# HELP base_REST_request_total The number of invocations and total response
   time of this RESTful resource method since the start of the server.
# TYPE base_REST_request_total counter
base_REST_request_total{class="quarkus.accounts.AccountResource",
   method="transact_javax.ws.rs.core.HttpHeaders_java.lang.Long_java.
   math.BigDecimal"} 24.0
# TYPE base_REST_request_elapsedTime_seconds gauge
base_REST_request_elapsedTime_seconds{class="quarkus.accounts.
   AccountResource",method="transact_javax.ws.rs.core.HttpHeaders_
   java.lang.Long_java.math.BigDecimal"} 0.767486469
# HELP base_classloader_loadedClasses_count Displays the number of classes
   that are currently loaded in the Java virtual machine.
# TYPE base_classloader_loadedClasses_count gauge
base_classloader_loadedClasses_count 13925.0
...
```

> **NOTE** If no scope is specified, then all available metrics are returned. In OpenMetrics format, metric names are preceded by their scope. In this example, all metrics are preceded with `base_`.

MICROPROFILE METRICS–SUPPORTED TYPES

The OpenMetrics and JSON-formatted outputs reference metric types, like gauge. MicroProfile Metrics offers support for the commonly used metric types outlined in table 10.3.

Table 10.3 Metric types (as defined in the specification)

Metric	Annotation	Description
Counter	`@Counter`	A monotonically increasing numeric value.
Concurrent gauge	`@ConcurrentGauge`	Incrementally increasing or decreasing value.
Gauge	`@Gauge`	Metric sampled to obtain its current value.
Meter	`@Metered`	Tracks mean throughput and 1-, 5-, and 15-minute exponentially weighted moving-average throughput.
Metric	`@Metric`	This is not a metric type but an annotation that contains the metadata information when requesting a metric to be injected or produced.
Histogram	N/A	Calculates the distribution of a value.
Timer	`@Timed`	Aggregates timing durations and provides duration statistics, plus throughput statistics.

Metric annotations accept a number of parameters, as shown in table 10.4.

Table 10.4 MicroProfile Metrics specification annotation field descriptions

Metric field	Description
`name`	Optional. Sets the name of the metric, like `concurrentBlockingCalls`. If not explicitly given, the name of the annotated object is used, such as `newTransaction` when the annotated object is the `newTransaction` method.
`absolute`	If `true`, uses the given name as the absolute name of the metric, like `newTransaction_current`. If `false`, prepends the package name and class name before the given name, like `io_quarkus_transactions_TransactionResource_newTransaction_current`. The default value is `false`. The metric names can get quite long, so it is more readable to set `absolute` to `true` when there is no risk of metric name collision across multiple objects within an application. Base metrics are `absolute`. Quarkus vendor metrics are also `absolute`. By default, metrics in the application scope are not `absolute`.
`displayName`	Optional. A human-readable display name for metadata. Useful metadata for third-party tooling to consume.
`description`	Optional. A description of the metric. Useful metadata for third-party tooling to consume.
`unit`	Unit of the metrics, like gigabytes, nanoseconds, and percent. Check the `MetricUnits` class for a set of predefined units.
`tags`	A list of key-value pairs. We will describe tags in more detail later.

With a list of available metrics in hand, the next step is to instrument the Account service with a useful metric.

10.2.3 *Instrumenting the Account service*

A useful place to start is to count the number of times the `ExceptionMapper` is called. Based on the count, perhaps a frontend web UI could be improved or the API enhanced. The `Counter` metric will count `ExceptionMapper` invocations, as shown in the next code snippet.

Listing 10.17   AccountResource.java

Injects a metric. If the metric does not exist, then it will be created.

Specifies the metric name

Specifies the metric description

The injected metric is a counter.

Increments the counter

```
@Provider
public static class ErrorMapper implements ExceptionMapper<Exception> {
  @Metric(
    name = "ErrorMapperCounter",
    description = "Number of times the AccountResource ErrorMapper is invoked"
  )
  Counter errorMapperCounter;

    @Override
    public Response toResponse(Exception exception) {
      errorMapperCounter.inc();

      ...
  }
}
```

Invoking an endpoint with an invalid value will increment the counter. The next two code listings pass an invalid account number to invoke the `ErrorMapper` and show the output.

Listing 10.18   Incrementing `ErrorMapper` counter

```
curl -i localhost:8080/accounts/234/balance
```

Listing 10.19   `ErrorMapper` output

```
HTTP/1.1 404 Not Found
Content-Length: 109
Content-Type: application/json

{"exceptionType":"javax.ws.rs.WebApplicationException",
 "code":404,
 "error":"Account with 234 does not exist."
}
```

To validate the counter has been incremented, along with validating the counter metadata is available, run the following code.

Listing 10.20   Validating `ErrorMapper` counter output

```
curl localhost:8080/q/metrics | grep ErrorMapper
```

> **Gets only the ErrorMapper metrics output. Using grep is often easier than remembering the format to access the metric directly as was done in listing 10.11. To access the metric directly, use curl localhost:8080/q/metrics/application/quarkus.accounts.AccountResource\$ErrorMapper.ErrorMapperCounter.**

Listing 10.21   `ErrorMapper` counter output

The MicroProfile metric description maps to the OpenMetrics HELP metadata.

```
# HELP application_quarkus_accounts_AccountResource_ErrorMapper_ErrorMapper_
  total Number of times the AccountResource ErrorMapper is invoked
# TYPE application_quarkus_accounts_AccountResource_
  ErrorMapper_ErrorMapper_total counter
application_quarkus_accounts_AccountResource_ErrorMapper_
  ErrorMapper_total 1.0
```

The MicroProfile metric type maps to the OpenMetrics TYPE metadata.

The metric name and value. When creating a metric using the @Metric annotation, the metric name uses the MicroProfile Metrics Annotated Naming Convention, which prefixes the scope, package, and class name to the metric name.

The `ErrorMapperCounter` is the only Account service custom metric. In the next section, we heavily instrument the Transaction service.

10.2.4 *Instrumenting the TransactionService*

MicroProfile Metrics stores metrics and their metadata like the `ErrorMapperCounter` in a `MetricRegistry`. There is a metric registry for each scope: base, vendor, and application. Custom metrics created by the developer are stored in the application scope. A unique `MetricID`, consisting of the metric name and an optional list of tags, identifies a metric in the `MetricRegistry`.

Metric tags are key-value pairs that add a dimension to metrics that share a commonality. Metrics with tags can be queried by tag or holistically (in aggregate). For example, consider the TransactionServiceFallbackHandler.java, which maps Java exceptions to HTTP response codes. It is useful to track the overall number of fallback invocations ("holistically") and track each exception type resulting in a fallback.

The next listing updates TransactionServiceFallbackHandler.java to use a `fallback` metric and the `MetricRegistry` to track fallbacks by the resulting HTTP status code.

Injects the MetricRegistry into a metric-Registry variable

```
public class TransactionServiceFallbackHandler implements
    FallbackHandler<Response> {

    @Inject
    @RegistryType(type = MetricRegistry.Type.APPLICATION)
    MetricRegistry metricRegistry;
```

Specifies the registry type to inject. MetricRegistry .Type.APPLICATION is used because the metric is specific to this application.

```
    @Override
    public Response handle(ExecutionContext context) {
        Logger LOG =
 Logger.getLogger(TransactionServiceFallbackHandler.class);

        Response response;
        String name;

        if (context.getFailure().getCause() == null) {
            name = context.getFailure().getClass().getSimpleName();
        } else {
            name = context.getFailure().getCause().getClass().getSimpleName();
        }

        switch (name) {
        case "BulkheadException":
            response = Response.status(Response.Status.TOO_MANY_REQUESTS)
                    .build();
            break;

        case "TimeoutException":
            response = Response.status(Response.Status.GATEWAY_TIMEOUT)
                    .build();
            break;

        case "CircuitBreakerOpenException":
        case "ConnectTimeoutException":
        case "SocketException":
            response = Response.status(Response.Status.SERVICE_UNAVAILABLE)
                    .build();
            break;

        case "ResteasyWebApplicationException":
        case "WebApplicationException":
        case "HttpHostConnectException":
            response = Response.status(Response.Status.BAD_GATEWAY)
                    .build();
            break;

        default:
            response =
 Response.status(Response.Status.NOT_IMPLEMENTED).build();

        }

        metricRegistry.counter("fallback",
            new Tag("http_status_code",
                    "" + response.getStatus()))
            .inc();

        LOG.info("******** " + context.getMethod().getName() + ": " + name + "
********");

        return response;
    }
}
```

The tag value is the HTTP response status code.

Increments the counter

Counts the number of fallbacks using a counter metric named fallback. If the counter does not exist, the counter will be created.

Creates a metric using a Tag, which is a name-value pair. The tag name is http_status_code.

To test the fallback counter, run the next command.

Listing 10.23 Running the `overload_bulkhead.sh` script

```
metrics/scripts/overload_bulkhead.sh     ◁
```
**Overloads the local transaction-service started with mvn
quarkus:dev -Ddebug=5006 to generate BulkheadExceptions**

After the script has finished, run the following commands to see the metric output.

Listing 10.24 Getting `fallback_total` metric

**Uses the local Transaction
service listening on port 8088**

```
export TRANSACTION_URL=http://localhost:8088     ◁
curl -i -s $TRANSACTION_URL/q/metrics/application | grep -i fallback_total  ◁
```

**Requests application metrics from the metrics
endpoint, and narrows the output to fallback_total**

Listing 10.25 `fallback_total` metric output

```
# TYPE application_fallback_total counter
application_fallback_total{http_status_code="429"} 290.0     ◁
```

**The BulkheadException maps to HTTP status code 429 (TOO_MANY_REQUESTS) in TransactionFallback-
Handler.java. There were 290 BulkheadExceptions (after multiple runs of the overload_bulkhead.sh).**

Redeploy the Transaction service to Minikube with `mvn clean package -DskipTests`
`-Dquarkus.kubernetes.deploy=true`.

> **IMPORTANT** Attempting to redeploy an application already present in Kuber-
> netes with `mvn package -Dquarkus.kubernetes.deploy=true` will result in an
> error in Quarkus 2.x. Follow the issue at https://github.com/quarkusio/
> quarkus/issues/19701 for updates on a resolution. We can work around the
> problem by removing the application first with `kubectl delete -f /target/`
> `kubernetes/minikube.yaml`.

The next step is to generate failures and view the results in the Grafana dashboard.
First, generate `BulkheadExceptions`, resulting in an HTTP status code of `TOO_`
`MANY_REQUESTS`. Second, make requests to the `Transaction Service` while the Account
service is scaled to zero and then scaled back to one. Scaling the Account service in
this manner will trip the circuit breaker and result in exceptions like `Circuit-`
`BreakerOpenException` and `WebApplicationException`. These exceptions result in
`SERVICE_UNAVAILABLE` (HTTP status code: 503) and `BAD_GATEWAY` (HTTP status code:
502), respectively. We can accomplish these steps with the heavily commented
`force_multiple_fallbacks.sh`, which executes against the Transaction service running in Minikube, as shown in listings 10.26 and 10.27.

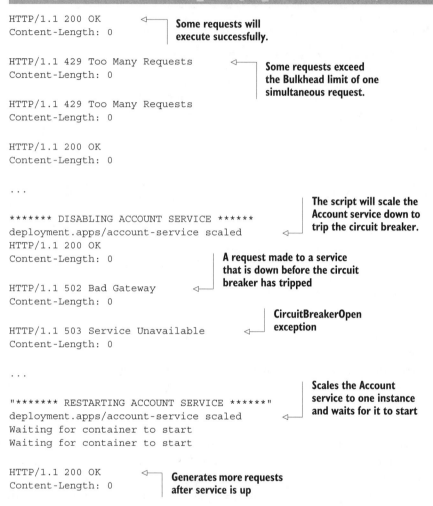

Listing 10.26   Running `force_multiple_fallbacks.sh`

```
export TRANSACTION_URL=`minikube service --url transaction-service`
metrics/scripts/force_multiple_fallbacks.sh
```

Listing 10.27   Shortened `force_multiple_fallbacks.sh` output

```
HTTP/1.1 200 OK                    ◁──┐   Some requests will
Content-Length: 0                      │   execute successfully.


HTTP/1.1 429 Too Many Requests     ◁──┐   Some requests exceed
Content-Length: 0                      │   the Bulkhead limit of one
                                       │   simultaneous request.
HTTP/1.1 429 Too Many Requests
Content-Length: 0


HTTP/1.1 200 OK
Content-Length: 0


...


                                            The script will scale the
                                            Account service down to
****** DISABLING ACCOUNT SERVICE ******    trip the circuit breaker.
deployment.apps/account-service scaled  ◁─┘
HTTP/1.1 200 OK
Content-Length: 0              A request made to a service
                              that is down before the circuit
HTTP/1.1 502 Bad Gateway   ◁──┘ breaker has tripped
Content-Length: 0
                                    CircuitBreakerOpen
HTTP/1.1 503 Service Unavailable  ◁─┘ exception
Content-Length: 0


...


                                            Scales the Account
                                            service to one instance
"****** RESTARTING ACCOUNT SERVICE ******"  and waits for it to start
deployment.apps/account-service scaled  ◁──┘
Waiting for container to start
Waiting for container to start


HTTP/1.1 200 OK     ◁──┐  Generates more requests
Content-Length: 0       │  after service is up
```

With forced fallbacks in place, the dashboard should update accordingly. Figure 10.6 show the fallbacks by type.

To demonstrate an additional metric, add the `@Timed` metric to the `Transaction-ServiceFallbackHandle.handle()` method shown in listing 10.28. This metric will track how much time is spent in the fallback handler and the number and rate of calls to the fallback handler.

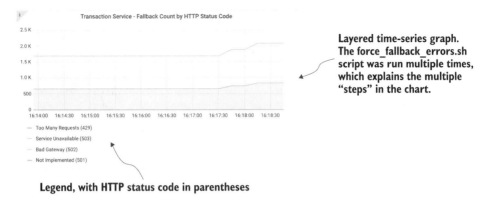

Layered time-series graph. The force_fallback_errors.sh script was run multiple times, which explains the multiple "steps" in the chart.

Legend, with HTTP status code in parentheses

Figure 10.6 Number of Transaction service fallbacks by HTTP status code

---

Listing 10.28 Timing the fallback handler

```
public class TransactionServiceFallbackHandler
        implements FallbackHandler<Response> {

    @Inject
    @RegistryType(type = MetricRegistry.Type.APPLICATION)
    MetricRegistry metricRegistry;

    @Timed(
        name = "fallbackHandlerTimer",
        displayName = "Fallback Handler Timer",
        description = "Time spent handling fallbacks",
        absolute = true,
        unit=MetricUnits.NANOSECONDS
    )
    @Override
    public Response handle(ExecutionContext context) {
        ...
    }
}

    ...
```

Sets the metric name

Optional—sets the metric display name

Optional—the timer counts in nanoseconds.

Tracks amount of time spent in the fallback handler

Optional—sets the metric description

Optional—the absolute parameter is true, which will remove the prepended class and method from the metric name because this is the only metric under this name.

The @Timed annotation tracks the frequency of invocations of the annotated object and how long it takes for invocations to complete. Sample OpenMetrics output of the @Timed annotation in listing 10.28 is shown here.

Listing 10.29 Timed fallback handler output

```
# TYPE application_fallbackHandlerTimer_rate_per_second gauge
application_fallbackHandlerTimer_rate_per_second 2.426100958072672
# TYPE application_fallbackHandlerTimer_one_min_rate_per_second gauge
application_fallbackHandlerTimer_one_min_rate_per_second 0.21734790157044565
# TYPE application_fallbackHandlerTimer_five_min_rate_per_second gauge
application_fallbackHandlerTimer_five_min_rate_per_second 1.1224561659490684
# TYPE application_fallbackHandlerTimer_fifteen_min_rate_per_second gauge
```

```
application_fallbackHandlerTimer_fifteen_min_rate_per_second 0.6479305746101738
# TYPE application_fallbackHandlerTimer_min_seconds gauge
application_fallbackHandlerTimer_min_seconds 1.35104E-4
# TYPE application_fallbackHandlerTimer_max_seconds gauge
application_fallbackHandlerTimer_max_seconds 0.05986594
# TYPE application_fallbackHandlerTimer_mean_seconds gauge
application_fallbackHandlerTimer_mean_seconds 3.792392736865503E-4
# TYPE application_fallbackHandlerTimer_stddev_seconds gauge
application_fallbackHandlerTimer_stddev_seconds 0.001681891771616228
# HELP application_fallbackHandlerTimer_seconds Time spent handling fallbacks
# TYPE application_fallbackHandlerTimer_seconds summary
application_fallbackHandlerTimer_seconds_count 768.0
application_fallbackHandlerTimer_seconds{quantile="0.5"} 2.78085E-4
application_fallbackHandlerTimer_seconds{quantile="0.75"} 3.65377E-4
application_fallbackHandlerTimer_seconds{quantile="0.95"} 6.51634E-4
application_fallbackHandlerTimer_seconds{quantile="0.98"} 8.98868E-4
application_fallbackHandlerTimer_seconds{quantile="0.99"} 0.001348871
application_fallbackHandlerTimer_seconds{quantile="0.999"} 0.004710182
```

Redeploy the application using `mvn clean package -DskipTests -Dquarkus.kuber-netes.deploy=true`. Once deployed, rerun `metrics/scripts/force_multiple_fallbacks.sh`.

The dashboard Transaction Service Fallback Call Rate Rolling One Minute Average gauge displays a sample `application_fallbackHandlerTimer_one_min_rate_per_second` metric value, which is the rate of method invocations, per second, over the last minute. Figure 10.7 shows sample requests per second over the last minute.

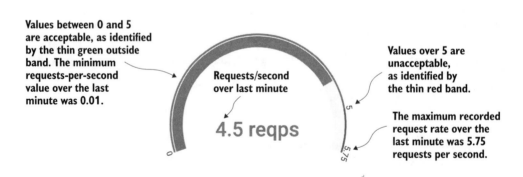

Figure 10.7   Grafana Transaction service fallback call rate

> **NOTE**   The "acceptable" and "unacceptable" requests per second are defined in the Grafana gauge configuration, not in the application code. These are hypothetical values to demonstrate the gauge.

Another approach to monitoring performance, perhaps tied to an SLA, is to track concurrent requests on a method. To see this in action, add the `@ConcurrentGauge` annotation to the `TransactionResource.newTransaction()` method as shown in the following listing.

Listing 10.30 Applying the `@ConcurrentGauge` annotation

Adds the @ConcurrentGauge to newTransaction() to track the number of concurrent requests to the method

The package and class name prefix will be removed from the metric name. There is no name conflict with another metric of the same name.

The metric name should be representative of intent.

```
@ConcurrentGauge(
    name = "concurrentBlockingTransactions",
    absolute = true,
    description = "Number of concurrent transactions using blocking API"
)
@POST
@Path("/{acctNumber}")
public Map<String, List<String>> newTransaction(@PathParam("acctNumber")
                                                Long accountNumber,
                                                BigDecimal amount) {
    try {
        updateDepositHistogram(amount);
        return accountService.transact(accountNumber, amount);
    } catch (Throwable t) {
        t.printStackTrace();
        Map<String, List<String>> response = new HashMap<>();
        response.put("EXCEPTION - " + t.getClass(),
        Collections.singletonList(t.getMessage()));
        return response;
    }
}
```

Provides a description representative of the metric intent

With the code updated, redeploy the application using `mvn clean package -Dskip-Tests -Dquarkus.kubernetes.deploy=true` and invoke each endpoint using the script shown next.

Listing 10.31 Generating concurrent requests to the blocking transaction endpoint

`metrics/scripts/concurrent.sh`

Scales the Transaction service to two replicas, and runs 8,000 requests (eight sets of 1,000 parallel requests). It will then scale the Transaction service to one replica, and run 8,000 requests (eight sets of 1,000 parallel requests).

Figure 10.8 shows the number of concurrent requests.

We have covered a lot of ground in this chapter, but we have one last code modification to make to the Transaction service: creating business metrics.

10.2.5 Creating business metrics

Metrics are not only about application performance; they can also encompass business performance. For example, it may be helpful to a business to have a live view of the distribution of customer deposits. It is better for the bank if customers tend

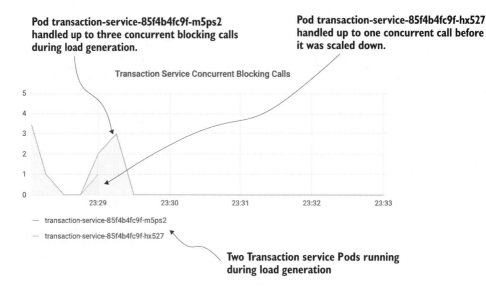

Pod transaction-service-85f4b4fc9f-m5ps2 handled up to three concurrent blocking calls during load generation.

Pod transaction-service-85f4b4fc9f-hx527 handled up to one concurrent call before it was scaled down.

Two Transaction service Pods running during load generation

Figure 10.8 Transaction service concurrent blocking calls graph

toward larger deposits. Accomplishing this is trivial with MicroProfile Metrics, as shown in the next listing.

Listing 10.32   TransactionResource.java

```
public class TransactionResource {

  @Inject
  @Metric(
    name = "deposits",
    description = "Deposit histogram"
  )
  Histogram  histogram;

  ...

  void updateDepositHistogram(BigDecimal dollars) {
    histogram.update(dollars.longValue());
  }

  ...

  @POST
  @Path("/{acctNumber}")
  public Map<String, List<String>> newTransaction(
        @PathParam("acctNumber") Long accountNumber, BigDecimal amount) {
    try {
      updateDepositHistogram(amount);
      return accountService.transact(accountNumber, amount);
    } catch (Throwable t) {
```

The Histogram class is not an annotation, although an instance can be injected. The Histogram metadata, name, and description are provided using the @Metric annotation.

Provides the updateDepositHistogram() method that adds a deposit amount to the histogram

A histogram can be updated only with integer and long values, which is accurate enough for this use case.

Updates newTransaction() to update the deposit histogram

```
        t.printStackTrace();
        Map<String, List<String>> response = new HashMap<>();
        response.put("EXCEPTION - " + t.getClass(),
          Collections.singletonList(t.getMessage()));
        return response;
      }
  }


  @POST
  @Path("/async/{acctNumber}")
  public CompletionStage<Map<String,
        List<String>>> newTransactionAsync(@PathParam("acctNumber") Long
    accountNumber,
      BigDecimal amount) {                    Updates newTransactionAsync()
      updateDepositHistogram(amount);    ◁── to update the deposit histogram
      return accountService.transactAsync(accountNumber, amount);
  }

@POST
 @Path("/api/{acctNumber}")
 @Bulkhead(1)
 @CircuitBreaker(
   requestVolumeThreshold=3,
   failureRatio=.66,
   delay = 1,
   delayUnit = ChronoUnit.SECONDS,
   successThreshold=2
 )
 @Fallback(value = TransactionServiceFallbackHandler.class)
 public Response newTransactionWithApi(@PathParam("acctNumber") Long
   accountNumber, BigDecimal amount)
     throws MalformedURLException {
   AccountServiceProgrammatic acctService =
     RestClientBuilder.newBuilder().baseUrl(new URL(accountServiceUrl))
       .connectTimeout(500, TimeUnit.MILLISECONDS).readTimeout(1200,
         TimeUnit.MILLISECONDS)
       .build(AccountServiceProgrammatic.class);

   acctService.transact(accountNumber, amount);
   updateDepositHistogram(amount);            ◁──  Updates newTransaction-
   return Response.ok().build();                    WithApi() to update the
  }                                                  deposit histogram
}
```

With the code updated, redeploy the application using `mvn clean package -Dskip-Tests -Dquarkus.kubernetes.deploy=true`, and invoke each endpoint using the script shown next.

Listing 10.33   Invoking each deposit endpoint

`metrics/scripts/invoke_deposit_endpoints.sh`

The Grafana Deposits Distribution panel should be updated with data, as shown in figure 10.9.

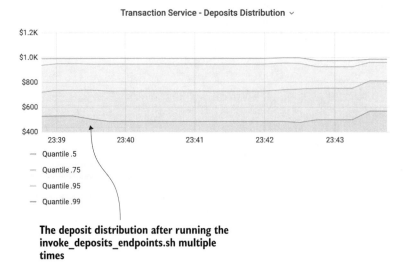

Transaction Service - Deposits Distribution ⌄

— Quantile .5
— Quantile .75
— Quantile .95
— Quantile .99

The deposit distribution after running the invoke_deposits_endpoints.sh multiple times

Figure 10.9   Grafana Deposits Distribution panel

In the next section, we discuss how MicroProfile Metrics integrates with other specifications to provide additional built-in metrics.

10.2.6   *MicroProfile Fault Tolerance and JAX-RS integration with MicroProfile Metrics*

MicroProfile Fault Tolerance automatically registers metrics for `@Retry`, `@Timeout`, `@CircuitBreaker`, `@Bulkhead`, and `@Fallback` annotations. The Transaction service uses all of these fault tolerance annotations. As a result, a plethora of metrics is available by probing the endpoint, as shown in the next listing, with the metrics output shown in listing 10.35.

Listing 10.34   Transaction Service fault tolerance metrics

Forces fallbacks   **Uses the Transaction service running in Minikube**

```
export TRANSACTION_URL=`minikube service --url transaction-service`
metrics/scripts/force_multiple_fallbacks.sh
curl -is $TRANSACTION_URL/q/metrics/application | grep ft | grep -v "^#"
```

Views the MicroProfile Fault Tolerance metrics only and without the metadata

Listing 10.35   Fault tolerance metrics output (output reduced)

```
...

application_ft_io_quarkus_transactions_TransactionResource_newTransactionWith
    Api_bulkhead_callsAccepted_total 110.0
application_ft_io_quarkus_transactions_TransactionResource_newTransactionWith
    Api_bulkhead_executionDuration_min 8816204.0
```

```
application_ft_io_quarkus_transactions_TransactionResource_newTransactionWith
    Api_bulkhead_executionDuration_max 1.28532238E8
application_ft_io_quarkus_transactions_TransactionResource_newTransactionWith
    Api_bulkhead_executionDuration_mean 1.4306619234752553E7
application_ft_io_quarkus_transactions_TransactionResource_newTransactionWith
    Api_circuitbreaker_callsSucceeded_total 110.0
application_ft_io_quarkus_transactions_TransactionResource_newTransactionWith
    Api_circuitbreaker_closed_total 1.038171586389E12
application_ft_io_quarkus_transactions_TransactionResource_newTransactionWith
    Api_circuitbreaker_halfOpen_total 0.0
application_ft_io_quarkus_transactions_TransactionResource_newTransactionWith
    Api_circuitbreaker_open_total 0.0
application_ft_io_quarkus_transactions_TransactionResource_newTransactionWith
    Api_invocations_total 110.0

...
```

A few notes about MicroProfile Fault Tolerance metrics integration follow:

- The metric names are not absolute and are in the application scope.
- The metrics are customized by the metric type. For example, the `@Bulkhead` metrics are a histogram covering the number of calls and the distribution of execution time in the method (not shown). The `@CircuitBreaker` metrics count the number of invocations for each state of the circuit breaker.
- To disable registration of fault tolerance metrics, set the property `MP_Fault_Tolerance_Metrics_Enabled=false`.

As an optional feature for MicroProfile implementations, JAX-RS can integrate with MicroProfile Metrics and provide time spent in REST endpoints and count REST endpoint invocations. To enable this feature in Quarkus, set the property `quarkus.smallrye-metrics.jaxrs.enabled=true`. REST metrics enabled in this manner are created in the base scope. Once the property is set, run the following commands.

Listing 10.36 Generating JAX-RS metrics

Uses the Transaction service running in Minikube   **Deploys the application**

```
mvn clean package -DskipTests -Dquarkus.kubernetes.deploy=true   ◁
export TRANSACTION_URL=`minikube service --url transaction-service`
metrics/scripts/invoke_deposit_endpoints.sh   ◁
curl -is $TRANSACTION_URL/q/metrics/base | grep base_REST
```

Deposits funds using the blocking, async, and client API endpoints

Views the JAX-RS metrics

Sample REST metric data is shown here.

Listing 10.37 REST metrics output

```
# HELP base_REST_request_total The number of invocations and total response
➥ time of this RESTful resource method since the start of the server.
# TYPE base_REST_request_total counter
base_REST_request_total{class="io.quarkus.transactions.TransactionResource",
➥ method="newTransactionAsync_java.lang.
```

```
  Long_java.math.BigDecimal"} 10.0
  # TYPE base_REST_request_elapsedTime_seconds gauge
  base_REST_request_elapsedTime_seconds{class="io.quarkus.transactions.
  TransactionResource",method="newTransactionAsync_java.lang.
  Long_java.math.BigDecimal"} 0.231018078
  base_REST_request_total{class="io.quarkus.transactions.TransactionResource",
  method="newTransactionWithApi_java.lang.Long_java.math.BigDecimal"}
  610.0
  base_REST_request_elapsedTime_seconds{class="io.quarkus.transactions.
  TransactionResource",method="newTransactionWithApi_java.lang.Long_java.
  math.BigDecimal"} 6.058761321
  base_REST_request_total{class="io.quarkus.transactions.TransactionResource",
  method="newTransaction_java.lang.Long_java.math.BigDecimal"} 10.0
  base_REST_request_elapsedTime_seconds{class="io.quarkus.transactions.
  TransactionResource",method="newTransaction_java.lang.Long_java.math.
  BigDecimal"} 0.193222971
```

**A gauge is available for each REST endpoint that
samples the time spent in a REST endpoint (latency).**

**A counter is available for each REST endpoint that counts
the number of REST invocations on that endpoint.**

Before wrapping up, Quarkus not only supports MicroProfile Metrics, it also supports
Micrometer metrics. The next section will explain the difference and why both
Quarkus and MicroProfile Metrics are moving towards Micrometer.

10.2.7 *Micrometer metrics*

Since Quarkus 1.8, Micrometer (https://micrometer.io/) is included as an alternative approach to metrics. Micrometer was popularized with widespread use within
Spring and Spring Boot projects but also has wide adoption within the broader Java
ecosystem.

   Why another metrics implementation? Though Micrometer does not implement
the MicroProfile Metrics specification, its use is a de facto standard within the Java
ecosystem. This is an important factor to consider. When operations or site reliability
engineers monitor many Java services, it's critical for metrics to be named alike to
enable the aggregation of data across instances. MicroProfile Metrics defines a hierar-
chical naming scheme, whereas Micrometer utilizes a dimensional naming scheme
with labels, or tags, associated with a name for additional context. With the popularity
of Micrometer, it's important for Quarkus to provide identically named metrics in
environments with many Java frameworks in deployments. For this reason, Quarkus
recommends the use of the Micrometer extension for exposing metrics.

> **NOTE** At the time of this writing, MicroProfile Metrics is considering adop-
> tion of Micrometer as the engine under the MicroProfile application API.

Let's see Micrometer in action. Open the book source to the /chapter10/micrometer-
account-service directory. The example comes from the active record in chapter 4.
Only one additional dependency is needed, as shown next.

Listing 10.38   Quarkus Micrometer Prometheus registry extension dependency

```
<dependency>
  <groupId>io.quarkus</groupId>
  <artifactId>quarkus-micrometer-registry-prometheus</artifactId>
</dependency>
```

The `quarkus-micrometer-registry-prometheus` dependency brings in the base Micrometer extension, as well as the Micrometer Prometheus registry dependency. This dependency activates the `/q/metrics` endpoint with metrics in the Prometheus format.

> **NOTE** Alternative metrics backends are available with Micrometer and Quarkus. Check the additional registries in the Quarkiverse at https://github.com/ quarkiverse/quarkus-micrometer-registry.

Time to see the Micrometer extension in action! Run the commands shown in listings 10.39 and 10.40.

Listing 10.39   Deploying `account-service-micrometer`

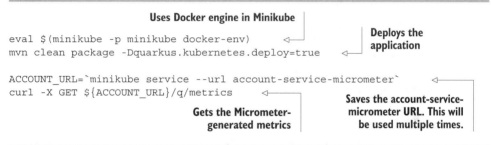

```
                Uses Docker engine in Minikube
eval $(minikube -p minikube docker-env)        ⊲─┘         Deploys the
mvn clean package -Dquarkus.kubernetes.deploy=true  ⊲───   application


ACCOUNT_URL=`minikube service --url account-service-micrometer`  ⊲─
curl -X GET ${ACCOUNT_URL}/q/metrics    ⊲──
                         Gets the Micrometer-      Saves the account-service-
                         generated metrics         micrometer URL. This will
                                                   be used multiple times.
```

Listing 10.40   Micrometer metrics output (sample)

```
...
jvm_threads_live_threads 11.0        ⊲──    It is immediately evident that the Micrometer
jvm_threads_daemon_threads 7.0              metrics are not following the MicroProfile
process_uptime_seconds 322.512              naming convention, with metric names like
jvm_threads_peak_threads 11.0               jvm_threads_live_threads missing the
...                                         MicroProfile Metrics scope.
```

With no requests having executed on the endpoints, there are no metrics covering HTTP requests. Let's change that now, as shown in the next code listing and a sample of the metrics output in listing 10.42.

Listing 10.41   Invoking HTTP endpoints to get accounts

```
curl -X GET ${ACCOUNT_URL}/accounts
curl -X GET ${ACCOUNT_URL}/accounts/87878787
curl -X GET ${ACCOUNT_URL}/q/metrics
```

Listing 10.42   Account service sample metrics output

```
# HELP http_server_requests_seconds
# TYPE http_server_requests_seconds summary
http_server_requests_seconds_count{method="GET",outcome="SUCCESS",status="200
     ",uri="/accounts/{acctNumber}",} 2.0
http_server_requests_seconds_sum{method="GET",outcome="SUCCESS",status="200",
     uri="/accounts/{acctNumber}",} 0.015225187
http_server_requests_seconds_count{method="GET",outcome="SUCCESS",status="200
     ",uri="/q/",} 1.0
http_server_requests_seconds_sum{method="GET",outcome="SUCCESS",status="200",
     uri="/q/",} 0.052366224
http_server_requests_seconds_count{method="GET",outcome="SUCCESS",status="200
     ",uri="/accounts",} 2.0
http_server_requests_seconds_sum{method="GET",outcome="SUCCESS",status="200",
     uri="/accounts",} 0.285417871
# HELP http_server_requests_seconds_max
# TYPE http_server_requests_seconds_max gauge
http_server_requests_seconds_max{method="GET",outcome="SUCCESS",status="200",
     uri="/accounts/{acctNumber}",} 0.011469553
http_server_requests_seconds_max{method="GET",outcome="SUCCESS",status="200",
     uri="/q/",} 0.052366224
http_server_requests_seconds_max{method="GET",outcome="SUCCESS",status="200",
     uri="/accounts",} 0.277971268
```

Without adding anything other than a dependency, the service is now producing many useful metrics using Micrometer!

We have covered a lot of content in this chapter. Before finishing up, let's simulate a busy production environment that generates a lively dashboard.

10.2.8 Simulating a busy production system

The `run_all.sh` script runs the commands and scripts used in this chapter to generate load. The result is a busy Grafana dashboard that looks like a busy production system. From the top-level chapter10/ directory, run the following command.

Listing 10.43   From chapter10 directory, running the `run_all.sh` script

```
metrics/scripts/run_all.sh

# Press CTRL-C to stop
```

Figure 10.10 shows the overall Grafana dashboard after running the metrics/scripts/run_all.sh command for five minutes.

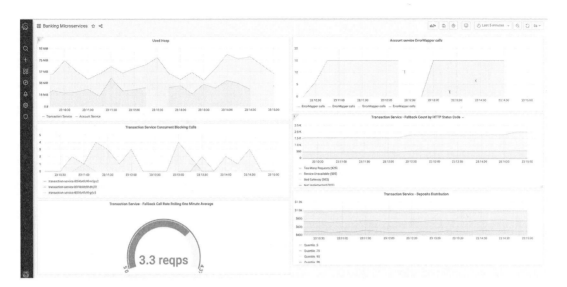

Figure 10.10   Grafana Deposits Distribution panel

Summary

- MicroProfile Metrics offers multiple types of metrics to address varying performance use cases, like counters, histograms, gauges, meters, and timers.
- MicroProfile Metrics separates metrics into scopes: base, vendor, and application.
- MicroProfile Fault Tolerance and (optionally) JAX-RS integrate with MicroProfile Metrics.
- MicroProfile Metrics exports metrics in JSON and OpenMetrics formats.
- Quarkus supports JSON and OpenMetrics output formats.
- Metrics output can be observed live using external tools like Prometheus and Grafana.
- Quarkus supports MicroProfile Metrics and Micrometer.

Tracing microservices

11

This chapter covers

- Using tracing between microservices
- Viewing traces with the Jaeger UI
- Injecting a tracer to customize attributes on a span
- Tracing beyond HTTP

Any form of application observability requires tracing execution paths within a distributed system. With the rise of distributed systems, developers can no longer debug and step through code because they are now dealing with many services. Tracing is the new debugging when dealing with distributed systems. In addition, being able to visualize the bottlenecks in services by observing higher execution times is critical. By no means does this discount the importance of observing metrics, discussed in chapter 10, but it is often necessary to drill deeper into a specific execution path to determine the root of a problem.

In essence, tracing is a key tool in the operations toolbox for observing a running production system. It is the best means of debugging the execution path of a distributed system.

In this chapter, we update the example architecture from chapter 8 to include tracing to highlight the impact of tracing across different communication mechanisms.

These include HTTP calls, both into a service and to another service, database interactions, and sending or receiving messages from Apache Kafka.

For a reminder of the services from chapter 8 and how they interact, see figure 11.1.

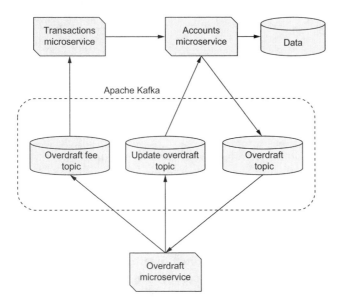

Figure 11.1 Microservice architecture

In this chapter, we won't change any of the functionality with respect to how the services interact, but instead we focus on tracing the existing interactions.

11.1 How does tracing work?

When tracing a specific service, or even a series of services within a single monolith, there is no need to propagate trace information because all calls are within a single JVM process. Every service within the single monolith can access a tracer, creating or ending spans as necessary without regard to service boundaries. That's not the case when dealing with distributed systems, or even two services in different JVMs calling each other. Propagating the trace context is required.

Whether it's HTTP, Apache Kafka, or another transportation protocol, each provides the ability to include headers along with the payload being sent. Figure 11.2 shows both these pieces of content on a request as it passes between services. In the header of such a request, there could be a header representing an existing trace created by the caller. If no tracing header is already present, the receiving service presumes no trace exists and will create one if tracing is enabled.

Figure 11.2 also highlights what happens to a trace when a service call completes. In the case of service A or service B, when processing is complete, any trace and span information that was captured will be passed to a collector. The *collector* might be known by different names, depending on the tracing implementation, but its purpose

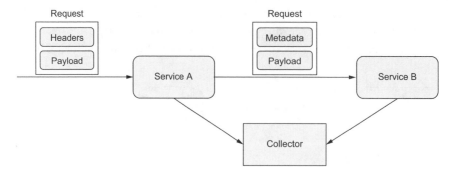

Figure 11.2   Tracing headers

is to receive trace information from any service that has captured traces throughout a distributed system. Once collected, all the trace information can be combined to provide a visualization of the trace execution path between services.

11.2   Jaeger

Jaeger (www.jaegertracing.io/) is a distributed tracing system that facilitates creating a view of the interaction between services within a distributed system. It's not the only tracing system available—Zipkin (https://zipkin.io/) is another. In this chapter, we use Jaeger in the examples for visualizing traces. Irrespective of the distributed tracing system used, they all provide the ability to visualize a trace through a system.

Before delving into some examples, it's worth mentioning the terms that are related to tracing to familiarize the reader with them. The execution path through a system captured by Jaeger is a *trace*, because it traces a path through different services. Each trace comprises one or more *spans*. A span represents a single unit of work within a trace.

Collecting traces does require time to gather the information a service captured during execution and time to send the tracing data to the collector in an external service. Depending on what's captured in a trace, large pieces of data could require memory as well. When handling several dozen requests, the extra time and memory requirements are likely minimal, but when dealing with thousands, or tens of thousands, of requests, the extra time and memory requirements to capture every execution can significantly impact service response times and throughput.

Because the collection of traces can be expensive in time and memory, compared to metrics, Jaeger provides the ability to define a *sampling rate* to indicate how many traces should be captured.

> **IMPORTANT**   Though the examples in this chapter have a sampling rate of 1, meaning to capture every trace, doing so in a production situation is appropriate only when the throughput is low enough to not be impacted. Or, if an application is critical, it's necessary to trace every execution if something goes wrong.

11.2.1 Trace sampling

The previous section introduced the concept of a sampling rate and how it can impact the cost of collecting traces. Understanding the sampling of traces is important, because each type of sampling has different features. The type of sampling chosen impacts the number of traces captured within an application.

Jaeger offers the following sampling options:

- *Constant*—The *constant* sampler always makes the same decision for every possible trace. All traces are sampled when set to `1`, or ignored when set to `0`. Most demo applications use a constant sampler with a value of `1` to capture all traces. For production, using constant sampling is beneficial only for applications that don't have many requests; otherwise, the cost of storing the traces grows too quickly.
- *Probabilistic*—The *probabilistic* sampler uses weighting to determine the likelihood of sampling a trace. Given a value of `0.2`, for example, approximately two traces will be sampled out of 10 traces.
- *Rate limiting*—A *leaky bucket* rate limiter ensures traces are sampled at a constant rate. A value of `4.0` informs Jaeger to sample requests at a rate of four traces every second.
- *Remote*—*Remote* is the default sampling type used if no other configuration is set. The Jaeger agent provides the sampling type remotely, as defined by the configuration in the Jaeger backend.

11.2.2 Setting up the Minikube environment

Chapter 8 contains all the details of how to set up Minikube with Apache Kafka, a PostgreSQL database, the Account service, and the Overdraft service. We use Apache Kafka and PostgreSQL in the later tracing examples. The steps to deploy everything, details of which are available in chapter 8, follow.

Listing 11.1 Environment setup

```
minikube start --memory 4096
kubectl create namespace kafka
kubectl apply -f 'strimzi-cluster-operator-0.25.0.yaml' -n kafka
kubectl apply -f kafka_cluster.yml -n kafka
kubectl wait kafka/my-cluster --for=condition=Ready --timeout=300s -n kafka
kubectl apply -f kafka_topics.yml -n kafka
kubectl apply -f postgresql_kubernetes.yml
```

Identical to listing 8.14, except for having one replica of Apache Kafka instead of two

11.2.3 Installing Jaeger

Jaeger has several installation options, depending on the environment it will run in. In this chapter, we use the Jaeger operator to install it into Minikube.

NOTE An operator is a software extension to Kubernetes for managing applications and their components. Operators can perform many varied tasks in

Kubernetes. In this case, the Jaeger operator performs the installation of the collector, UI, and dependent services.

With Minikube started, run the following commands to install the Jaeger operator.

Listing 11.2   Jaeger operator installation

```
                     Creates an observability namespace              Installs the CRDs
                        for the Jaeger components                  (custom resource
kubectl create namespace observability     ◄─┐           definitions) for Jaeger
kubectl create -f https://raw.githubusercontent.com/jaegertracing/
➥ jaeger-operator/master/deploy/crds/
➥ jaegertracing.io_jaegers_crd.yaml                        ◄──────────────┘
kubectl create -n observability -f https://raw.githubusercontent.com/
➥ jaegertracing/jaeger-operator/master/deploy/service_account.yaml
kubectl create -n observability -f https://raw.githubusercontent.com/
➥ jaegertracing/jaeger-operator/master/deploy/role.yaml
kubectl create -n observability -f https://raw.githubusercontent.com/
➥ jaegertracing/jaeger-operator/master/deploy/role_binding.yaml    Creates
kubectl create -n observability -f https://raw.githubusercontent.com/  the Jaeger
➥ jaegertracing/jaeger-operator/master/deploy/operator.yaml  ◄─┘ operator
```

With the commands complete, run `kubectl get deployment jaeger-operator -n observability` to verify the Jaeger operator is present and ready to create instances. To be ready, the `jaeger-operator` needs to be in a `READY` state of `1/1`.

The Jaeger operator creates an ingress route for Kubernetes, enabling access to the Jaeger console. Ingress routes are the Kubernetes means for exposing a service to the outside world. Because Minikube doesn't include ingress providers by default, one needs to be installed, as follows:

```
minikube addons enable ingress     ◄─┐  Installs the ingress add-on for Minikube. minikube
                                        addons list shows all the available add-ons.
```

To simplify the deployment of Jaeger, we use the all-in-one image (all-in-one combines all the pieces needed for using Jaeger, without having to deploy storage, query, and UI components separately), as shown next:

```
kubectl apply -n observability -f - <<EOF
apiVersion: jaegertracing.io/v1
kind: Jaeger
metadata:
  name: simplest
EOF
```

Use `kubectl get pods -n observability` to see when all the Jaeger components have started successfully.

> **IMPORTANT**   The all-in-one image is not recommended for production usage. There is no single image available for production, because it requires working through the necessary storage requirements, collectors, and querying.

With all the components started, the URL of the Jaeger console is available by querying the `ingress` object, as follows:

```
kubectl get -n observability ingress
NAME              CLASS    HOSTS   ADDRESS         PORTS   AGE
simplest-query    <none>   *       192.168.64.18   80      65s
```

Open a browser at http://192.168.64.18 to see the Jaeger console, shown in figure 11.3.

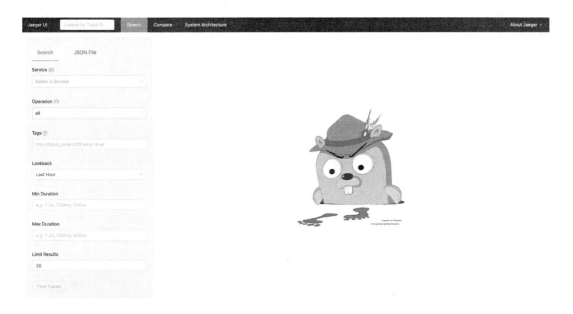

Figure 11.3 The Jaeger console

Now that Jaeger is installed, in the next section, we trace the microservices, showing how they appear in the Jaeger console.

11.2.4 *Microservice tracing with Jaeger*

Distributed tracing is difficult to describe; it's far easier to see the traces that are produced and how they change as a service is altered. To that end, let's deploy all the microservices from figure 11.1 to see what's traced, as shown in the next code listing.

Listing 11.3 Microservice deployment

```
eval $(minikube -p minikube docker-env)
/chapter11/account-service> mvn verify -Dquarkus.kubernetes.deploy=true
/chapter11/overdraft-service> mvn verify -Dquarkus.kubernetes.deploy=true
/chapter11/transaction-service> mvn verify -Dquarkus.kubernetes.deploy=true
```

Before proceeding, verify the three services are up and running by executing `kubectl` `get pods`. The terminal returns three Pods, one for each service, in the state of `RUN-` `NING`. Once they're ready, withdraw funds from an account, making it overdrawn, as shown here:

```
TRANSACTION_URL=`minikube service --url transaction-service`
curl -H "Content-Type: application/json" -X PUT -d "600.00"
      ${TRANSACTION_URL}/transactions/123456789/withdrawal
```

A JSON response is returned, showing the new account balance of –49.22. In the browser, refresh the Jaeger console page, and select the Service drop-down menu. Figure 11.4 shows the services available for selection.

Figure 11.4   **Jaeger console service selection**

We expected `account-service` and `transaction-service`, but what's `jaeger-query`? `jaeger-query` is the service the Jaeger console interacts with when the console is refreshed or a tracing search is made. When the Jaeger console was first loaded in figure 11.3, `jaeger-query` wasn't present because there hadn't been any queries issued until the page was actually loaded. In figure 11.4, select `transaction-service` from the dropdown and click Find Traces.

Figure 11.5 explains the parts of the Jaeger UI seen. The left-hand pane labeled Search includes different parameters that can be used to retrieve available traces.

In the usage so far, we've used only the Service drop-down menu, but if we have hundreds of traces for a particular service, we can use additional parameters to filter the results. Parameters include Operation name, any Tags on a trace, over what period to search for traces, Min Duration and Max Duration of a trace—which is helpful when trying to find problematic traces taking too long to execute—and Limit Results to a specific number of traces. Depending on the number of traces found, the top portion of the right-hand side of the page displays a dot for every trace found over time based on the search. Dots, or traces, toward the top of the page had a higher duration than lower-placed dots, and traces are spread left to right from oldest to most recent. As has already been seen, the bottom part of the page is the list of all the traces found from a search.

Figure 11.5 Transaction service trace results

Figure 11.5 shows all the traces currently found, which is only a single trace resulting from the withdrawal consisting of three spans. To see more detail about the captured trace, and the included spans, click the trace.

Figure 11.6 includes useful information about the request. The very top of the page highlights the method that triggered the creation of the trace—in this case, PUT—against the `transaction-service` that resulted in `TransactionResource.withdrawal` being called.

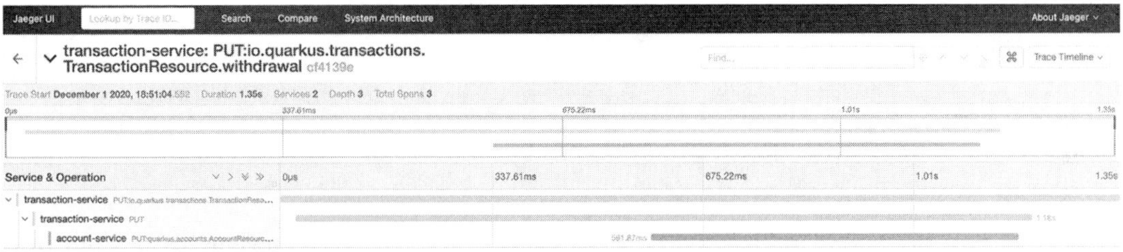

Figure 11.6 Transaction service trace detail

Below the header is pertinent information on the trace, including the date and time it started, total duration of the trace, number of services in the trace, total trace depth, and the number of spans. Each span is visualized as a separate horizontal bar. The bar's length indicates the time a span took to complete. Its position shows when it began and ended, and its color indicates which service the span belongs to. In figure 11.6, spans in the `transaction-service` appear in one color (yellow when viewed in the browser), whereas the `account-service` span is a different color (a blue-green color).

The bottom half of figure 11.6, under Service & Operation, lists every span within the trace, broken down by which service and methods within a service were called.

The timeline on the right provides a visualization of each span and its execution within the overall trace. For instance, the span for the `account-service` took 591.87 ms to complete but didn't commence until about 600 ms into processing on the `transaction-service`.

When looking at figure 11.6, clicking the first `transaction-service` span heading expands it to provide further information such as that in figure 11.7, after expanding each section.

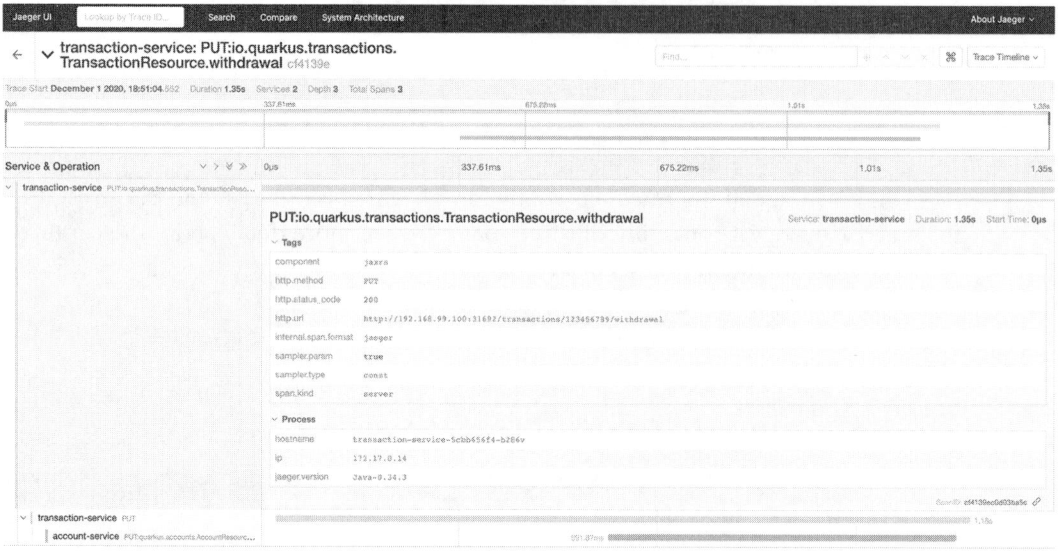

Figure 11.7   Transaction service span detail

Figure 11.7 shows the list of all the Tags present on the trace and the Process information that was collected. The Tags present will be dependent on the component being traced. In this instance, Tags include `jaxrs` for the type of component, HTTP method, HTTP status code response, HTTP URL being executed, and details on the sampling. Process captured the Kubernetes Pod name as the hostname, the IP address, and the version of Jaeger being used. The span ID is displayed in the bottom right-hand corner.

Figure 11.8 includes similar information as figure 11.7 but for the `account-service`.

Figure 11.8   Account service span detail

The Tags and Process sections are collapsed by default, but a particular tag and information are shown as a single line until it's expanded. Examining figure 11.8, we see the actual time at which the `account-service` span began on the right-hand edge. Spend some time exploring the different parts of the Jaeger console to understand the different pieces of information available and where they can be found.

From the Jaeger console search page, select `account-service` from the Service drop-down menu and click Find Traces. It should return the same trace but from the perspective of the Account service. In the list of available services to search on, there are no traces from the Overdraft service! No services or spans are being captured after the message is sent to Kafka. The trace is not being propagated from one side of Kafka to the other. We discuss how to implement propagation with Kafka in section 11.4.4.

Figure 11.9 highlights where the trace and spans fall in terms of the Banking architecture. What's interesting to note is that a single service, the Transaction service, contains multiple spans. Multiple spans within a single service can be a good way to break down the various pieces of work that are performed in a single request to better visualize where time is spent.

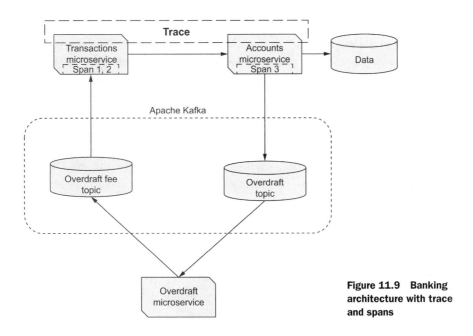

Figure 11.9 Banking architecture with trace and spans

In view of the traces in the Jaeger console from a transaction withdrawal request, what was necessary to make that possible?

Each of the services needs the dependency for OpenTracing in Quarkus. This dependency includes the OpenTracing APIs, discussed in section 11.3.1, and the tracing implementation from Jaeger, shown next:

```
<dependency>
  <groupId>io.quarkus</groupId>
  <artifactId>quarkus-smallrye-opentracing</artifactId>
</dependency>
```

It's not necessary to add a dependency for the Jaeger implementation—it is transitively brought in through OpenTracing. With an implementation present, Jaeger needs to be informed about where to send traces collected during execution. The following updates to application.properties are needed:

URL for the Jaeger collector. Microservices send any traces to the collector. Defining it as a production configuration means the default URL, http://jaeger-collector:14268/api/traces, will work running locally with Docker.

```
%prod.quarkus.jaeger.endpoint=
http://simplest-collector.observability:14268/api/traces
quarkus.jaeger.service-name=account-service
quarkus.jaeger.sampler-type=const
quarkus.jaeger.sampler-param=1
```

Any traces passing through the service will use this name on spans.

The type of sampling to perform. Options include const, probabilistic, rate-limiting, and remote.

Value used in conjunction with sampler-type

The configuration for Jaeger needs to be included in all the services, along with the quarkus-smallrye-opentracing dependency. Don't forget to change the service-name value when copying it between the files. If it's not changed, every trace will be from account-service, making it very confusing to understand what has actually been traced.

Those are all the changes that we made to capture a trace. Though it still misses the use of the Overdraft service, the trace was correctly propagated from Transaction service to Account service without any intervention from developers to make it happen. For that matter, other than adding a dependency and configuration, developers don't need to add any code to begin tracing what their application is doing!

The next section provides details on the various specifications for tracing, explaining how they're related and which ones are used in Quarkus.

11.3   *Tracing specifications*

This section provides details on the key projects and specifications related to tracing, both inside and outside of MicroProfile, while also providing some insight into what's coming with OpenTelemetry.

11.3.1   *OpenTracing*

OpenTracing (https://opentracing.io/) consists of an API specification and frameworks and libraries implementing the specification for various languages. OpenTracing itself is not a standard, because it is not part of any official standards body. The OpenTracing project is part of the Cloud Native Computing Foundation (CNCF) (https://www.cncf.io/).

OpenTracing began in 2015 with a goal of enabling application and framework developers to include instrumentation for tracing within their projects, but without being tied to a specific tracing vendor. Without this ability, there is no guarantee that a trace started in one application will be correctly propagated down the chain of execution.

Jaeger is one possible backend that can accept traces created with OpenTracing. OpenTracing and Jaeger have seen wide adoption within the open source community and within enterprises needing to trace their services.

11.3.2 What is MicroProfile OpenTracing?

MicroProfile OpenTracing chose to build upon the foundations of OpenTracing and not define its own API for creating or interacting with traces. The beauty of this approach is any trace format OpenTracing supports will be supported by MicroProfile OpenTracing. Additionally, the mere inclusion of a MicroProfile OpenTracing implementation facilitates the capturing and propagation of traces without any interaction on the part of a developer in their application code.

Implementations enable *no code* propagation of traces by extracting `SpanContext` information from incoming JAX-RS requests. No code instrumentation, where every JAX-RS resource method has a new `Span` of its execution, ensures tracing of every JAX-RS endpoint in a microservice by default. MicroProfile OpenTracing adds the `@Traced` annotation for developers to indicate that specific methods, or all methods on a class, should have a `Span` created to represent the processing of the method. `@Traced` can be used on non-JAX-RS resource methods to have spans created, and the creation of a `Span` can be prevented by adding `@Traced(value = false)` onto a method.

`@Traced` can modify the default span name for any traced method. The default for inbound requests follows:

```
<HTTP-method>:<package-name>.<class-name>.<method-name>
```

However, the span name can be overridden with `@Traced(operationName = "my-method")`.

11.3.3 OpenTelemetry

In March 2019, members of the OpenTracing and OpenCensus communities decided to merge under a single project named OpenTelemetry. Both projects focus on unifying application instrumentation to make observability a built-in feature for modern applications. However, each project tackled a different aspect. OpenTracing implements tracing APIs, whereas OpenCensus has APIs for metrics. Combining the two into a single project for all observability is the right approach.

Because both OpenCensus and OpenTracing are well-established projects in their own right, it takes time to combine them into a single project while ensuring each project is considered equally. In early 2021, OpenTelemetry released tracing APIs as

GA (generally available). The release included finalized tracing features. As of August 2021, Metrics is close to being finalized, but Logging is not expected until 2022.

Readers might be wondering why we discuss OpenTelemetry if it will not be final for a while. The reason is the MicroProfile community is only beginning to explore OpenTelemetry. In particular, how it will impact the existing Metrics and OpenTracing specifications, what becomes of MicroProfile Metrics and OpenTracing, and whether an OpenTelemetry specification should be added to the MicroProfile platform will be discussed in 2022.

Quarkus has initial support for OpenTelemetry already. However, because the book focuses on MicroProfile functionality, we won't cover the OpenTelemetry features.

11.4   *Customizing application tracing*

We have several ways to customize what's traced, both in terms of what's being captured in a trace but also what is being traced. The following sections detail how each of these can be achieved with existing services.

11.4.1   *Using @Traced*

As we described in a previous section, `@Traced` enables developers to customize the name of the span to provide more meaning to the name. Let's modify `Account-Resource` by adding the following annotation to the `withdrawal` method:

```
@Traced(operationName = "withdraw-from-account")
```

With the change made, redeploy the Account service as follows:

```
mvn verify -Dquarkus.kubernetes.deploy=true
```

Once it's deployed, make a withdrawal from an account, as shown next:

```
curl -H "Content-Type: application/json" -X PUT -d "2500.00"
    ${TRANSACTION_URL}/transactions/111222333/withdrawal
```

Refresh the Jaeger console browser page, and search for `account-service` traces. Click the most recent trace result, and expand the `account-service` span section. The reader will see content similar to figure 11.10, showing the span name is now `withdraw_from_account`.

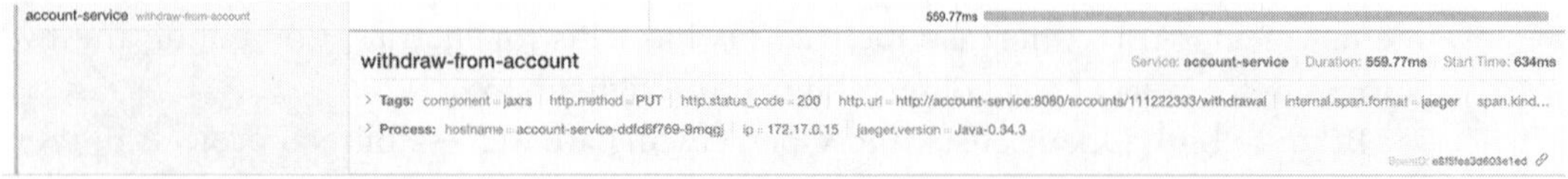

Figure 11.10   Account service: custom span name

Exercise for the reader
Try out different scenarios with `@Traced`, such as changing span names, disabling tracing, and making withdrawal and deposit requests. Take a look at how they appear in the Jaeger console.

11.4.2 Injecting a tracer

Let's take the customization a step further. Injecting a `Tracer` instance provides the ability to interact with the trace and span through an API. Modify `AccountResource`.`withdrawal` to inject a tracer, and modify the span to have the account number as a tag and the withdrawal amount as a baggage item, as shown in the next listing. A *baggage item* enables propagation of state across process boundaries within a trace.

Listing 11.4 `AccountResource`

```
public class AccountResource {        Injects an          Sets a tag on the currently
    @Inject                           OpenTracing         active span with a key of
    Tracer tracer;            ◀       Tracer instance     accountNumber

    public CompletionStage<Account> withdrawal(@PathParam("accountNumber") Long
        accountNumber, String amount) {
        ...
        tracer.activeSpan().setTag("accountNumber", accountNumber);       ◀
        tracer.activeSpan().setBaggageItem("withdrawalAmount", amount);        ◀
        ...
    }                                    Sets a baggage item on the current
}                                        span with a key of withdrawalAmount
```

With the changes made, redeploy the Account service. When the deployment is ready, withdraw money from an account as follows:

```
curl -H "Content-Type: application/json" -X PUT -d "950.00"
    ${TRANSACTION_URL}/transactions/87878787/withdrawal
```

With the response received, reload the Jaeger console in the browser. Search for `account-service` traces, and select the most recent one to see the details.

Figure 11.11 shows the span with the new tag and baggage item that were added. All the tags seen on previous spans are still there, but the span now includes the tag added directly through the tracer API.

11.4.3 Tracing database calls

Having seen how it's possible to modify details of the span operation and customize the tags and baggage items on the span with the API, now let's trace the database interactions. Although knowing how long a particular method takes to execute is important for diagnosing performance issues, it doesn't provide enough of a picture when a method interacts with many other methods or services, such as a database.

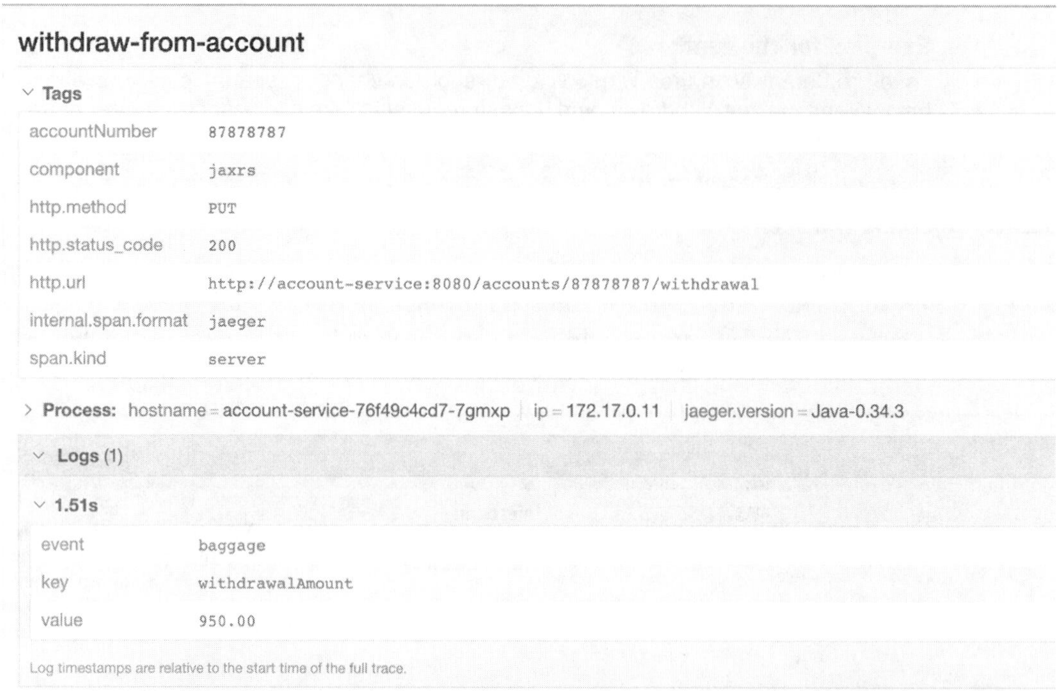

withdraw-from-account

∨ **Tags**

accountNumber	87878787
component	jaxrs
http.method	PUT
http.status_code	200
http.url	http://account-service:8080/accounts/87878787/withdrawal
internal.span.format	jaeger
span.kind	server

> **Process:** hostname = account-service-76f49c4cd7-7gmxp   ip = 172.17.0.11   jaeger.version = Java-0.34.3

∨ **Logs** (1)

∨ **1.51s**

event	baggage
key	withdrawalAmount
value	950.00

Log timestamps are relative to the start time of the full trace.

Figure 11.11 Account service: modify span content

Maybe a method takes two seconds to complete, but most of that occurs performing database operations. Data needs to be of the correct granularity to be useful; otherwise, it is just as likely to be harmful as helpful.

We need to make a few modifications to be able to trace database calls. First we add a tracing dependency for JDBC as shown here:

```
<dependency>
  <groupId>io.opentracing.contrib</groupId>
  <artifactId>opentracing-jdbc</artifactId>
</dependency>
```

The JDBC tracer from OpenTracing sits between a service and the database. For that to work, an application needs to know the tracer must be used instead of the driver for a specific database. It's also necessary to inform Hibernate which database is being used, because it's no longer possible to deduce it from the JDBC driver. That's a lot of pieces! Thankfully, all it means is a few changes to the application.properties of the Account service:

```
%prod.quarkus.datasource.db-kind=postgresql
%prod.quarkus.datasource.username=quarkus_banking
```

```
%prod.quarkus.datasource.password=quarkus_banking
%prod.quarkus.datasource.jdbc.url=
    jdbc:tracing:postgresql://postgres.default:5432/quarkus_banking
%prod.quarkus.datasource.jdbc.driver=io.opentracing.contrib.jdbc.TracingDriver    ◁─┐
%prod.quarkus.hibernate-orm.dialect=org.hibernate.dialect.PostgreSQL10Dialect      ◁─┐
```

Adds tracing to the JDBC URL from previous chapters

Informs Hibernate that the underlying database type is PostgreSQL. Without this configuration property, Quarkus is unable to determine the database type from the chosen driver.

Specifies the JDBC driver for tracing. With multiple JDBC drivers on the class path, PostgreSQL, and Tracing, it's necessary to specify which one to use.

All the properties for the database are set to the prod profile. Doing so prevents the tracing driver from interfering with Dev Services starting the PostgreSQL database.

With the changes made, redeploy the service. When the deployment is ready, withdraw money from an account as follows:

```
curl -H "Content-Type: application/json" -X PUT -d "900.00"
    ${TRANSACTION_URL}/transactions/987654321/withdrawal
```

Once the response has been received, head back to the Jaeger console in the browser, and search for account-service. A new trace will be retrieved from the most recent request, similar to that shown in figure 11.12, where the number of spans for the account-service has increased from one to three.

Figure 11.12   Account service traces

Click the trace with the new spans from figure 11.12.

The Jaeger console should show details like those in figure 11.13. There are now two additional spans in the trace that were not previously present. Named Query and Update, they represent the two database interactions that were performed during the request.

Looking at the AccountResource.withdrawal() method, the first line calls Account.findByAccountNumber(accountNumber), which is the Query. Though it's within the persistence framework handling inside Quarkus, and not in application code, Update results from committing the transaction to the database.

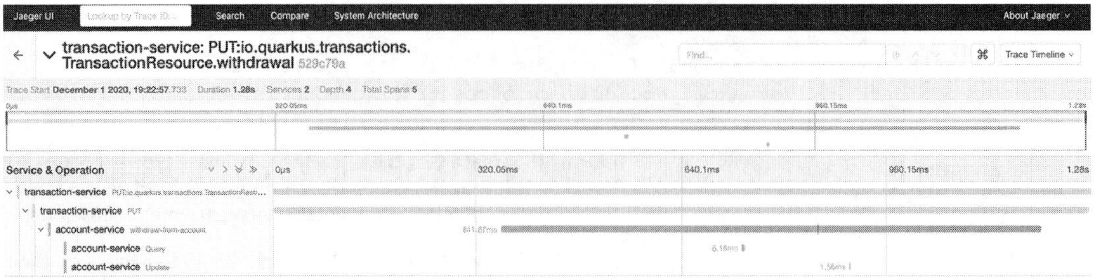

Figure 11.13   Account service trace with a database call

Let's take a look at what the detail for each of them contains. Figure 11.14 includes details of the database interaction that retrieved the account, including the database type and the SQL select statement used to retrieve the account.

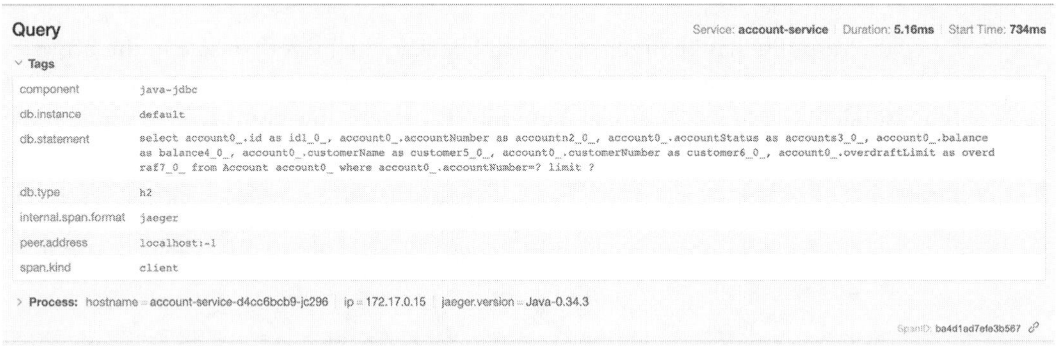

Figure 11.14   Database query trace detail

Though this particular select executed in 5.16 ms, having the ability to know the called SQL enables us to investigate whether the statement is as efficient as it can be when the execution time is longer.

Figure 11.15 shows the Update database transaction trace. As with figure 11.14, we see information about the database the trace connected to and the SQL statement executed to update the record.

The traces being collected now include information about the database calls, but there's still nothing from the pesky Overdraft service. Time to fix that! In the next section, we explain how to propagate OpenTracing traces with Kafka, filling the gap in tracing end to end with the example code.

| Update | | Service: **account-service** | Duration: **1.56ms** | Start Time: **902ms** |

✓ Tags

component	java-jdbc
db.instance	default
db.statement	update Account set accountNumber=?, accountStatus=?, balance=?, customerName=?, customerNumber=?, overdraftLimit=? where id=?
db.type	h2
internal.span.format	jaeger
peer.address	localhost:-1
span.kind	client

> **Process:** hostname = account-service-d4cc6bcb9-jc296   ip = 172.17.0.15   jaeger.version = Java-0.34.3

SpanID: 3b50312894a5b9bb 🔗

Figure 11.15   Database update trace detail

11.4.4 Tracing Kafka messages

At the moment, some spans exist for JAX-RS resource methods and database calls, but nothing for the producing and consuming of messages with Kafka! Let's fix that right now. For both the Account service and Overdraft Service, add the following dependency to pom.xml:

```
<dependency>
  <groupId>io.opentracing.contrib</groupId>
  <artifactId>opentracing-kafka-client</artifactId>
  <version>0.1.15</version>
</dependency>
```

Similar to the dependency for JDBC tracing, this dependency is an extension to Open-Tracing for Kafka. With the dependency in place, the tracing interceptors for Kafka need to be identified to the connectors for consuming and producing messages. The necessary changes to application.properties for the Account service follow:

The connector to the account-overdrawn topic will use the TracingProducerInterceptor when producing messages.

```
mp.messaging.outgoing.account-overdrawn.interceptor.classes=
  ➥ io.opentracing.contrib.kafka.TracingProducerInterceptor
```

```
mp.messaging.incoming.overdraft-update.interceptor.classes=
  ➥ io.opentracing.contrib.kafka.TracingConsumerInterceptor
```

Consuming messages from the overdraft-update topic uses the TracingConsumerInterceptor for consuming messages.

> **NOTE** Existing mp.messaging properties were left out for brevity, because they were not altered.

The required interceptor configuration for the Overdraft service is shown next:

```
mp.messaging.incoming.account-overdrawn.interceptor.classes=
    io.opentracing.contrib.kafka.TracingConsumerInterceptor
```

```
mp.messaging.outgoing.overdraft-fee.interceptor.classes=
    io.opentracing.contrib.kafka.TracingProducerInterceptor

mp.messaging.outgoing.overdraft-update.interceptor.classes=
    io.opentracing.contrib.kafka.TracingProducerInterceptor
```

Without adding anything more than a dependency and configuration, redeploy the Account service and Overdraft service as follows:

```
/chapter11/account-service> mvn verify -Dquarkus.kubernetes.deploy=true
/chapter11/overdraft-service> mvn verify -Dquarkus.kubernetes.deploy=true
```

Once they're both deployed and running, verify with `kubectl get pods` that each service has a Pod running, and withdraw funds from an account as follows:

```
curl -H "Content-Type: application/json" -X PUT -d "400.00"
    ${TRANSACTION_URL}/transactions/5465/withdrawal
```

Once the response is received, open the Jaeger console in the browser and refresh the page.

When selecting the Service drop-down menu, we now see an entry for `overdraft-service` when there wasn't one before, as seen in figure 11.16. Getting back to the earlier problem of not having traces from the Overdraft service, the answer is that the execution being performed is around Kafka and not JAX-RS.

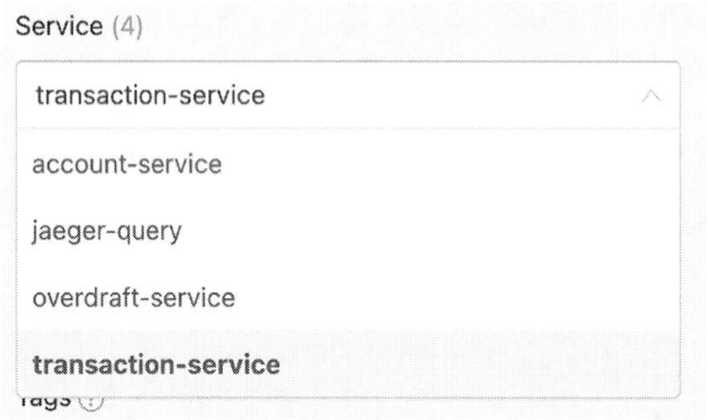

Service (4)

transaction-service

account-service

jaeger-query

overdraft-service

transaction-service

Tags

Figure 11.16   The Jaeger console service list

Though the methods interacting with Kafka are on `OverdraftResource`, a JAX-RS resource, without a JAX-RS incoming request, there is nothing for it to trace. With the Kafka interceptor installed, traces are now present. Search for traces for the `account-service`, and for now, it will find traces such as those depicted in figure 11.17.

Comparing these with previous traces, the main trace of five spans containing the call from Transaction service to Account service still exists. However, we now have a new trace named `account-service: To_overdrawn` with spans in the Account service and Overdraft service. Select the trace to take a closer look.

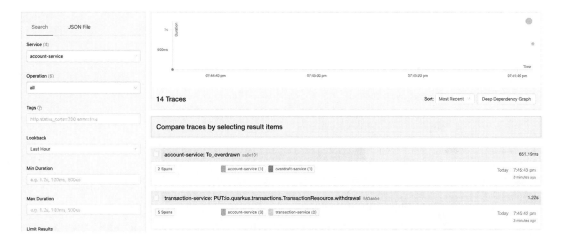

Figure 11.17 Traces for Account service

Figure 11.18 shows two spans in the trace—one span for producing a message to a Kafka topic, and another span to consume the message.

Figure 11.18 Account service trace detail

The tags on the `To_overdrawn` span provide details as to what's happening, such as `message_bus.destination`, `peer.service`, and `span.kind`. The `From_overdrawn` span provides additional information, because it's a consumer, such as `offset` and `partition`. All these tags are Kafka-specific and are present only on spans connecting to Kafka topics.

Searching for `overdraft-service` traces shows two traces; see figure 11.19. One is the trace from figure 11.18, but there is also a trace for putting a message onto the `account-fee` topic.

Figure 11.19   Traces for the Overdraft service

Figure 11.20 is a representation of the traces in Jaeger so far. Currently, there are three separate traces, but it's all from one request!

1 Call from the Transaction service to the Account service, including the database call in the Account service
2 Message passed from the Account service to Kafka, which is consumed by the Overdraft service
3 An overdraft fee message from Overdraft service to Kafka

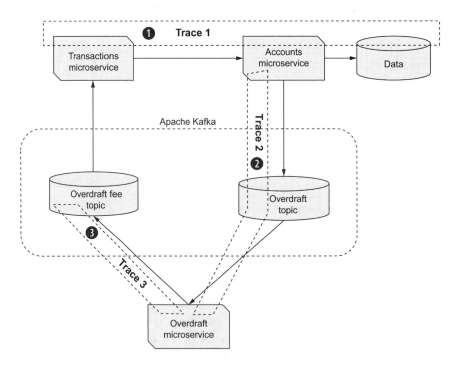

Figure 11.20   Microservice architecture traces

Having separate traces makes it difficult to manually correlate which traces are *actually* part of the same request. As a developer, the preference would be for all the spans in each of the three traces to be within a single trace. Notice the points where trace continuation breaks is when moving from JAX-RS to Kafka, and also between receiving a Kafka message and sending out another one.

Now that we know what the problems are, let's look at fixing them. The first step is propagating the trace from JAX-RS to Kafka. Instead of calling `emitter.send(payload)`, we need to add information about the trace to the Kafka message, as shown next.

Listing 11.5 `AccountResource`

Creates an instance of Kafka RecordHeaders. The headers are added to the Kafka message, enabling the information on them to be available in consumers.

Uses the TracingKafkaUtils utility class to inject the details of the trace and span into the RecordHeaders instance created inthe previous line

```
public class AccountResource {
    @Inject
    Tracer tracer;

    public CompletionStage<Account> withdrawal(@PathParam("accountNumber") Long
        accountNumber, String amount) {
      ...
        RecordHeaders headers = new RecordHeaders();
        TracingKafkaUtils.inject(tracer.activeSpan().context(), headers, tracer);
        OutgoingKafkaRecordMetadata<Object> kafkaMetadata =
          OutgoingKafkaRecordMetadata.builder()
            .withHeaders(headers)
            .build();
        CompletableFuture<Account> future = new CompletableFuture<>();
        emitter.send(Message.of(payload, Metadata.of(kafkaMetadata),
            ... ack handler,
            ... nack handler
        );
        return future;
      ...
    }
}
```

Emits a new Message containing the payload and OutgoingKafkaRecordMetadata instance

Creates an OutgoingKafkaRecordMetadata instance and sets the RecordHeaders instance on it. This metadata instance can be used to set Kafka-specific metadata on an outgoing message.

On the other side of the Kafka topic, the Overdraft service needs to retrieve the span information. Doing so involves two steps: extracting the span information from Kafka headers, and then creating a child span for additional method calls, as shown in the next code listing.

Listing 11.6 `OverdraftResource` creating a child span

Verifies there is IncomingKafka-RecordMetadata in the metadata; otherwise doesn't handle traces

Builds a new span named process-overdraft-fee

```
public class OverdraftResource {
    @Inject
    Tracer tracer;

    public Message<Overdrawn> overdraftNotification(Message<Overdrawn> message) {
      ...
        RecordHeaders headers = new RecordHeaders();
        if (message.getMetadata(IncomingKafkaRecordMetadata.class).isPresent()) {
            Span span = tracer.buildSpan("process-overdraft-fee")
```

Makes the new span a child of the span extracted from the Kafka message on the next line ⟶

```
.asChildOf(
    TracingKafkaUtils.extractSpanContext(
        message.getMetadata(IncomingKafkaRecordMetadata
            .class).get().getHeaders(),
            tracer))
    .start();
try (Scope scope = tracer.activateSpan(span)) {
    TracingKafkaUtils.inject(span.context(), headers, tracer);
} finally {
    span.finish();
}
}
OutgoingKafkaRecordMetadata<Object> kafkaMetadata =
    OutgoingKafkaRecordMetadata.builder()
        .withHeaders(headers)
        .build();


    return message.addMetadata(customerOverdraft).addMetadata(kafkaMetadata);
    }
}
```

Extracts the SpanContext from the incoming Kafka message

Utilizes a Scope within a try-with-resources block, so the scope closes automatically at the end of the code block

Retrieves the current span context, and injects it into RecordHeaders

In addition to the metadata about the customer overdraft, also attaches metadata for OutgoingKafkaRecordMetadata containing the trace headers

Listing 11.6 extracts the encoded span information from the Kafka headers. The span is recreated within the `Tracer` instance of the Overdraft service, as if it had been called from within the same service. To ensure the trace continues, we need to create a new child span to handle further processing.

There's one more change that needs to be made to propagate the trace back into Kafka. `ProcessOverdraftFee.processOverdraftFee` needs to return `Message<Account-Fee>` instead of just `AccountFee`. Changing the return type enables the trace information in the metadata to be propagated by returning `message.withPayload(feeEvent)`. Using `message.withPayload` retains all the metadata within the message but uses a different payload for the outgoing message.

Redeploy the Account service and Overdraft service to enable the changes, as shown here:

```
/chapter11/account-service> mvn verify -Dquarkus.kubernetes.deploy=true
/chapter11/overdraft-service> mvn verify -Dquarkus.kubernetes.deploy=true
```

Once they're both deployed and running, withdraw funds from an account as follows:

```
curl -H "Content-Type: application/json" -X PUT -d "500.00"
    ${TRANSACTION_URL}/transactions/78790/withdrawal
```

Now to see how the traces look! Open the Jaeger console in the browser, and refresh the page. Select `transaction-service` from the drop-down menu, and click Find Traces.

Figure 11.21 shows a trace containing nine spans—success!

Figure 11.21   Trace for the Transaction service

All the previous traces containing spans are now present within a single trace. With all the spans properly connected, developers can now accurately observe traces through the entire distributed system. Let's dive in and click the trace to see the details.

In figure 11.22, we now have a visualization of all the pieces of a single request through the entire system. This is fantastic!

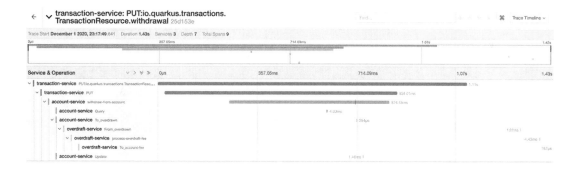

Figure 11.22   Transaction service trace detail

It might have taken some time to put all the pieces into place to enable a full single trace through it all, but the benefits of doing so are worth it. Diagnosing slow execution in a request is now possible with the wider context of all methods being called.

Exercise for the reader
As an exercise for the reader, modify the Transaction service processing of messages from the `account-fee` topic to extract the trace from metadata. Execute a withdrawal from an account, and see the captured trace include the span for handling the fee in the Transaction service.

Summary

- Including the `quarkus-smallrye-opentracing` dependency and Jaeger configuration to define the sampling type and rate is all that's necessary to achieve traces within JAX-RS resources.

- By adding `@Traced` to a method, it's possible to customize the name of the span, or to not trace the method at all.
- Injecting a `Tracer` into application code enables the addition of custom tags to the span or adding objects into `Baggage` for propagation to later services.
- Similar to out-of-the-box tracing, database transactions can be traced with a dependency and Hibernate configuration changes to indicate the new JDBC driver to use.
- Use Kafka interceptors for OpenTracing to handle spans when producing and consuming messages from Kafka.

API visualization 12

This chapter covers

- Generating OpenAPI (previously known as Swagger UI) specifications for a project
- Accessing OpenAPI project specifications
- Visually inspecting project endpoints with the Swagger UI
- Utilizing the design-first approach to developing APIs—the process of creating an API design before implementing it with code

Originally developed in 2010 as a way for defining machine-readable interfaces to describe RESTful services, in 2016, the *Swagger specification* was rebranded as the *OpenAPI specification* under a new OpenAPI initiative sponsored by the Linux Foundation. Other benefits to an OpenAPI specification of a service follow:

- Creating interactive documentation of a service
- Automation of test cases based on a specification
- Generating clients or services aligned with a specification

The ability to visualize an API, including its definition and expected behavior, can be tremendously helpful when a developer wants to interact with an external

257

service, particularly when the service is developed by another team or another company entirely. Why? How does it help?

When a developer must communicate with another service, they need to know about the service, everything from expected inputs and return types to possible error responses. Sometimes it's possible to review the implementation code to elicit the needed information, but doing so is not ideal and leads to misinterpretation. In particularly complex implementations, it could require detailed knowledge of the implementation to determine all possible response types and their exceptions.

Other times a developer can speak with the team implementing the service to ask necessary questions. However, though such an approach is feasible with a few teams wanting to use a service, it quickly becomes impossible for the implementors of a service to meet the demands of questions from clients of the service as the number of clients grows.

A single source of truth for a service defining the behavior and expected outcomes is the only way to effectively communicate to developers of external clients how a service operates. The *OpenAPI specification* (OAS) is designed for such a purpose. The version of the specification is currently v3. In the remainder of the chapter, we refer to it as "OpenAPI specification" only, and not the "OpenAPI specification v3."

The code for both examples in this chapter uses the chapter 2 Account service as a starting point. Follow along with the changes throughout the chapter by copying the source from /chapter2/account-service. The two completed versions of the chapter examples are in the /chapter12 folder of the book source code.

12.1 *Viewing OpenAPI documents with Swagger UI*

We cover two features in this chapter: providing an OpenAPI specification file, and visualizing it with Swagger UI. Without the former, the latter has nothing to show. Using Swagger UI is a great way to provide a means of testing an API from a browser if there isn't a UI for the application already present.

Time to get started! Copy the code from /chapter2/account-service to another location for updating to use OpenAPI and Swagger UI as the code starting point for the chapter.

12.1.1 *Enabling OpenAPI*

With the source code in place, let's add the following dependency needed for OpenAPI:

```
<dependency>
  <groupId>io.quarkus</groupId>
  <artifactId>quarkus-smallrye-openapi</artifactId>
</dependency>
```

An alternative way to add the dependency is by using the Quarkus Maven plugin, as shown here:

```
mvn quarkus:add-extension -Dextensions="quarkus-smallrye-openapi"
```

That's it! With the addition of one dependency, the Account service will have an OpenAPI document produced from the code. Let's try it out.

Start the service in live coding mode as follows:

```
mvn quarkus:dev
```

When started, access http://localhost:8080/q/openapi either with a browser or `curl`. The default format for the OpenAPI document is YAML. If the OpenAPI document was accessed in a browser, it will download a file with the following content.

Listing 12.1 The Account service–generated OpenAPI document

```
openapi: 3.0.3                              ◁─────      Version of the OpenAPI
info:                                       ◁─────      specification with which
  title: Generated API                                  the document conforms
  version: "1.0"
paths:                                      ◁─────      Information about the service. In this
  /accounts:                                            case, there isn't any information
    get:                                                because it was generated.
      responses:
        "200":                                          The paths, or API endpoints,
          description: OK                               exposed by the service
          content:
            application/json:
              schema:
                $ref: '#/components/schemas/SetAccount'
    post:
      requestBody:
        content:
          application/json:
            schema:
              $ref: '#/components/schemas/Account'
      responses:
        "200":
          description: OK
  /accounts/{accountNumber}:
    get:
      parameters:
      - name: accountNumber
        in: path
        required: true
        schema:
          format: int64
          type: integer
      responses:
        "200":
          description: OK
          content:
            application/json:
              schema:
                $ref: '#/components/schemas/Account'
    delete:
      parameters:
```

```
          - name: accountNumber
            in: path
            required: true
            schema:
              format: int64
              type: integer
          responses:
            "200":
              description: OK
....
components:
  schemas:                 ◁──────────    All the entities that the API endpoints
    SetAccount:                           require and the schema for each,
      uniqueItems: true                   defining their structure
      type: array
      items:
        $ref: '#/components/schemas/Account'
    Account:
      type: object
      properties:
        accountNumber:
          format: int64
          type: integer
        accountStatus:
          $ref: '#/components/schemas/AccountStatus'
        balance:
          type: number
        customerName:
          type: string
        customerNumber:
          format: int64
          type: integer
        status:
          $ref: '#/components/schemas/AccountStatus'
    AccountStatus:
      enum:
      - CLOSED
      - OPEN
      - OVERDRAWN
      type: string
```

NOTE Some methods were removed from the OpenAPI document shown
here for brevity. Viewing the document locally will also include the API methods for withdrawal and deposit.

The same OpenAPI document can be served in JSON format instead by accessing
http://localhost:8080/q/openapi?format=json. If explicitness is desired, the YAML
format can be used as well: http://localhost:8080/q/openapi?format=yaml.

NOTE Instead of using query parameters on a URL, the desired format of the
OpenAPI document can be specified with the Accept HTTP request header.
Setting it to application/json will retrieve JSON instead of YAML.

It's by no means a great OpenAPI document to use with clients, but it's a good first representation of what the Account service offers and is far better than no OpenAPI document at all.

Readers may have noticed when the service was started earlier that the console output didn't show only `smallrye-openapi` as a feature. There is also `swagger-ui`. With Quarkus, Swagger UI is packaged as part of the OpenAPI extension. Let's take a look at Swagger UI in the next section.

12.1.2 *Swagger UI*

As mentioned earlier, with the OpenAPI extension, Swagger UI is automatically included. There is one caveat, though. The Swagger UI is present only during live coding and testing, not as part of a final, packaged build. Quarkus views Swagger UI as beneficial during development and testing with the application directly, but for production, it is recommended to use a separate Swagger UI instance that can be properly secured using the OpenAPI document produced from a service.

> **WARNING** The default behavior can be overridden by adding `quarkus.swag-ger-ui.always-include=true` to application.properties. However, the configuration is for build time only, which means the configuration value can not be altered once a service is built. Setting this property for production use is not recommended.

Open http://localhost:8080/q/swagger-ui in a browser, as shown in figure 12.1.

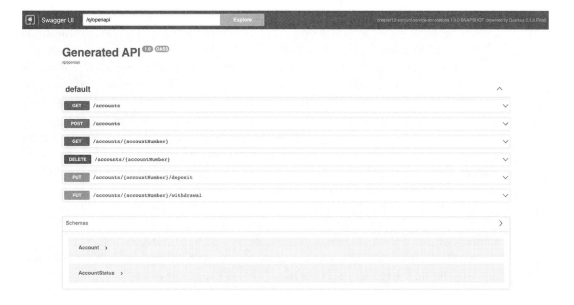

Figure 12.1   The Account service OpenAPI document in Swagger

Clicking on the GET /accounts section header expands the details for that particular endpoint, as illustrated in figure 12.2.

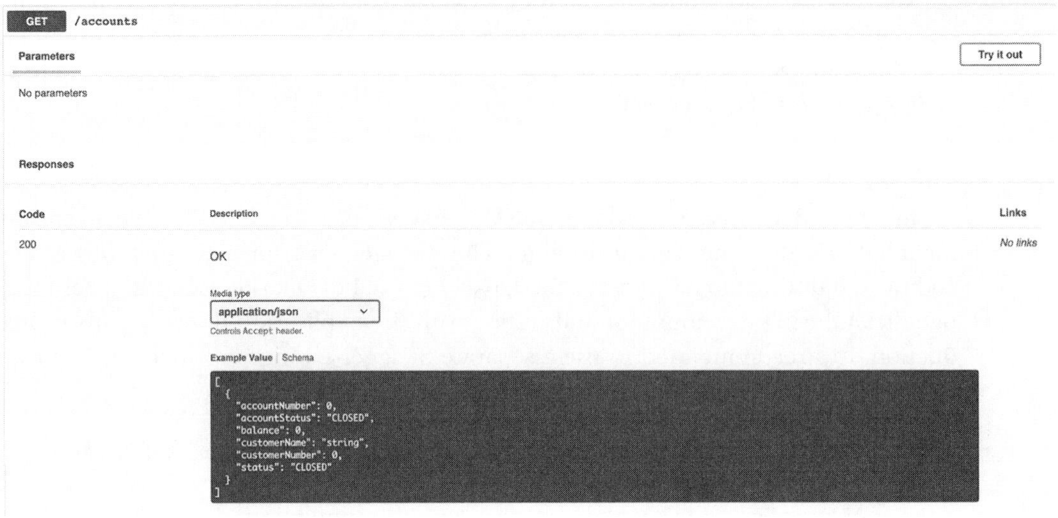

Figure 12.2   Get all Accounts details

With an endpoint section detail expanded, click Try It Out. In this case, the endpoint doesn't require any parameters to be passed, so click Execute.

Figure 12.3 shows the response received when executing the API endpoint to retrieve all accounts. Swagger UI shows the request URL it executed and also the equivalent command for use with `curl`. Below the request details, the response received is detailed, including the HTTP response code, response body, and response headers.

Take some time to explore the content of the OpenAPI document in the Swagger UI and learn how it works. Looking through the endpoints, the only response code defined for any of them is 200, which means OK. Why is that? The OpenAPI document right now is generated based on the methods on the JAX-RS resource class. Though it's possible to make reasonable assumptions about what the methods do, such as returning an HTTP response code of 200 if they work, anything beyond that is more effort than what would be offered.

For instance, expand the POST endpoint to see the response code documented there. The code returns a 201 for the response, but the documentation shows a 200. This is a problem wiith the generation assuming an OK response is always 200.

We need to make some modification to the automatically generated OpenAPI document! The next section explains how we can add customizations.

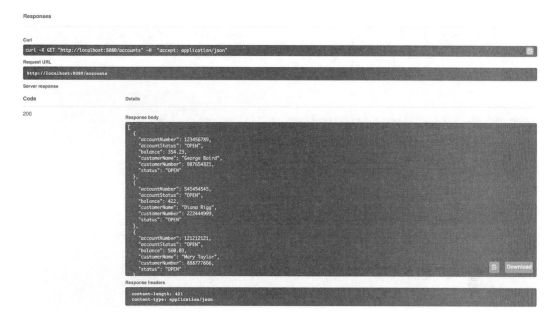

Responses

Curl

```
curl -X GET "http://localhost:8080/accounts" -H  "accept: application/json"
```

Request URL

```
http://localhost:8080/accounts
```

Server response

Code   Details

200   Response body

```
[
  {
    "accountNumber": 123456789,
    "accountStatus": "OPEN",
    "balance": 354.23,
    "customerName": "George Baird",
    "customerNumber": 987654321,
    "status": "OPEN"
  },
  {
    "accountNumber": 545454545,
    "accountStatus": "OPEN",
    "balance": 422,
    "customerName": "Diana Rigg",
    "customerNumber": 222444999,
    "status": "OPEN"
  },
  {
    "accountNumber": 121212121,
    "accountStatus": "OPEN",
    "balance": 560.03,
    "customerName": "Mary Taylor",
    "customerNumber": 888777666,
    "status": "OPEN"
  }
```

                Response headers

```
content-length: 421
content-type: application/json
```

Figure 12.3 Get all Accounts response

12.2 *MicroProfile OpenAPI*

The MicroProfile OpenAPI specification provides annotations, making it easier for Java developers to customize the contents of an OpenAPI document from existing code. The specification does not replace the OpenAPI specification or seek to alter how an OpenAPI document is defined. It *does* provide annotations, configurations, and a programming model for customizing OpenAPI documents.

12.2.1 *Application information*

Quarkus allows the setting of most of the application information with configuration, going beyond what is offered in MicroProfile OpenAPI. This approach has the added benefit of allowing different values, depending on the selected configuration profile. Add the following code to application.properties.

Listing 12.2 Application properties

```
mp.openapi.extensions.smallrye.info.title=Account Service
%dev.mp.openapi.extensions.smallrye.info.title=Account Service (development)
mp.openapi.extensions.smallrye.info.version=1.0.0
mp.openapi.extensions.smallrye.info.description=Service for maintaining
    accounts,\
    their balances, and issuing deposit and withdrawal transactions
mp.openapi.extensions.smallrye.info.license.name=Apache 2.0
mp.openapi.extensions.smallrye.info.license.url=https://www.apache.org/
    licenses/LICENSE-2.0.html
```

Let's see what it looks like. Figure 12.4 has the Swagger UI showing the new information added by the configuration in application.properties, including a customized application name for development!

Account Service (development) 1.0.0 OAS3

/q/openapi

Service for maintaining accounts, their balances, and issuing deposit and withdrawal transactions

Apache 2.0

default

| GET | /accounts |

| POST | /accounts |

Figure 12.4   Swagger output with application information

Stop the application with Ctrl-C, update application.properties with `quarkus.swagger-ui.always-include=true`, run the `mvn package`, then start the service as follows:

```
java -jar target/quarkus-app/quarkus-run.jar
```

Open Swagger UI to see the application name using the production profile value!

It's also possible to use an annotation to define the same information. `@Open-APIDefinition` enables the inclusion of information about an application such as title, version, license, and contact information, as well as tags defining the application. To work, the annotation must be added to a JAX-RS application class, as shown in the next listing.

Listing 12.3   AccountServiceApplication

```
@OpenAPIDefinition(
    tags = {
        @Tag(name = "transactions",
            description = "Operations manipulating account balances."),
        @Tag(name = "admin",
            description = "Operations for managing accounts.")
    },
    info = @Info(
        title = "Account Service",
```

Defines any tags for grouping methods or operations within the OpenAPI document

Information about the service such as title, description, version, and license. There is additional data available to capture with @Info that wasn't used here.

```
        description = "Service for maintaining accounts, their balances,
and issuing deposit and withdrawal transactions",
        version = "1.0.0",
        license = @License(
            name = "Apache 2.0",
            url = "https://www.apache.org/licenses/LICENSE-2.0.html"
        )
    )
)
public class AccountServiceApplication extends Application {     ◁──────
}
```

> An empty JAX-RS application
> class with no methods

Listing 12.3 has the same information as listing 12.2, with the addition of @Tag. Use Swagger UI to see how the OpenAPI document changed when tags were included.

By default, all methods in an OpenAPI document are under a *default* tag as seen previously in Swagger UI. Using @Tag enables developers to group different methods into a similar category. Adding them to the application allows a common description to be applied to all methods with the same tag without copying the description in each of them.

Though @OpenAPIDefinition supports tag definition, which is not possible currently in application.properties, it adds a class that isn't needed. Tags can be included with alternative approaches, which we cover later in the chapter.

12.2.2 *Customizing the schema output*

In Swagger UI the automatically generated schemas are for SetAccount, Account-Status, and Account. SetAccount refers to the Set<Account> returned by retrieving all accounts. We discuss SetAccount further in section 12.7. Looking at AccountStatus, it describes an enumeration with values of CLOSED, OPEN, and OVERDRAWN. Everything looks good.

Now for Account. Though the presented information is accurate, it doesn't provide detailed information on the type. There also is a weird problem of the status enum being represented twice!

First off, use @Schema to customize the POJO itself and also the fields, as shown in the next listing.

Listing 12.4 Account

Customizes the field in the schema—specifying it is required—with a minimum length of 8, provides an example value, and defines its type as **INTEGER**

Defines the POJO name and description to be included in the schema and its object type

```
@Schema(name = "Account", description = "POJO representing an account.",
    type = SchemaType.OBJECT)
public class Account {
  @Schema(required = true, example = "123456789", minLength = 8, type =
    SchemaType.INTEGER)
  public Long accountNumber;
  @Schema(required = true, example = "432542374", minLength = 6, type =
    SchemaType.INTEGER)
```

```
    public Long customerNumber;
    @Schema(example = "Steve Hanger", type = SchemaType.STRING)   ◁──┐  Provides an
    public String customerName;                                        example, because
    @Schema(required = true, example = "438.32")                       it's not a
    public BigDecimal balance;                                         required field,
    @Schema(required = true, example = "OPEN")                         and specifies the
    public AccountStatus accountStatus = AccountStatus.OPEN;           STRING type
}
```

Though the generator does a good job of identifying the type of field for the schema, explicitly setting it—as opposed to staying with the default of no type—ensures there isn't a mistake in the generation that is missed. It never hurts to be more explicit than necessary in defining schemas.

> **NOTE** In a real application, a `customerName` would be required. However, listing 12.4 states it is not required to enable Swagger UI to show the difference between required and not-required fields.

Now the schema definition is looking better, but the `enum` field is still there twice. What's going on?

Taking a look at `Account`, the getter method to retrieve the account status is named `getStatus()`. Although a shorter method name for convenience works, in this case, the generator believes it's a different field on `Account`. Change the method name to `getAccountStatus()` and see how Swagger UI adjusts.

A nice side effect of providing example values for the `Account` POJO is that Swagger UI now shows example values that are more meaningful, as opposed to empty strings or zeroed values.

12.2.3 *Defining operations*

`@Operation` defines the details of a particular endpoint method. Developers can provide a `summary` message of what the endpoint does, as well a detailed `description` with additional details, possibly even example usage. The most important value to set on `@Operation` is `operationId`, because this provides a unique name for an endpoint in the entire OpenAPI document.

It's also possible to mark a method as `hidden` from the OpenAPI document. Try adding `@Operation(hidden = true)` to a method, then check out what the OpenAPI document and Swagger UI show. Nothing! Any method marked as hidden is completely removed. This is needed for methods on a JAX-RS resource that shouldn't be executed by clients but are required by the maintainers of the service. Depending on the service, a better approach could be an entirely separate JAX-RS resource that is hidden in the OpenAPI document, instead of hiding specific methods on the same resource.

Quarkus provides a means of defaulting the `operationId` for all endpoints using the following configuration property:

```
mp.openapi.extensions.smallrye.operationIdStrategy=METHOD
```

The METHOD strategy uses the Java method name as the operationId name. Other available strategies are CLASS_METHOD and PACKAGE_CLASS_METHOD. With the setting in place, look at the OpenAPI document to see the generated operationId generated for each method. In Swagger UI, there isn't a visible way to see the name, but if a method is selected, the operationId will be part of the new URL used to view a particular method's information.

What happens if further customization is needed? Is the operationIdStrategy setting ignored? No, developers do not need to replicate the name when wanting to specify additional operation information. Add an @Operation to createAccount specifying a description, as shown here:

```
@Operation(description = "Create a new bank account.")
public Response createAccount(Account account) {}
```

Notice operationId was not set with @Operation. The OpenAPI document still contains the operationId naming defined by the chosen strategy, while allowing descriptions or other customizations to be made. Take a look at the OpenAPI document and Swagger UI to see the new description.

12.2.4 *Operation responses*

Time to ensure all possible HTTP responses are properly documented in OpenAPI. Right now every method only defines a 200 response, which is a good start, but it doesn't cover all scenarios.

Let's begin! Looking at GET /accounts, a Set is returned, but there is no possibility for other response codes because there are no exceptions or custom responses defined. However, the odd-looking SetAccount schema type is being generated. It could be left as is, but there is no real need for a referencable schema type because it's the only method needing it.

Let's add an @APIResponse as shown next to remove the autogenerated schema type.

Listing 12.5 AccountResource.allAccounts()

```
@APIResponse(responseCode = "200", description = "Retrieved all Accounts",   ◁──┐
    content = @Content(                       ◁────────── Indicates the        Defines the 200
        schema = @Schema(              ◁──────── response           response with a
            type = SchemaType.ARRAY,                content            description
            implementation = Account.class)
    )
)
public Set<Account> allAccounts() {
    return accounts;
}
```

Specifies the schema for the response is an **ARRAY** with Account types within it

It's not necessary to include mediaType = "application/json" for @Content because the method has @Produces(MediaType.APPLICATION_JSON), meaning only a single media type for the response is possible. If the method supported multiple media types, multiple @Content values would be needed for each supported media type.

Head over to Swagger UI, refresh it, and see the updated GET /accounts detail and the removal of the SetAccount autogenerated schema.

Moving on to POST /accounts, AccountResource.createAccount, the response code, is wrong for a success because 200 cannot happen. It also misses the 400 that could be returned. To properly document the method, we need a couple of @API-Response entries, shown in the next listing.

Listing 12.6   `AccountResource.createAccount()`

Details the content of a response for code 201, an instance of Account in JSON format

A valid APIResponse for code 201 when successfully creating an account

```
@APIResponse(responseCode = "201", description = "Successfully created a new
    account.",
  content = @Content(
      schema = @Schema(implementation = Account.class))
)
@APIResponse(responseCode = "400",
    description = "No account number was specified on the Account.",
  content = @Content(
      schema = @Schema(
         implementation = ErrorResponse.class,
         example = "{\n" +
           "\"exceptionType\": \"javax.ws.rs.WebApplicationException\",\n" +
           "\"code\": 400,\n" +
           "\"error\": \"No Account number specified.\"\n" +
           "}\n")
     )
  )
public Response createAccount(Account account) {
}
```

Shows a failed response of 400 when no account number was provided

The type to represent the failed response. We cover ErrorResponse momentarily.

Provides an example of the JSON error response with actual values—this appears nicely in Swagger UI, as well as provides good detail for consumers of the OpenAPI document.

Those following along will have noticed that right now the code doesn't compile! The 400 failed response said it uses the ErrorResponse type as the schema, but it doesn't exist yet. With the custom exception mapper in AccountResource, a type is needed to represent the JSON output the failed response can provide. Let's add it now, as illustrated in the next listing.

Listing 12.7   `ErrorResponse`

```
private static class ErrorResponse {
    @Schema(required = true, example = "javax.ws.rs.WebApplicationException")
    public String exceptionType;
    @Schema(required = true, example = "400", type = SchemaType.INTEGER)
    public Integer code;
    public String error;
}
```

Because the ErrorResponse type is not needed by any actual code, it was added to the existing AccountResource as a private class.

IMPORTANT In the recently released MicroProfile OpenAPI 2.0, a new annotation, @SchemaProperty, was introduced to support inline schema type definitions. Once the release is available in Quarkus, ErrorResponse can be replaced with @SchemaProperty for each property of ErrorResponse.

Head over to Swagger UI to see how the POST method changed. The autogenerated 200 response is gone, replaced with the two valid responses added to createAccount.

NOTE Whether to use multiple @APIResponse annotations or place them all inside a single @APIResponses annotation is entirely a matter of personal choice for a developer. The OpenAPI document does not change based on which approach is chosen.

Moving on to GET /accounts/{accountNumber}, we need to make the following changes:

- @APIResponse for 200 and 400 HTTP response codes
- Document the accountNumber path parameter

Let's add them, as shown next.

Listing 12.8 AccountResource.getAccount()

```
@APIResponse(responseCode = "200",                          ◁── 200 response
    description = "Successfully retrieved an account.",          for successfully
    content = @Content(                                          retrieving an
        schema = @Schema(implementation = Account.class))        Account
)
    @APIResponse(responseCode = "400",
        description = "Account with id of {accountNumber} does not exist.",
        content = @Content(
            schema = @Schema(
                implementation = ErrorResponse.class,
                example = "{\n" +
                    "\"exceptionType\":
\"javax.ws.rs.WebApplicationException\",\n" +
                    "\"code\": 400,\n" +
                    "\"error\": \"Account with id of 12345678 does not
exist.\"\n" +
                    "}\n")
        )
    )
    public Account getAccount(
        @Parameter(
            name = "accountNumber",
            description = "Number of the Account instance to be retrieved.",
            required = true,
            in = ParameterIn.PATH                           ◁──
        )
        @PathParam("accountNumber") Long accountNumber) {
}
```

400 response when failing to find an Account, with an example exception response content

Adds @Parameter to document the @PathParam parameter of accountNumber. @Parameter needs to be added next to @PathParam for the generation to know they're related.

Specifies the parameter is a path parameter and doesn't come from a query string, header, or cookie

Indicates accountNumber is a required parameter. If it wasn't required, a different endpoint could potentially be matched instead.

With listing 12.8 added, refresh Swagger UI and the OpenAPI JSON document to verify the changes. Try out the method call in Swagger UI to make sure the defined responses align with what is actually received by a request.

Let's move on to PUT /accounts/{accountNumber}/deposit, shown next.

Listing 12.9 AccountResource.deposit()

```
@APIResponse(responseCode = "200", description = "Successfully deposited
    funds to an account.",
        content = @Content(
            schema = @Schema(implementation = Account.class))    Names the attribute
    )                                                            where the body of
                                                                 the request will be
    @RequestBody(                                                passed into the
        name = "amount",                                         method
Adds the OpenAPI  description = "Amount to be deposited into the account.",
definition of the required = true,              Passing an amount is
HTTP request body content = @Content(          definitely required.
the method should   schema = @Schema(
receive                 name = "amount",       Defines the possible content
                        type = SchemaType.STRING,  of the request body
                        required = true,
   Example             minLength = 4),         Schema of the request body. In this
   value of a          example = "435.61"      case a String with a minimum length
   request         )                           of 4. The minimum deposit is 1.00.
   body        )
                                               @Parameter similar to the one
    public Account deposit(                    on getAccount(), with a modified
        @Parameter(                            description for this method
            name = "accountNumber",
            description = "Number of the Account to deposit into.",
            required = true,
            in = ParameterIn.PATH
        )
        @PathParam("accountNumber") Long accountNumber,
        String amount) {
    }
```

Where the @RequestBody annotation is placed is a little flexible. It can be above the method name, as here, or inside the top of the method itself. Developer's preference is the only deciding factor. With listing 12.9, the content is always application/json because the method is annotated with a @Consumes. If it wasn't, multiple @Content sections with different examples should be added for each media type.

Check out the changes in Swagger UI, shown in figure 12.5, noticing the @RequestBody section is now marked required and has a meaningful example as well.

Exercise for the reader
As an exercise for the reader, add the necessary OpenAPI annotations to closeAccount() and withdrawal() on AccountResource. Verify it did what was expected in Swagger UI and the OpenAPI document.

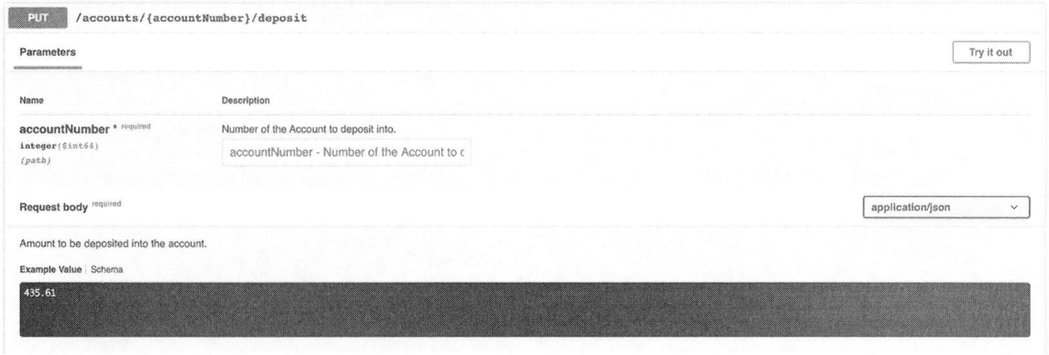

Figure 12.5 Swagger: `AccountResource.deposit` **method**

12.2.5 *Tagging operations*

Earlier in section 12.4, `@OpenAPIDefinition` included multiple `@Tag` annotations within the definition. When switching to using application.properties, it wasn't possible to include `@Tags`. How can we add these back in?

First, add the `@Tag` entries from previously to the top of the `AccountResource` as follows:

```
@Tag(name = "transactions",
    description = "Operations manipulating account balances.")
@Tag(name = "admin",
    description = "Operations for managing accounts.")
public class AccountResource {}
```

Two tags are defined: for transactions and admin. Looking at Swagger right now, we see all methods duplicated under each tag group—not what we want at all.

What is needed is adding either `@Tag(name = "admin")` or `@Tag(name = "transactions")` to each method on `AccountResource` to indicate which group a method falls into. With that done, it should look something like figure 12.6.

If all methods within a JAX-RS resource fall under a single grouping, or `@Tag`, it's not necessary to add a `@Tag` to each method. There needs to be only a single instance on the class. If it's possible to split methods across different resource classes, aligned with their grouping, it saves having to add `@Tag` to every method!

We haven't covered all possible annotations, such as `@Header`, `@Callback`, and `@Link`. Take some time to review them in the MicroProfile OpenAPI specification (http://mng.bz/xXD7), and try them out.

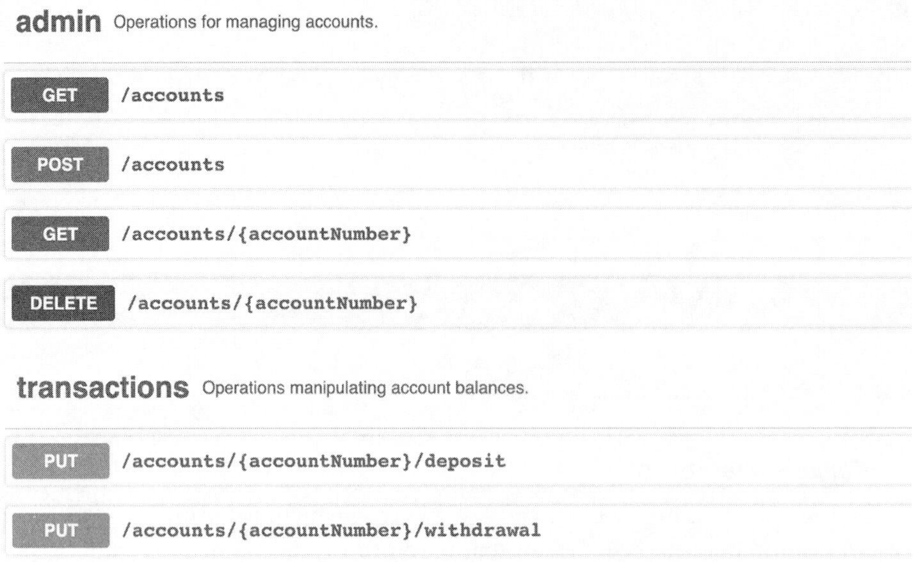

admin Operations for managing accounts.

| GET | /accounts |

| POST | /accounts |

| GET | /accounts/{accountNumber} |

| DELETE | /accounts/{accountNumber} |

transactions Operations manipulating account balances.

| PUT | /accounts/{accountNumber}/deposit |

| PUT | /accounts/{accountNumber}/withdrawal |

Figure 12.6   Swagger: endpoints grouped by `@Tag`

12.2.6 *Filtering OpenAPI content*

The MicroProfile OpenAPI specification provides a way to customize the generated OpenAPI document before it's returned. Developers can implement `OASFilter` to perform customizations. Let's see how that works in the next listing.

Listing 12.10   `OpenApiFilter`

OpenApiFilter implements OASFilter from MicroProfile OpenAPI.

The method to filter Operation instances present in the OpenAPI document

```
public class OpenApiFilter implements OASFilter {
  @Override
  public Operation filterOperation(Operation operation) {
    if (operation.getOperationId().equals("closeAccount")) {
      operation.setTags(List.of("close-account"));
    }
    return operation;
  }
}
```

Makes a change only when the operationId is closeAccount. Change the Tag to be called close-account.

With the filter written, it needs to be activated with a change to application.properties. Add the following configuration:

```
mp.openapi.filter=quarkus.accounts.OpenApiFilter
```

Refresh the Swagger UI page and see the new method grouping the filter created.

We can customize and tailor any aspects of an OpenAPI document as needed. Look through OASFilter to see all the methods that can be implemented. One thing to bear in mind: it's not possible to *add* new elements into an OpenAPI document with a filter. Though listing 12.10 added a new tag name into the document, it wasn't possible to set a description for the tag.

12.3 *Design-first development*

Design-first development, also known as *contract-first* development, is when an OpenAPI document is created by describing the service being developed before writing any code. This approach can be a good way of validating whether an API *makes sense* before writing any code. Once validated, an OpenAPI generator can then be used to generate the service based on the OpenAPI document as a starting point for implementing a service.

One point of note with generation is it is a *one-way* process. When service methods are generated from an OpenAPI document, once the methods are implemented, there is no way to regenerate the method signatures without losing the implementation. It's not entirely the end of the world—developers need to make sure they're generating service methods only after the OpenAPI document isn't expected to change anymore. If it does, it becomes a manual process of keeping the service implementation in sync with an OpenAPI document as methods are added, removed, or modified.

We have many tools for designing an API using the OpenAPI specification without code, including Swagger Editor (https://swagger.io/tools/swagger-editor/) (from the creators of the OpenAPI Specification), Apicurio Studio (https://www.apicur.io/studio/), and many others.

With an OpenAPI document in hand, we can use a generator such as https://openapi-generator.tech/ to generate code from it, though using a generator is not the focus of this chapter.

12.3.1 *OpenAPI file base*

To show how to use an existing OpenAPI document with a service in Quarkus, we copied the Account service from earlier in the chapter to /chapter12/account-service-external-openapi. The main difference is all references to MicroProfile OpenAPI annotations were removed from AccountResource and Account classes—the OpenAPI definitions will come from an external file—and the configuration in application .properties was removed. In addition, OpenApiFilter was removed because what it does is already present in the OpenAPI document.

With the source code in place, either by generation or removing previously existing annotations, where does the OpenAPI definition come from for the service?

First, we need the OpenAPI document as a separate file. Download the YAML of the Account service from earlier in the chapter at http://localhost:8080/q/openapi. Rename the downloaded file from openapi to openapi.yaml, then move it into the /src/main/resources/META-INF directory of the new project.

Adding `mp.openapi.scan.disable=true` to application.properties will ensure the static OpenAPI document in the project will be served "as is." Without this setting, Quarkus will generate an OpenAPI document combining the static document with the model generated from the application code.

Start the service with `mvn quarkus:dev`, and verify the OpenAPI document and Swagger UI look and behave as expected. The service should behave exactly the same as the alternative version from earlier in the chapter.

12.3.2 *Mixing the file and annotations*

We have a few options for combining a static file with annotations in code. The OpenAPI document could be the main source of truth, with minor modifications made to annotations in code. Or an OpenAPI document could contain common schema definitions, with code annotations referencing them.

First, remove the `mp.openapi.scan.disable` configuration from application .properties. Doing so enables the annotations in code to mix with the static OpenAPI document.

Add `@Tag(name = "all-accounts", description = "Separate grouping because we can")` to `AccountResource.allAccounts()`, and see how Swagger UI adjusts, as shown in figure 12.7.

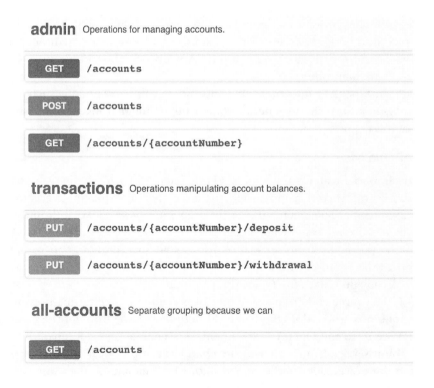

Figure 12.7   Swagger: mixing a static OpenAPI document and annotations

12.4 Code first or OpenAPI first?

In this chapter, we explored different ways to integrate OpenAPI documents with code. Code-first requires adding annotations to code for @APIResponse, @Request-Body, @Parameter, @Operation, @Tag, and others, to customize the content of a generated OpenAPI document. Design-first defines an OpenAPI document representing the desired service and references the static file for serving the document. What's the best option? It depends! (All developers' favorite saying.)

Some situations where OpenAPI first could be the better option follow:

- Nondevelopers are defining the API and are therefore more likely to be using an OpenAPI tool to create it.
- Some teams need to implement the service, whereas other teams will be communicating with the service as clients. If the service isn't already implemented, working on a shared API definition before either team begins developing can help prevent issues later.

How about when to use code first? Some scenarios include the following:

- When services are already implemented, it is often easier to autogenerate the OpenAPI document and add annotations to customize it as needed.
- If the exact structure and content of an API isn't already known and requires prototyping, it's hard to define an OpenAPI document if it's unknown what the API needs to be.

Another factor to consider when choosing whether to use annotations in code is the impact it has on the code itself. Comparing AccountResource content between the two services, the version with annotations in the code is almost double the size. That's a large impact both to the size of the code and also the readability of the code with all the extra annotations present.

> **Exercise for the reader**
> As an exercise for the reader, deploy the service to Minikube and view the OpenAPI document. Try accessing Swagger UI—it shouldn't be present by default.

Summary

- Including the quarkus-smallrye-openapi dependency is all that's required to generate an OpenAPI document automatically from code.
- OpenAPI documentation of a service is available by accessing http://localhost: 8080/q/openapi.
- While live coding, use Swagger UI at http://localhost:8080/q/swagger-ui for visualizing the OpenAPI document content, but also to try out the API with the actual service.

- Use MicroProfile OpenAPI annotations, such as `@OpenAPIDefinition` and `@Operation`, to customize the generated OpenAPI document.
- When using a design-first approach, you modify a service to serve a static version of the OpenAPI document instead of generating it.

Securing a microservice

This chapter covers

- Securing microservices with authentication and authorization
- Quarkus authentication and authorization options
- Utilizing Quarkus file-based user and role definitions during development to secure REST endpoints
- Utilizing Keycloak and OpenID Connect to authenticate users and generate JWT tokens
- Securing microservices using MicroProfile JWT
- Quarkus features that facilitate unit testing

Enterprises require secure applications to prevent unauthorized access to information. This chapter focuses on authentication and authorization as two primary application security measures. This chapter updates the Bank service, Account service, and Transaction service with new endpoints that require authenticated users. The new, secured endpoints will exist alongside the existing insecure endpoints so services can easily switch between them. These services will also require a user to belong to a specific role to access new, secured REST endpoints. Existing REST endpoints will continue to work so the reader can compare the approaches.

13.1 *Authorization and authentication overview*

Let's define a the following terms before continuing to figure 13.1:

- *Authentication*—A user has validated that they are who they say they are by providing credentials like a username and password or a validated JWT token. Authenticated users can be assigned roles, like Bank `customer` and Bank `teller`.
- *Authorization*—The act of granting access to a resource. In figure 13.1, only authenticated users assigned to the proper role have access to the secure endpoints.
- *Identity provider*—A facility that manages user identities, like LDAP, a file, a database, or Keycloak.
- *Security context*—The application contains a security context for each request that includes an authenticated user's assigned roles.

Figure 13.1 depicts the Bank application identity providers (application.properties, Keycloak) and the credential flow (e.g., username and role) used to access new, secure REST endpoints added in this chapter.

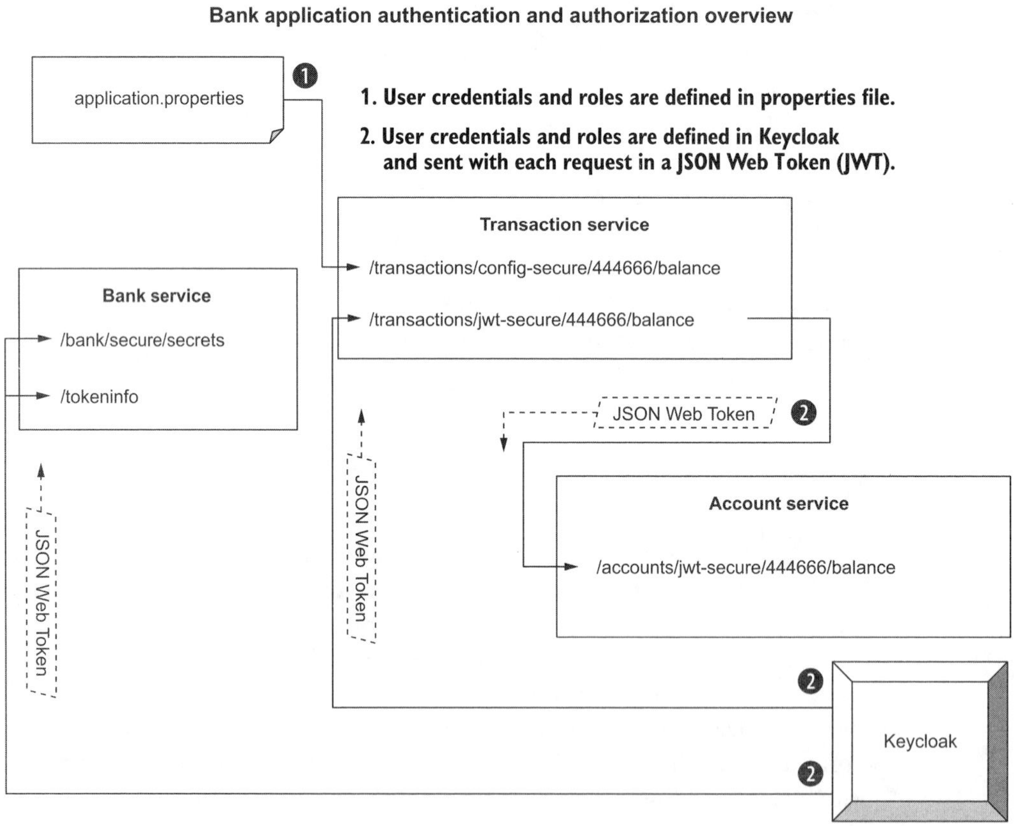

Bank application authentication and authorization overview

Figure 13.1   Authentication and authorization overview

The next listing illustrates a simple code example of securing access to a method within an application using a Java annotation. Additional authorization mechanisms, like defining roles using Java properties, are covered as well.

Listing 13.1 Authorizing Java method access

```
@RolesAllowed("customer")
public void getBalance() {
    // ...
}
```

◁— The getBalance() method authorizes access only to users assigned the customer role.

Tables 13.1 and 13.2 list supported Quarkus authentication and authorization mechanisms, respectively. Mechanisms identified with an asterisk (*) are covered in detail throughout the remainder of the chapter.

Table 13.1 Quarkus authentication mechanisms

Mechanism	Description
Basic*	An HTTP user agent (e.g., web browser) requests user credentials.
Form	Presents a web form (e.g., HTML) to obtain user credentials.
Mutual TLS	Authenticates users based on their X.509 certificate.
OpenID Connect (OIDC)*	An industry standard authentication layer that builds on OAuth 2.0. Delegates authentication to an OpenID Connect provider like Keycloak. Quarkus supports the OIDC Authorization Code and Implicit Flows.
MicroProfile JWT*	Supports a JSON Web Token (JWT) bearer token containing a verified user identity.
LDAP	LDAP server requests user credentials.

Table 13.2 Quarkus authorization mechanisms

Mechanism	Description
OAuth 2.0	An industry standard protocol for granting a third-party authorization to access a user's protected resources
Configuration*	Specifies application authorization rules using configuration properties
Annotations*	Specifies application authorization rules using security-related annotations from the Jakarta Annotations specification's (https://eclipse-ee4j.github.io/common-annotations-api/apidocs/) @PermitAll and @RolesAllowed

13.2 Using file-based authentication and authorization

One approach to securing the Transaction service uses the Quarkus built-in HTTP policy configuration and a file-based identity provider. This approach is both effective and highly productive when developing a microservice. To add support for defining user credentials and roles using configuration properties, add the quarkus-elytron-security-properties-file extension as shown in the next listing.

Listing 13.2 Adding the quarkus-elytron-security-properties-file extension

```
cd transaction-service
mvn quarkus:add-extension -Dextensions=quarkus-elytron-security-properties-file
```

Next, create a method in TransactionResource.java to be secured by file security as shown next.

Listing 13.3 Adding a new method to TransactionResource.java

```
@GET
@Path("/config-secure/{acctnumber}/balance")
@Produces(MediaType.APPLICATION_JSON)
@Consumes(MediaType.APPLICATION_JSON)
public Response secureConfigGetBalance(@PathParam("acctnumber") Long
      accountNumber) {
  return getBalance(accountNumber);
}
```

secureConfigGetBalance() has the same functionality and method signature as getBalance() but is available at a different REST subpath that will be secured using configuration properties.

The Quarkus built-in HTTP request authorization implementation uses configuration properties. Add the properties in the following listing to the Transaction service application.properties.

Listing 13.4 Configuring the HTTP policy and file users

Refines the customer permission to allow only authenticated users to access the secured endpoint

Defines a customer permission that defines an endpoint to secure

```
# Security using Quarkus built-in policy controls

quarkus.http.auth.permission.customer.paths=/transactions/config-secure/*
quarkus.http.auth.permission.customer.methods=GET
quarkus.http.auth.permission.customer.policy=authenticated

# Security - Embedded users/roles (File realm)

%dev.quarkus.security.users.embedded.enabled=true
%dev.quarkus.security.users.embedded.plain-text=true
%dev.quarkus.security.users.embedded.users.duke=duke
%dev.quarkus.security.users.embedded.roles.duke=customer
%dev.quarkus.security.users.embedded.users.quarkus=quarkus
%dev.quarkus.security.users.embedded.roles.quarkus=teller

# Enable HTTP basic authentication, which this application uses
# only during development

%dev.quarkus.http.auth.basic=true
```

Authorizes GET requests on the endpoint

Creates user duke with a password of duke

Assigns user duke the customer role

Creates user quarkus with a password of quarkus

Assigns user quarkus the bank teller role

Enables HTTP basic authentication. The user is prompted to provide a username and password when using a web browser. When using the curl command, user credentials are provided using the --user command line option, like --user duke:duke.

Enables clear-text passwords. If set to false or omitted, then the password is assumed to be an MD5 password hash. Only clear-text and MD5 hashed passwords are currently supported.

Enables embedded users and roles. Defining users, roles, and passwords using properties is useful when in development mode.

NOTE Using configuration files is generally too limiting for production but is useful during development and testing.

Before testing authentication and authorization, start the required services as shown in the following listing.

Listing 13.5   Starting the database, Account service, and Transaction service

```
minikube start        ◁──────── Starts minikube

kubectl apply -f postgresql_kubernetes.yml    ◁──┐
kubectl port-forward service/postgres 5432:5432    ◁──┐

mvn quarkus:dev    ◁────────────────┐
mvn clean quarkus:dev -Ddebug=5006    ◁──┘
```

From the chapter top-level directory, deploys the Postgres database to Kubernetes if it is not already running

Proxies the Postgres database to localhost so it can be used by local services

In a new window, starts the Transaction service from the transaction-service subdirectory

In a new window, starts the Account service from the account-service subdirectory

Manually test the endpoint using `curl` as shown in the next listing, with the output shown in the subsequent listing.

Listing 13.6   Testing a secured endpoint using built-in permissions

```
TRANSACTION_URL=http://localhost:8088

curl -i \        ◁──────┐
  -H "Accept: application/json" \
  $TRANSACTION_URL/transactions/config-secure/444666/balance
```

Accesses the secured endpoint without specifying a user

Listing 13.7   Testing a secured endpoint output without specifying a user

```
HTTP/1.1 401 Unauthorized        ◁──┐
www-authenticate: basic realm="Quarkus"
content-length: 0
```

The result is HTTP/1.1 401 Unauthorized when no authenticated user is provided.

Test the endpoint with an authenticated user using `curl` as shown in the following listing, with the output in listing 13.9.

Listing 13.8   Testing a secured endpoint with an authenticated user

```
curl -i \
  -H "Accept: application/json" \
  --user duke:duke \        ◁──
  $TRANSACTION_URL/transactions/config-secure/444666/balance
```

Specifies user duke with a password of duke. Because duke is an authenticated user defined using file configuration properties, the method call is allowed (listing 13.9).

Listing 13.9   Validating user output

```
HTTP/1.1 200 OK        ◁──┐
Content-Length: 7
Content-Type: application/json
```

Grants access and returns a result when an authenticated user, duke, is provided

3499.12

Test the endpoint with second authenticated user using `curl` as shown in listing 13.10 with the output in listing 13.11.

Listing 13.10   Testing a secured endpoint using built-in permissions with embedded users

```
curl -i \
  -H "Accept: application/json" \
  --user quarkus:quarkus \
  $TRANSACTION_URL/transactions/config-secure/444666/balance
```

Specify user quarkus with a password of quarkus.

Listing 13.11   Testing secured endpoint output with second authenticated user

```
HTTP/1.1 200 OK
Content-Length: 7
Content-Type: application/json

3499.12
```

User quarkus is also an authenticated user, and access is allowed.

To limit access to customers in a specific role, replace the `authenticated` authorization policy with the one shown in the following listing.

Listing 13.12   Testing a secured endpoint output

Applies the customer-policy policy to the customer permission

Creates a policy, customer-policy, that grants access to users that are assigned the customer role

```
quarkus.http.auth.policy.customer-policy.roles-allowed=customer
quarkus.http.auth.permission.customer.paths=/transactions/config-secure/*
quarkus.http.auth.permission.customer.methods=GET
quarkus.http.auth.permission.customer.policy=customer-policy
# quarkus.http.auth.permission.customer.policy=authenticated
```

Comments out the prior authenticated policy

Manually test `customer-policy` by using `curl` to invoke the endpoint with a user in the `customer` role and a user in the `teller` role, as shown in the next code, with the expected output in listing 13.14.

Listing 13.13   Testing a secured endpoint output

Tests with user quarkus, who is assigned the teller role. The request returns an HTTP Forbidden response (listing 13.14) because user quarkus is assigned the teller role and not the customer role.

```
curl -i \
  -H "Accept: application/json" \
  --user quarkus:quarkus \
  $TRANSACTION_URL/transactions/config-secure/444666/balance

curl -i \
  -H "Accept: application/json" \
  --user duke:duke \
  $TRANSACTION_URL/transactions/config-secure/444666/balance
```

Tests with user duke, who is assigned the customer role. The HTTP OK response and the account balance (listing 13.14) is returned because user duke is assigned the customer role.

Listing 13.14 Testing a secured endpoint output

```
HTTP/1.1 403 Forbidden
content-length: 0

HTTP/1.1 200 OK
Content-Length: 7
Content-Type: application/json

3499.12
```

Using curl is a convenient way of testing code while making rapid iterative changes during development. However, Quarkus makes testing secured endpoints easy as well. Quarkus supports testing secured endpoints by defining users and roles with the @TestSecurity annotation. To use the @TestSecurity annotation, add the quarkus-test-security dependency in the test scope to the Transaction service pom.xml as follows.

Listing 13.15 Adding a dependency to Transaction service pom.xml

```xml
<dependency>
  <groupId>io.quarkus</groupId>
  <artifactId>quarkus-test-security</artifactId>
  <scope>test</scope>
</dependency>
```

Create SecurityTest.java in the transaction-service/test/java/io/quarkus/transactions directory to be used to test the Transaction service security. See the next listing.

Listing 13.16 Testing roles and security

@TestSecurity defines a user, duke, in the customer role. Because it is applied to the TestSecurity class, it will be applied to all test methods in the class. This duke user applies only when running tests, whereas the embedded duke user defined in application.properties applies only during development.

```java
import static io.restassured.RestAssured.given;
import static org.hamcrest.CoreMatchers.containsString;

@QuarkusTest
@QuarkusTestResource(WiremockAccountService.class)
@TestSecurity(user = "duke", roles = { "customer" })
public class SecurityTest {
    @Test
    public void built_in_security() {
        given()
          .when()
          .get("/transactions/config-secure/{acctNumber}/balance", 121212)
        .then()
          .statusCode(200)
          .body(containsString("435.76"));
    }
}
```

SecurityTest uses the mocked AccountService, introduced in an earlier chapter, to return predefined values for Account service HTTP endpoints.

Gets the balance using the config-secure endpoint

Validates the balance

Stop the Account service to avoid a port conflict with `WireMockAccountService` by pressing CTRL-C to stop the Account service running in development mode. Next, follow the steps shown in the next listing.

Listing 13.17   Running the security test

```
mvn test \
    -Dtest=SecurityTest    ◁─┐
```
Only runs SecurityTest to speed up the testing.
Optionally, run all tests by omitting this line.

13.3   *Authentication and authorization with OpenID Connect*

In this section, we use OpenID Connect (OIDC) to access new secure REST endpoints in the Bank service.

13.3.1   *Introduction to OpenID Connect (OIDC)*

OAuth 2.0 is an industry standard authorization protocol for how a third-party application can obtain limited access to another application.

> *OAuth 2.0 is the industry-standard protocol for authorization. OAuth 2.0 focuses on client developer simplicity while providing specific authorization flows for web applications, desktop applications, mobile phones, and living room devices.*
>
> —OAuth2 website

Although Quarkus supports OAuth 2.0, detailed coverage is beyond the scope of this chapter. OIDC adds an identity layer on OAuth 2.0 that supports authentication and controlled access to user identity. Historically, a service might have to present the user's login information, like a username and password, to a third-party service to gain access to its user data and functionality. This would result in the third-party service having the user credentials and coarse-grained access to the user's data provided by that service. Imagine having a third-party payment-processing service requiring a user's Bank service username and password!

For the remainder of the chapter, we focus on using OIDC to authenticate a user and provide enough user identity—and their role, in particular—to access secure endpoints.

13.3.2   *OIDC and Keycloak*

OIDC is a layer on OAuth 2.0 that adds authentication flows. This chapter focuses on the following flows:

- *Authorization Code Flow*—An unauthenticated user trying to access a protected resource is first redirected to an OpenID Connect provider to authenticate.
- *Implicit Flow*—A service accesses an OpenID Connect provider directly to obtain a token to access protected resources.

In preparation for securing services using OIDC, let's review the following points:

- First, this chapter uses Keycloak as an identity provider. Running Keycloak alongside services supporting other chapters, like Prometheus and Grafana, requires at least 5 GB of memory.
- The two options follow:
  - Start Minikube with more memory as shown in the next listing.

Listing 13.18   Starting Minikube with more memory

```
minikube delete
minikube start --memory=5120
```
Deletes the current Minikube cluster, which also deletes any work done in previous chapters

Starts Minikube with 5 GB of memory

- If the desktop does not have enough memory to allocate 5 GB of memory, delete the monitoring namespace created in chapter 10, as shown in listing 13.19. Metrics are still available by accessing a service's `/q/metrics` endpoint directly. The monitoring namespace can be recreated by following the steps in chapter 10.

Listing 13.19   Deleting the monitoring namespace

```
kubectl delete ns monitoring
```

After ensuring enough memory is available, install Keycloak using the Keycloak Operator (https://github.com/keycloak/keycloak-operator) as shown in listing 13.20. A Kubernetes *Operator* manages the life cycle of a service, and the Keycloak Operator manages the Keycloak life cycle. The installation uses version 14.0.0 of the Keycloak Operator.

Listing 13.20   Installing Keycloak into the Kubernetes `keycloak` namespace

Adds the host keycloak.local to /etc/hosts so Keycloak host lookups resolve to the Minikube IP address. The hosts file on Windows 10 is at C:\Windows\System32\drivers\etc\hosts.

```
echo "$(minikube ip) keycloak.local" | sudo tee -a /etc/hosts
scripts/install_keycloak.sh
```
Runs this command from the top-level chapter13 directory. The script is heavily commented.

NOTE   Installing Keycloak can take several minutes depending on RAM, processor speed, and internet connection. Several "pods keycloak-0 not found" messages may appear during installation. Explaining the Keycloak installation is beyond the scope of this chapter, but the script is heavily commented.

Also beyond the scope of this chapter, Keycloak console access can be useful when problems occur. The console is available at http://keycloak.local/auth/admin/. The username is admin. To obtain the password, run the command in the next code.

Listing 13.21   Getting the Keycloak admin password

```
kubectl get secret credential-bank-keycloak \
        -n keycloak \
        -o go-template='{{range $k,$v := .data}}{{printf "%s: " $k}}
        ⮕ {{if not $v}}{{$v}}{{else}}{{$v | base64decode}}{{end}}
        ⮕ {{"\n"}}{{end}}'
```

The Keycloak *bank realm* defines four users and their assigned roles as outlined in table 13.3.

Table 13.3   Quarkus authorization mechanisms

Username	Password	Role
admin	admin	bankadmin
duke	duke	customer
jwt	jwt	customer
quarkus	quarkus	teller

13.3.3   *Accessing a protected resource with OpenID Connect*

OIDC Authorization Code Flow defers user authentication to an authentication server, Keycloak, in this case. Figure 13.2 explains the flow.

To explain with more detail:

1   The user accesses a protected resource, perhaps protected by the built-in HTTP security policy or @RolesAllowed.
2   The Bank service will redirect the user to the OIDC provider specified with the quarkus.oidc.auth-server-url property. The OIDC provider used in this chapter is Keycloak.
3   The OIDC provider presents the user with an authentication form to enter a username and password. This step is covered in more detail later.
4   Upon successful authentication, Keycloak returns a JWT token and an HTTP redirect to the originally requested resource. We explain JWT's role in the authorization shortly.
5   The browser is redirected to the protected resource.
6   The service successfully returns the resource contents.

To use OIDC with Quarkus, add the Quarkus OIDC extension to the Bank service and start the service as follows.

Listing 13.22   Adding the OIDC extension and starting the Bank service

```
cd bank_service
mvn quarkus:add-extension -Dextensions="quarkus-oidc"    ⟵  Adds the OIDC
                                                              extension
```

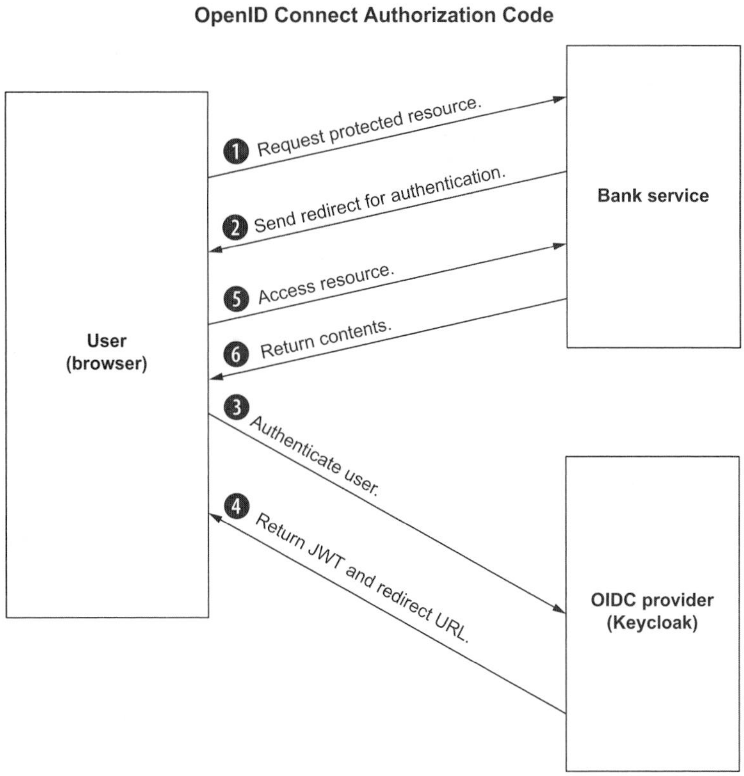

OpenID Connect Authorization Code

Figure 13.2 Authorization Code Flow

After adding the OIDC extension, configure the Bank service to interoperate with the OIDC server (Keycloak) as shown in the next code listing.

Listing 13.23 Bank service application.properties

**The OIDC extension will compare the token issuer with this issuer,
ensuring the token came from the proper, trusted source.**

```
# Security
quarkus.oidc.enabled=true
quarkus.oidc.tls.verification=none
quarkus.oidc.token.issuer=https://keycloak.local/auth/realms/bank
%dev.quarkus.oidc.auth-server-url=https://keycloak.local/auth/realms/bank
%prod.quarkus.oidc.auth-server-url=https://keycloak:8443/auth/realms/bank
quarkus.oidc.client-id=bank
```

**Enables OIDC
authentication**

**Disables TLS verification of
the self-signed certificate
installed by the Keycloak
Operator**

**The URL for
Keycloak as
an OpenID
identity
provider in
production.**

**The OIDC client ID. An OIDC client ID typically has
an associated client secret (e.g., password),
the credentials for a client to access an
identity provider. To keep things simple, the
bank client does not have a client secret.**

**The URL for Keycloak as an
OIDC authorization server
when running locally. The bank
realm is specified in the URL.**

```
quarkus.oidc.application-type=web-app
username=admin
password=secret
```

Uses the Authorization Code Flow (web app). The OIDC extension redirects the user to a Keycloak-provided login screen.

The Bank service, copied from chapter 3, requires the username and password properties to be defined. These properties are not used in this example.

Update the Bank service to add a `BankResource.getSecureSecrets()` method to secure access to the `/bank/secure/secrets` endpoint so only an administrator can view them, as shown here.

Listing 13.24   Securing the existing `BankResource.getSecureSecrets()` method

```
@RolesAllowed("bankadmin")
@GET
@Produces(MediaType.APPLICATION_JSON)
@Path("/secure/secrets")
public Map<String, String> secureGetSecrets() {
    return getSecrets();
}
```

Secures the endpoint with @RolesAllowed so only users in the bankadmin role can access the /bank/secure/secrets endpoint

Creates a new method named secureGetSecrets()

The method calls the existing getSecrets method.

Start the Bank service as shown in the next listing.

Listing 13.25   Starting the Bank service

```
mvn quarkus:dev -Ddebug=5008 -Dquarkus.http.port=8008
```

Starts the Bank service. The mvn command specifies the debug and HTTP ports to avoid potential port conflicts with the Account service and Transaction service.

With the Bank service up and running, browse to http://localhost:8008/bank/secure/secrets. As shown in figure 13.3, attempting to access /bank/secure/secrets will redirect the browser to Keycloak to obtain user credentials.

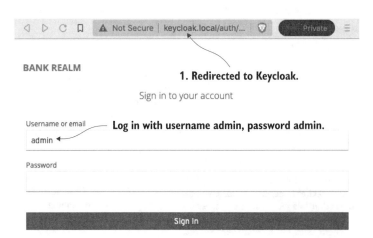

Figure 13.3   Redirect to Keycloak for user authentication

After logging in with a username (admin) and password (admin), Keycloak redirects the browser back to the original /bank/secure/secrets endpoint to display the secrets as shown next.

Listing 13.26   Output of the `/bank/secure/secrets` endpoint

```
{"password":"secret","db.password":"secret","db.username":"admin","username":
    "admin"}
```

> **IMPORTANT**   The browser will likely not trust the Keycloak self-signed certificate. However, the self-signed certificate must be trusted by "agreeing to proceed" to test Keycloak authentication and access the secured REST endpoint. This is the final browser-related exercise, so feel free not to trust the certificate and skip testing this functionality.

Having to run Keycloak to unit test the Code Authorization Flow is heavy and tedious. The following section introduces the `OidcWiremockTestResource` to replace Keycloak as an OIDC authorization server for unit testing.

13.3.4   Testing the Code Authorization Flow

Keycloak has been the authentication and authorization server behind supporting the OIDC Code Authorization Flow. Quarkus offers an OIDC WireMock that can replace a Keycloak instance during a test of the Bank service. To use the OIDC WireMock, add the dependency shown in the next listing to pom.xml.

Listing 13.27   The Bank service pom.xml WireMock dependency

```
<dependency>
    <groupId>io.quarkus</groupId>
    <artifactId>quarkus-junit5</artifactId>        <-- Adds JUnit5 testing support
    <scope>test</scope>
</dependency>
<dependency>
    <groupId>io.rest-assured</groupId>
    <artifactId>rest-assured</artifactId>          <-- Tests REST endpoints using the RESTassured framework
    <scope>test</scope>
</dependency>
<dependency>
    <groupId>io.quarkus</groupId>
    <artifactId>quarkus-test-oidc-server</artifactId>  <-- The dependency that includes the Quarkus OIDC WireMock server
    <scope>test</scope>
</dependency>
<dependency>
    <groupId>net.sourceforge.htmlunit</groupId>
    <artifactId>htmlunit</artifactId>              <-- UI-less web browser. The testing uses HtmlUnit to browse through the Keycloak login UI.
    <version>2.36.0</version>
    <scope>test</scope>
</dependency>
```

Next, add a `src/test/java/io/quarkus/bank/BankTest.java` class to the Bank service to test the Code Authorization Flow as follows.

Listing 13.28 `src/test/java/io/quarkus/bank/BankTest.java`

Utilizes the OidcWiremockTestResource class to simulate an OIDC authorization server like Keycloak. The life cycle of the WireMock is bound to the life cycle of the BankTest.java class.

Creates a WebClient, which is the entry point into HtmlUnit

```java
import static org.junit.jupiter.api.Assertions.assertTrue;


@QuarkusTest
@QuarkusTestResource(OidcWiremockTestResource.class)
public class BankTest {
  @Test
  public void testGetSecrets() throws IOException {
    try (final WebClient webClient = createWebClient()) {
      webClient.getOptions().setRedirectEnabled(true);
      HtmlPage page =
        webClient.getPage("http://localhost:8081/bank/secure/secrets");

      HtmlForm loginForm = page.getForms().get(0);

      loginForm.getInputByName("username").setValueAttribute("admin");
      loginForm.getInputByName("password").setValueAttribute("admin");

      UnexpectedPage json = loginForm.getInputByValue("login").click();

      Jsonb jsonb = JsonbBuilder.create();
      HashMap<String, String> credentials =
        jsonb.fromJson(json.getWebResponse().getContentAsString(),
                    HashMap.class);
      assertTrue(credentials.get("username").equals("admin"));
      assertTrue(credentials.get("password").equals("secret"));
    }
  }

  private WebClient createWebClient() {
    WebClient webClient = new WebClient();
    webClient.setCssErrorHandler(new SilentCssErrorHandler());
    return webClient;
  }
}
```

Enables HTTP redirect in the WebClient for OIDC web authentication

Accesses the /bank/secure/secrets endpoint, which results in a redirect to the WireMocked Keycloak login page

Loads the Keycloak login page

Sets the username as admin

Sets the password as admin

Gets the result as a string, parses it as JSON, and stores it in a HashMap

Asserts the returned password is secret

Asserts the returned username is admin

Clicks the Submit button, which has a form value parameter of login. The result is of type UnexpectedPage because the response is JSON and not an HTML page.

Returns an HtmlUnit WebClient as the entry point into the HtmlUnit framework

The application needs to be configured properly to use the mocked OIDC server. The next code listing updates the test configuration to properly utilize the mocked server.

Listing 13.29 The Bank service application.properties

```
%test.quarkus.oidc.auth-server-url=${keycloak.url}/realms/quarkus    ◁──┐
```

Directs the test framework to the mocked OIDC server. OidcWiremockTestResource.class replaces ${keycloak.url} with the host and port of the mocked OIDC server. OidcWiremockTestResource.class also preconfigures a quarkus realm.

Run the test as shown in the following listing.

Listing 13.30 Running the test

Sets the role to be stored in the generated token. The role is set to bankadmin because that is the role required to access the /bank/secure/secrets endpoint.

```
mvn test \
  -Dquarkus.test.oidc.token.admin-roles="bankadmin" \    ◁──
  -Dquarkus.test.oidc.token.issuer=https://keycloak.local/auth/realms/bank    ◁──

# Test should pass
```

Defines the token issuer, overriding the default value (see table 13.4)

Listing 13.30 shows the `OidcWiremockTestResource` settings that can be overridden using system properties. Table 13.4 shows the overridable `OidcWiremockTestResource` properties. These properties must be set as system properties and are not currently configurable using MicroProfile Config.

Table 13.4 `OidcWiremockTestResource` **properties**

Property	Default Value
quarkus.test.oidc.token.user-roles	user
quarkus.test.oidc.token.admin-roles	user, admin
quarkus.test.oidc.token.issuer	https://server.example.com
quarkus.test.oidc.token.audience	https://server.example.com

`OidcWiremockTestResource` also defines two users. The first is user `admin`, with a password of `admin` and assigned role of `admin`. The second is user `alice`, with a password of `alice` and assigned role of `user`. Listing 13.30 overrides the default `admin` roles with `bankadmin`, which is required by the `/bank/secure/secrets` endpoint. The default token issuer is https://server.example.com and is overridden in listing 13.30 with https://keycloak.local/auth/realms/bank.

The OIDC Code Authorization Flow uses a JSON Web Token (JWT) for authentication and authorization. The following section discusses JWT, the MicroProfile JWT API, and how JWT allows access to the secured endpoint.

13.4 *Json Web Tokens (JWT) and MicroProfile JWT*

Like the Bank example used throughout this book, a microservices architecture often revolves around REST APIs, which in turn require REST security. REST microservices tend to be stateless, so they benefit from the stateless security approach offered by JWT. The security state is encapsulated in lightweight JSON Web Tokens (JWT) defined in RFC 7519 (https://datatracker.ietf.org/doc/html/rfc7519). Because JWTs are lightweight, they are propagated efficiently through a chain of REST service calls.

A JWT contains three sections—a header, a payload, and a signature—with a dot separating each section ("."). For example, a sample token is shown in listing 13.31 in the raw form. The *italicized* text is the JWT header, the **bold** text is the JWT payload, and the underlined text is the JWT signature, which, if valid, verifies that the token has not been tampered with.

Listing 13.31 Sample Base64-encoded JWT

```
eyJhbGci0iJSUzI1NiIsInR5cCIgOiAiSldUIiwia2lkIiA6ICJHNjZaUWxsTmNoOWVLVVB3VGp
nVWJTcTB1eTN6aFJmeFZiOUItTUxNOG9FIn0.eyJleHAiOjE2MjM1NTM5MjIsImlhdCI6MTYyM
zU1MzYyMiwiYXV0aF90aW1lIjoxNjIzNTUzNjE3LCJqdGkiOiI3NWI5MmZhZi02ZTVkLTRlMjItY
WFlYi02NWYyOTJjMzU2YWMiLCJpc3MiOiJodHRwczovL2tleWNsb2FrLmxvY2FsL2F1dGgvcmVhb
G1zL2JhbmsiLCJzdWIiOiJlZGJiMzlkMC1jNmZhLTQyMTEtYTc1Yy03MGQ5MzQwMzE2MjAiLCJ0e
XAiOiJCZWFyZXIiLCJhenAiOiJiYW5rIiwic2Vzc2lvbl9zdGF0ZSI6IjJjYTJiNGYwLWE0NjAtN
DliMi04MTkzLWI0YzNlYTg3ZTAxYSIsImFjciI6IjEiLCJhbGxvd2VkLW9yaWdpbnMiOlsiaHR0c
DovLzEyNy4wLjAuMTo4MDA4IiwiaHR0cDovL2xvY2FsaG9zdDo4MDA4IiwiaHR0cDovL2xvY2Fsa
G9zdDo4MDgxIiwiaHR0cDovL2xvY2FsaG9zdDo4MDExIiwiaHR0cDovL2xvY2FsaG9zdDo4MDg4I
iwiaHR0cDovL2xvY2FsaG9zdDo4MDg4Il0sInJlYWxtX2FjY2Vzcyi6eyJyb2xlcyI6WyJjdXN0b
21lciJdfSwic2NvcGUi0iJvcGVuaWQgcHJvZmlsZSBtaWNyb3Byb2ZpbGUtand0IGVtYWlsIHBob
251IiwidXBuIjoiZHV0ZSIsImJpcnRoZGF0ZSI6IkZlYnJ1YXJ5IDMwLCAyMDAwIiwiZW1haWxfd
mVyaWZpZWQiOnRydWUsIm5hbWUiOiJEdWtlIEN1c3RvbWVyIiwiZ3JvdXBzIjpbImN1c3RvbWVyI
l0sInByZWZlcnJlZF91c2VybmFtZSI6ImR1a2UiLCJnaXZlbl9uYW1lIjoiRHVrZSIsImZhbWlse
V9uYW1lIjoiQ3VzdG9tZXIiLCJlbWFpbCI6ImR1a2VAYWNtZTIuY29tIn0.QrM
```
```
Su9_9VE47xih2J9t-LhSDC-JPN2ptKip0OMCE3wl_bT3-IQoaX_TPuHz9elGrUQUYNjpnUuML8D2
yQmvt5QNaXjMvmxTFyEQgob2pxzbLkrQqIHhg7eSXKPLeJZtko3uWoiWDghYHFE_QBOk6iIZFY4c
YUQgxOiFTk4M73L2lkcy94fyv6Mgr4y5UQnTJqERVTfOQCybPy-B2nuRcpAcwB0eRTMgVsXAUsEI
camVjwwe1rkaHAdJvV6Z5Y8ouafSqdDMxRElmzkwnvWOfeNthVduiqba8YK0rkmvJhj0WS7Ehq74
UTtmHe5fMPvciVCSIMPVfDGKyVc45LYC2sA
```

13.4.1 *JWT header*

Each JWT section is Base64-encoded, including the header, so any tool that can decode a Base64 representation can view the header contents.

> **IMPORTANT** Because JWTs are not encrypted, it is highly recommended that JWTs are transferred over a secure transport layer, like HTTPS.

The `base64` command in listing 13.31 decodes the header matching JWT *italicized* text shown earlier to prove this point. Listing 13.32 shows the decoded header claims. A *claim* is a key-value pair that makes a statement about the entity (e.g., the user or token). The header claims are explained in table 13.5.

Listing 13.32 Displaying the contents of the JWT header

```
echo "eyJhbGciOiJSUzI1NiIsInR5cCIgOiAiSldUIiwia2lkIiA6ICJHNjZaUWxsTmNoOWVLVV
➥ B3VGpnVWJTcTB1eTN6aFJmeFZiOUItTUxNOG9FIn0" | base64 -d    ◁
```

> **Decodes the JWT header. Not all systems have base64 preinstalled. The following section decodes the entire JWT using a website, so installing base64 is not necessary.**

Listing 13.33 Decoded JWT header (formatted)

```
{"alg":"RS256",
 "typ" : "JWT",
 "kid" : "G66ZQllNch9eKUPwTjgUbSq0uy3zhRfxVb9B-MLM8oE"
```

Table 13.5 JWT header claims (all three required by MicroProfile JWT)

Claim	Description
alg	The cryptographic algorithm used to sign the JWT. MicroProfile JWT requires this to be RS256, which uses a public/private key pair to verify the token contents have not been tampered with.
typ	Media type, MicroProfile JWT requires this header claim to be defined as JWT.
kid	Hint indicating the key used to secure the JWT. This claim is useful when multiple keys are available to choose from, or to recognize if a key has changed between requests.

13.4.2 *JWT payload*

A JWT payload consists of a collection of standardized claims defined by RFC 7519. MicroProfile JWT extends these standardized claims, and developers can also add custom claims if needed.

To view the token claims returned from Keycloak, add TokenResource.java to the Bank service as shown in the next listing.

Listing 13.34 Viewing the contents of a token returned from OIDC Authorization Flow

```
@Authenticated        ◁
@Path("/token")
public class TokenResource {
    /**
     * Injection point for the Access Token issued
     * by the OpenID Connect Provider
     */
    @Inject
    JsonWebToken accessToken;     ◁

    @GET
    @Path("/tokeninfo")
    @Produces(MediaType.APPLICATION_JSON)    ◁
    public Set<String> token() {
        HashSet<String> set = new HashSet<String>();    ◁
        for (String t : accessToken.getClaimNames()) {
```

> **A Quarkus-specific annotation that allows access only to an authenticated user. This annotation, and any protective security annotation, will trigger the Authorization Code Flow and token creation for a successful authentication.**

> **Injects the token into a MicroProfile JsonWebToken instance**

> **Returns the token contents as a JSON object**

> **Token contents will be added to a Java collection (set)**

```
            set.add(t + " = " + accessToken.getClaim(t));    ◁──┐  Adds each claim
        }                                                          and its value to
        return set;      ◁──┐  Returns the                        the collection
    }                       │  claims
}
```

Next, access the token endpoint in a browser using http://localhost:8008/token/
tokeninfo, and log in using username duke and password duke. Use of an incognito
window is recommended to ensure a prior cookie is not used.

TIP Keycloak uses cookies to track the Authorization Code Flow. Browser
incognito or *private* windows will delete cookies when closed, which makes testing code as simple as closing and opening a new incognito browser window.

The (formatted) output will be a JSON token similar to the next listing.

Listing 13.35 Decoded JWT header (formatted for readability)

```
[
  "realm_access = {\"roles\":[\"customer\"]}",
  "preferred_username = duke",
  "jti = 75b92faf-6e5d-4e22-aaeb-65f292c356ac",
  "birthdate = February 30, 2000",
  "iss = https://keycloak.local/auth/realms/bank",
  "scope = openid profile microprofile-jwt email phone",
  "upn = duke",
  "principal = duke",
  "typ = Bearer",
  "name = Duke Customer",
  "azp = bank",
  "sub = edbb39d0-c6fa-4211-a75c-70d934031620",     The raw token is too long
  "email_verified = true",                          to list but is identical to the
  "raw_token = <too long to list>",    ◁──────────  token listed in listing 13.31.
  "family_name = Customer",
  "exp = 1623553922",
  "session_state = 2ca2b4f0-a460-49b2-8193-b4c3ea87e01a",
  "groups = [customer]",
  "acr = 1",
  "auth_time = 1623553617",
  "iat = 1623553622",
  "allowed-origins = [\"http://127.0.0.1:8008\",\"http://localhost:8008\",
➥  \"http://localhost:8081\",\"http://127.0.0.1:8081\",\"http://127.0.0.
➥  1:8088\",\"http://localhost:8088\"]",
  "email = duke@acme2.com",
  "given_name = Duke"
]
```

Table 13.6 explains the claims that are shown in listing 13.35.
    The groups claim is the only one of interest to the application functionality
because its value determines method access.

Table 13.6   Payload JWT claims (*required by MicroProfile JWT)

Claim	Description
typ	Declares the token media type.
iss*	Issuer of the MicroProfile JWT.
sub*	Identifies the principal that is the subject of the JWT.
exp*	JWT expiration time, at which point the JWT is considered invalid, in seconds since January 1, 1970.
iat*	The time a JWT was issued, in seconds since January 1, 1970.
jti*	JWT unique identifier; can be used to prevent a JWT from being replayed.
upn*	A human-readable MicroProfile JWT custom claim that uniquely identifies the subject or user principal of the token across all services that will access the token. This claim is the user principal name in `java.security.Principal`. `JsonWebToken` extends `java.security.Principal`, so it can be used by existing frameworks that support `java.security.Principal`. If this claim is missing, MicroProfile JWT will fall back to the `preferred_username` claim. If `preferred_username` is missing, the `sub` claim is used.
groups*	MicroProfile JWT custom claim that lists the groups the principal belongs to.
unlisted here	The remaining claims have been configured by the Keycloak administrator and are not directly relevant to MicroProfile JWT.

13.4.3 *JWT signature*

Each JWT is signed using the algorithm defined in the header `alg` claim to ensure it has not been tampered with. An easy way to view the token header claims and payload claims and verify the signature is to paste the contents of the `raw_token` claim in listing 13.35 into the form available at https://jwt.io/#encoded-jwt, as shown in figure 13.4.

1 Paste the JWT into the encoded form. The JWT header and payload sections display the claim values.

2 JWT header. The header claims, although not necessarily their values, will match claims in listing 13.33.

3 JWT payload. The claims, although not necessarily their values, will match the claims in listing 13.35.

4 The signature is not validated because the public key has not been provided.

To obtain the public key, run the command in the next listing, which should result in an output similar to that shown in listing 13.37.

Listing 13.36   Getting the public key

```
scripts/createpem.sh
```
Prints the public key in Privacy-Enhanced Mail (PEM) format

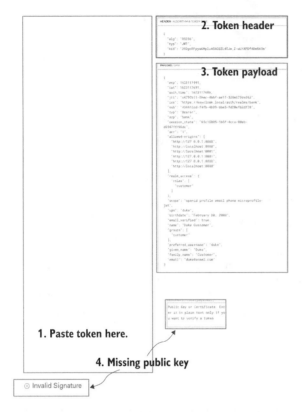

1. Paste token here.

4. Missing public key

⊙ Invalid Signature

Figure 13.4   jwt.io decoded JWT

Listing 13.37   Public key

```
-----BEGIN PUBLIC KEY-----
MIIBIjANBgkqhkiG9w0BAQEFAAOCAQ8AMIIBCgKCAQEAjJ/GYpCkgfYT1HYpa96AP8djbKiv25Yh
VlZcHcIt2QX4VZPJM/qntF2m7ubPSz3zHHNQUOWYl+3xIo4EFfCcTPTBgL0aSlCsuT5+0RuajsFj
ejLGa19p3eKuBjtB0buqI4SbxpitvZj4L4beBdFj+r2NZZNxeFFMrd9lORW3b4cUmk8tS6ZrgbTK
Ij3adjlVMYHOkGQNNGBf1KJkdbi8UQtXaATuyFHiQCCYY/ENWGGomu+dXqvqnRRsdWBndsUcCNe+
NPwT1z3lbfYoXkldWFVvXjBnNme/f8mCMWuKBz4fGZUkt7Sdc5FPnFpsbT+0inarxIov3puDxHbB
gNJ9xwIDAQAB
-----END PUBLIC KEY-----
```

Paste the public key into the jwt.io form public key field as shown in figure 13.5.

> **IMPORTANT**   The public key in listing 13.37 validates the token in listing 13.31. The token and public key for any other installation will differ. Attempting to use the public key in listing 13.37 to validate a token from another installation will fail.

In the next section, we utilize a JWT to secure a Transaction service REST endpoint.

Figure 13.5 Verified JWT

13.5 Securing the Transaction service using MicroProfile JWT

With a firm understanding of JWT and the MicroProfile JWT API, the next step is to secure the Transaction service with MicroProfile JWT. Before writing code, add the `quarkus-smallrye-jwt` extension as shown next.

Listing 13.38 Adding MicroProfile JWT support to the Transaction service

```
cd transaction_service
mvn quarkus:add-extension -Dextensions="io.quarkus:quarkus-smallrye-jwt"

# If the transaction service is not running, start it
mvn clean quarkus:dev -Ddebug=5006
```

> Adds the Quarkus extension that supports MicroProfile JWT. If the Transaction service is already running, an error message likely appears because two required MicroProfile JWT properties are missing.

The next step is to update application.properties with the public key, as shown in the following code snippet.

Listing 13.39 Configuring the MicroProfile JWT

Verifies the trusted token issuer is Keycloak

Pastes the public key obtained in listing 13.36, without the BEGIN PUBLIC KEY and END PUBLIC KEY lines (the Base64-encoded string only)

```
# Configure MicroProfile JWT

mp.jwt.verify.publickey=<INSERT PUBLIC KEY HERE>
mp.jwt.verify.issuer=http://keycloak.local/auth/realms/bank
```

Add the method in listing 13.40 to TransactionResource.java. This method adds a secure REST method endpoint intended to test that the JWT allows method access.

Listing 13.40 Adding `jwtGetBalance()` to TransactionResource.java

```
@GET
@RolesAllowed("customer")
```

> Only users in the customer role are allowed access to the method.

```
@Path("/jwt-secure/{acctnumber}/balance")
@Produces(MediaType.APPLICATION_JSON)
@Consumes(MediaType.APPLICATION_JSON)
public Response jwtGetBalance(
        @PathParam("acctnumber") Long accountNumber) {
  return getBalance(accountNumber);
}
```

◁── **Specifies a URL for the endpoint intended to be accessed using a JWT**

◁── **Calls the existing getBalance() method**

Finally, access the endpoint to verify access as shown here.

Listing 13.41   Testing endpoint access

```
# Start the account service in a new terminal window if it
# is not running

cd account-service
mvn quarkus:dev

# In a new window from the chapter top-level directory,
# restart the Transaction service

cd transaction-service
mvn clean quarkus:dev -Ddebug=5006

# In a new window from the chapter top-level directory

TOKEN=`scripts/gettoken.sh`
TRANSACTION_URL=http://localhost:8088

curl -i \
  -H "Accept: application/json" \
  -H "Authorization: Bearer "${TOKEN} \
    $TRANSACTION_URL/transactions/jwt-secure/444666/balance
```

Gets a token from Keycloak, simulating the OIDC Implicit Flow. The token will be valid for five minutes. To manually refresh the token after five minutes, rerun the command. The gettoken.sh script is heavily documented.

◁── **Specifies the top-level Transaction service URL**

◁── **Accesses the /jwt-secure/ endpoint to print the account balance**

Passes the token to the Transaction service using the Authorization header. The quarkus-smallrye-jwt extension recognizes and parses the token, creating a security context.

Listing 13.42   Testing endpoint access output

```
HTTP/1.1 200 OK
Content-Length: 7
Content-Type: application/json

3499.12
```

Accessing the endpoint without a valid bearer token, or using an expired token, will result in an HTTP/1.1 401 Unauthorized message as shown next.

Listing 13.43   Testing endpoint access

```
HTTP/1.1 401 Unauthorized
www-authenticate: Bearer {token}
content-length: 0
```

The Transaction service is now successfully using a JWT to access a secured endpoint. The following section propagates the token to the Account service to authorize access to a secured Account service endpoint.

13.6 Propagating the JWT

A request may travel across multiple secured microservices. The security context can travel with the request using a JWT to enable access to those secured microservices. The remainder of the JWT discussion switches from the OIDC Code Authorization Flow to the OIDC Implicit Flow, where the JWT is obtained directly from Keycloak and is propagated with HTTP requests. Before propagating the token, in the next section, we add a secured endpoint to the Account service.

13.6.1 Secure an Account service endpoint

The process for securing an Account service endpoint is the same as for securing a Transaction service endpoint.

First, a few Account service preparation steps are required, as shown next.

Listing 13.44 Adding MicroProfile JWT support to the Account service

> Adds the Quarkus extension that supports MicroProfile JWT. If the Account service is already running, an error message will likely appear because two required MicroProfile JWT properties are missing.

```
cd account_service
mvn quarkus:add-extension -Dextensions="io.quarkus:quarkus-smallrye-jwt"   ⊲─
```

The next step is to update the application.properties as follows.

Listing 13.45 Configuring the MicroProfile JWT

```
# Configure MicroProfile JWT
```
> Pastes the public key obtained in listing 13.36, without the **BEGIN PUBLIC KEY** and **END PUBLIC KEY** lines

```
mp.jwt.verify.publickey=<INSERT PUBLIC KEY HERE>        ⊲─
mp.jwt.verify.issuer=http://keycloak.local/auth/realms/bank   ⊲─
```
> **Verifies the trusted token issuer**

Next, add a secured method to get the bank balance, as shown in the next listing.

Listing 13.46 AccountResource.java: adding the secured endpoint

```
@RolesAllowed("customer")        ⊲─
@GET
@Path("/jwt-secure/{acctNumber}/balance")       ⊲─
public BigDecimal getBalanceJWT(
    @PathParam("acctNumber") Long accountNumber) {
  return getBalance(accountNumber);       ⊲─
}
```
> **Only users in the customer role are allowed access to the method.**
>
> **Specifies a URL for the endpoint intended to be accessed using a JWT**
>
> **Invokes the existing, unsecured, getBalance() method**

In the next section, we update the Transaction service to access the new secured endpoint.

13.6.2   *Propagating JWT from the Transaction service to the Account service*

The Transaction service uses the MicroProfile REST Client (via AccountService.java) to access the Account service. Therefore, add a new method to AccountService.java to invoke the new Account service secured endpoint as shown here.

Listing 13.47   Transaction service: AccountService.java

```
@GET
@Path("/jwt-secure/{acctNumber}/balance")
BigDecimal getBalanceSecure(@PathParam("acctNumber") Long accountNumber);
```

With the new MicroProfile REST Client method in place, update `Transaction-Resource.jwtGetBalance()` to invoke the new secure endpoint as follows.

Listing 13.48   Transaction service: AccountService.java

```
@GET
@RolesAllowed("customer")                         ◁——  Only users in the customer
@Path("/jwt-secure/{acctnumber}/balance")               role are allowed access to
@Produces(MediaType.APPLICATION_JSON)                   the method.
@Consumes(MediaType.APPLICATION_JSON)                        Invokes the secured
public Response jwtGetBalance(                            Account service endpoint
        @PathParam("acctnumber") Long accountNumber) {      using the REST Client
    String balance =
        accountService.getBalanceSecure(accountNumber).toString();  ◁——

    return Response.ok(balance).build();         ◁——  Returns the balance
}                                                      in JSON format
```

One last step is required for the Transaction service to access the Account Service securely. The JWT contains the user identity information, including the user's role. Therefore, the JWT must be propagated from the Transaction service to the Account service on each request, so the role is available to `AccountService.getBalanceJWT()`. This is as easy as updating the Transaction service application.properties to pass the `Authorization` header as shown in the following listing.

Listing 13.49   Propagate the `Authorization header`

```
org.eclipse.microprofile.rest.client.propagateHeaders=Special-
    Header,Authorization
```

Appends Authorization to the org.eclipse.microprofile.rest.client.propagateHeaders property, so the Authorization header containing the JWT (bearer) token is passed along with the REST calls

To test JWT propagation, run the commands in the next listing to receive the output in listing 13.51.

Listing 13.50 Testing JWT propagation

```
# If the account service is not running, start it
cd account-service
mvn clean quarkus:dev                          ◄─
```

Starts the Account service. The Transaction service should already be running.

Specifies the top-level Transaction service URL ─▷

```
TOKEN=`../scripts/gettoken.sh`                 ◄─
TRANSACTION_URL=http://localhost:8088

curl -i \
    -H "Accept: application/json" \
▷   -H "Authorization: Bearer "${TOKEN}
    $TRANSACTION_URL/transactions/jwt-secure/444666/balance   ◄─
```

Gets a token from Keycloak, simulating the OIDC Implicit Flow. The token will be valid for five minutes. To manually refresh the token after five minutes, rerun the command. The gettoken.sh script is heavily documented.

Accesses the /jwt-secure/ endpoint to print the account balance

Passes the token to the Transaction service using the Authorization header. The quarkus-smallrye-jwt extension recognizes and parses the token, creating a security context.

Listing 13.51 Testing JWT propagation

```
HTTP/1.1 200 OK
Content-Length: 7
Content-Type: application/json

3499.12
```

13.7 Running the services in Kubernetes

To deploy the services to Kubernetes, run the commands in the following listing to obtain the output shown in listing 13.53.

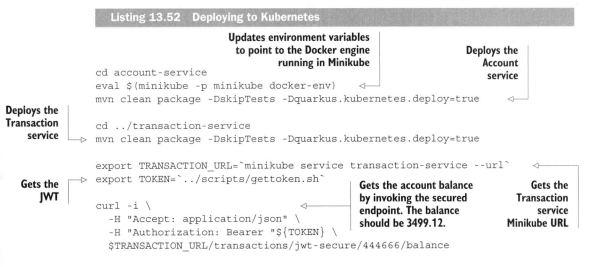

Listing 13.52 Deploying to Kubernetes

Updates environment variables to point to the Docker engine running in Minikube

Deploys the Account service

```
cd account-service
eval $(minikube -p minikube docker-env)        ◄─
mvn clean package -DskipTests -Dquarkus.kubernetes.deploy=true   ◄─
```

Deploys the Transaction service ─▷

```
cd ../transaction-service
mvn clean package -DskipTests -Dquarkus.kubernetes.deploy=true
```

Gets the JWT ─▷

```
export TRANSACTION_URL=`minikube service transaction-service --url`   ◄─
export TOKEN=`../scripts/gettoken.sh`

curl -i \                                      ◄─
    -H "Accept: application/json" \
    -H "Authorization: Bearer "${TOKEN} \
    $TRANSACTION_URL/transactions/jwt-secure/444666/balance
```

Gets the account balance by invoking the secured endpoint. The balance should be 3499.12.

Gets the Transaction service Minikube URL

IMPORTANT Attempting to redeploy an application already present in Kubernetes with mvn package -Dquarkus.kubernetes.deploy=true will result in an error in Quarkus 2.x. Follow the issue at https://github.com/quarkusio/quarkus/issues/19701 for updates on a resolution. We can work around the

problem by removing the application first with `kubectl delete -f /target/`
`kubernetes/minikube.yaml`.

Listing 13.53   Deploying to Kubernetes

```
HTTP/1.1 200 OK
Content-Length: 7
Content-Type: application/json

3499.12
```

At this point, the Bank service is using the OIDC Code Authorization Flow, and the
Transaction service is using the OIDC Implicit Flow and propagating the token to the
Account service.

Summary

- Authentication and authorization are necessary security strategies for web
  applications.
- Quarkus supports many authentication and authorization mechanisms.
- Defining users and authorization strategies in application.properties is a pro-
  ductive development approach.
- Quarkus offers productive features to simplify testing secured applications.
- OIDC Code Authorization Flow typically obtains user identity using a web form
  and returns a JWT.
- JWTs propagate user identity across services using the OIDC Implicit Flow.
- Quarkus enhances the OIDC testing experience with a WireMock OIDC autho-
  rization server.

index